# Studying Abroad 2014:
# A guide for UK students

## 2nd edition

## Cerys Evans

*Studying Abroad: A Guide for UK Students 2014*

This second edition published in 2013 by Trotman Publishing, a division of Crimson Publishing Ltd, Westminster House, Kew Road, Richmond, Surrey TW9 2ND

First edition published in 2012

Author: Cerys Evans

**British Library Cataloguing in Publication Data**
A catalogue record for this book is available from the British Library

ISBN 978 1 84455 520 8

Typeset by IDSUK (DataConnection) Ltd

Printed and bound in the UK by Ashford Colour Press, Gosport, Hants

# Acknowledgements

---

This book would not have been possible without the help of UK students at universities across the world who were happy to tell their stories. Many got involved in order to share their experience of a life-changing opportunity. Particular thanks go to Mark Huntington (A Star Future) and the many university staff who took the time to talk to me and who put me in touch with their students.

Finally, Matt, Alice and Oscar deserve my heartfelt thanks for their understanding and support.

# Contents

Contents

# Contents

Contents

# Introduction

Britain has had a long tradition of welcoming international students to its universities, yet far fewer UK students venture overseas to study. All that is changing and there has never been so much interest in the possibility of studying abroad.

The three-fold increase in tuition fees in England in 2012 prompted some young people to start looking for alternative, affordable ways to study. Many students are unaware of the degrees available to them overseas, taught in English and at a range of prices. Although fees outside England are subsidised, students from Wales and Northern Ireland will also be able to find comparably priced, and sometimes cheaper, opportunities than those available at home. Scottish students can find free courses available elsewhere in Europe, at undergraduate and even at postgraduate level.

But price alone is not enough to drive people to study overseas. A more competitive marketplace for graduate employment is leading students to make themselves more attractive to potential employers and studying overseas provides the opportunity to produce a more dynamic CV.

However, choosing to study overseas is not a decision that should be made lightly. There are many aspects to consider and many questions to ask before you get to that stage. Higher education is a global market and, although there is a lot of information available online, the challenge is making sense of it, ensuring that it is genuine and being able to make meaningful comparisons between the different options available.

This book will help you to determine whether studying a degree abroad is the right option for you. It will tackle the costs, risks and benefits of studying abroad. It will enable you to compare the merits of different countries and their education systems. You can read about the trials and the tribulations of a variety of students, as well as learning about their highlights of overseas study. The book will help you to navigate the plethora of information available, guiding you through the decision-making process by providing answers to the essential questions.

This book is only the starting point of what could be a life-changing educational and cultural adventure.

## Note

The following exchange rates were used throughout the book (sourced in November 2012).

- £1 to €1.25 (Euro)
- £1 to $1.59 (US Dollar)
- £1 to C$1.59 (Canadian Dollar)
- £1 to A$1.54 (Australian Dollar)
- £1 to NZ$1.96 (New Zealand Dollar)
- £1 to DKK9.29 (Danish Krone)
- £1 to CZK31.83 (Czech Koruna)
- £1 to NOK9.17 (Norwegian Krone)
- £1 to SEK10.76 (Swedish Krona)
- £1 to S$1.95 (Singapore Dollar)
- £1 to HK$12.31 (Hong Kong Dollar)

- £1 to ¥9.90 (Chinese Yuan Renminbi)
- £1 to JPY128.61 (Japanese Yen)
- £1 to ZAR14.11(South African Rand)
- £1 to MYR4.87 (Malaysian Ringgit)
- £1 to SAR5.95 (Saudi Arabian Riyal)
- £1 to QAR5.78 (Qatari Riyal)

## Student story
## Rebecca Jackson, Stenden University
## of Applied Sciences, the Netherlands

Rebecca Jackson's desire to experience different cultures was the starting point for her overseas study experience. 'I wanted to see the world and get out of the bubble that was created for me where I was. I also wanted to achieve something unusual, something even more challenging. This was to learn the Dutch language fluently during my study.'

Rebecca already had some knowledge of the Netherlands before she decided on it as a study destination. 'There is something about the culture and the Dutch which has always attracted me to the Netherlands. I always used to visit the Netherlands when I was a child and it's just such an open country with so many nationalities. It also helps that a vast majority of the Dutch are fluent English speakers.

'I knew I wanted a Bachelor of Education and, due to my limited Dutch, I needed an education course that I could learn in my language. This is when I found ITEPS (International Teacher Education for Primary Schools). The course is perfect for me. It will let me see the world, travel and earn money doing something I love.'

So after finding the perfect course, the next step for Rebecca was to look at the costs; she had some good news. 'There is an incredible difference. It is €7,500 (£6,018) cheaper per year compared to similar studies in the UK. ITEPS is not run yet in the UK but is run in the Netherlands and Denmark and soon to be in Sweden and Norway.

'I had to apply through a website called Studielink. This is much simpler than UCAS! To apply, you simply upload your information to create your profile and choose the university which you would like to enrol in. You send each course you apply for a letter of motivation which is relatively short and just describes why you would like to study that course. From there, the university sends you either an acceptance letter, a decline or, in some cases like with

Stenden, all participants are asked to attend an interview. This, I believe, can also be done on Skype.

'The application took approximately two months in total, from the initial set-up of Studielink to being told I was accepted. I got told I was accepted in March, which made it much more relaxing for me unlike for my friends. They seemed to have a hard time over the summer awaiting their grades. I was glad I didn't have to do any of that.'

Rebecca got plenty of help along the way. 'I had lots of help with the application process, from sending me information about how to set up Studielink to putting me in contact with people for housing. The university also set up an application for a bank account for me and translated everything into English. I also was offered a Dutch intensive course for the summer, paid for by the institution.

'There were a few international applicants in my course and the university helped with introducing me to another course member, a French girl, who attended the summer course with me, so we could fill the applications in together and help each other through the process.

'I also was sent a lot of information about moving to Holland and studying here in a brochure provided by Stenden. It was like a crash course in the Dutch culture and it was one of the most useful things that I received.'

The supportive approach didn't end when the course started. 'We have weekly tutor sessions in which educational or personal issues are discussed and the university helps in every way possible to find a solution to any problems we may have. I have also been offered Dutch tuition from the institution for four hours a week.'

The style of teaching at Stenden UAS is a bit different from that in UK universities. 'We're taught in a classroom. There are no lectures. The classes are very practical and laid back. I find the teaching style very personal as there are only up to 30 people in a class. We're really aided and guided.'

Adjusting to life in a new country presented some challenges for Rebecca. 'It can be difficult to find your way around a country when you don't know the language. The language is very difficult for the English.

'It's been a bit of a challenge trying to find a job due to hours at university and not having the NT2 Dutch (official Dutch as a second language qualification) exam yet. I have been given the opportunity to promote Stenden in a documentary for ITV, in the newspaper and at various study fairs all over the country. I get paid by the hour for this. The university has also put me in touch with people to help me find a job here in Meppel.

'Those have been my only difficulties, as the Dutch are very hospitable and really helped me. There are other international students here too, so that helps.'

## Rebecca's top tips

### Accommodation

'Use housing recommended by the university. It is hard to find a house for a similar or cheaper price that is of any better standard. They are usually relatively cheap and I love my house. But, be aware that, in Holland, male and female students often share houses or flats so it could be possible to be the only female or male in the house. You can speak to the university about this if there are any problems and they will help you.'

### Shopping

'Shop around. The price difference between foods in some shops is amazingly high. I shop at about four different shops. It can be a hassle but I eat well, just like I did at home, for €15 (£12) a week on average. I could get that down to €10 (£8) if I were struggling. Dutch food is pretty good, it's not too different from British food but I suppose it's a lot healthier. If you're a vegetarian, it's quite difficult to live cheaply here. The substitutes can be very expensive, so you'll need to be innovative!

'I'd bring toiletries with you in bulk as they're very expensive out here. I get to shop in Germany where there's sometimes a €3 (£2.40) price difference on a type of toothpaste. It's worth looking around.

## Insurance

'You must have medical insurance. I got mine from www.studentinsurance.com and it is relatively cheap.'

## Living costs

'Buy the 40% korting (discount) card if you don't have a job. It's €50 (£40) for the year and you save loads. A bike is also necessary, preferably not a mountain bike as it would most likely get stolen. Dutch bikes out here are very cheap second-hand. Try to avoid using a car unless you have to. Fuel is very expensive. I top up in Germany as it's €0.30 (24p) a litre cheaper.'

## Financial support for study

'I don't receive any financial support at all from the UK; however, you can take out a loan in the Netherlands for your fees. You can get grants and loans from the Dutch government.'

## Working while studying

'Working is difficult to do with my course because the timetable changes every three months. You need the NT2 Dutch course before being able to get a decent job. It's not compulsory, but is highly desired, especially in the part of Holland where I live. I don't live in a largely bilingual part of Holland so I look for cleaning and waitressing jobs. If you work for eight hours or more a week, you can receive around €250 (£200) a month to aid tuition and you are entitled to a loan and free travel across the whole country with an OV-Chip card (similar to the Oyster card in the UK).'

## Lifestyle and culture

'Holland is a proud nation – racism and nationalism are not accepted. Speaking Dutch is not always necessary, as most love to speak English, but it is always polite. Common stereotypes about the Dutch are laughed about but not always taken too well if they're commonly used. Keep an open mind and be on time. Not a minute late or a minute early, the Dutch are always on time and also finish directly on the hour. Apart from timekeeping, the Dutch are pretty laid back with their 'maaknietuit' (it doesn't matter) attitude. They are not a nation to rush or to cause any drama in the slightest. Being impolite or impatient does not fit in well here.

The Dutch are very hospitable also. If you stay at someone's house, you don't need to bring anything. It's a lovely culture.'

## Options for after you finish your studies

'My options are unlimited. Worldwide travel comes as standard, as I can teach at any international school or Dutch national school with my bachelor's degree. This Bachelor of Education is the same as the British bachelor's degree.'

When Rebecca's course ends in a couple of years' time, she's got some idea of what she'd like to do next. 'I'd like to travel the world, and eventually settle somewhere to retire. I don't want to be fixed. I want to see the world and make a difference. I won't be going back to the UK, that's for sure. Being abroad has caught on like a bug.'

*Stenden University of Applied Sciences (www.stenden.com/en) attracts local students as well as international students from over 60 countries.*

# Chapter 1

## Why study abroad?

UK students don't traditionally study abroad. Far more international students come to the UK than leave its shores to study. International study might be a new thing for UK students, but across much of the world it is far more common. In fact, the number of international students around the world just keeps growing. The Organisation for Economic Co-operation and Development (OECD) and United Nations Educational, Scientific and Cultural Organization's (UNESCO) Institute for Statistics tell us that 4.1 million international students were enrolled in higher education in 2010. The number of students going abroad to study has almost doubled since 2000 and looks set to soar.

But how many of these are UK students? OECD reveals that 35,308 UK students were enrolled at overseas tertiary institutions in 2012. Although this figure is low compared to the global numbers, it is worth knowing that this is almost a 60% increase since 2006–2007: things are certainly changing.

If you mention studying abroad, a common response is that we already have a world-class university system, so why look elsewhere? But there are benefits of moving country to go to university which is why UK students are starting to look elsewhere, and in increasing numbers. There are plenty of reasons why study abroad might be beneficial; maybe you want to avoid higher tuition fees, to have an amazing adventure or to gain a place at one of the top universities in the world.

There has been a flurry of interest in overseas study since the announcement of the fee increases in the UK. Studying abroad may be a hot topic, but is that enough of a reason to set sail for foreign shores? I don't think so. Things are changing so fast that it is hard to know what the economic, employment or educational landscape will look like in a year or two, while you might only be part-way through your overseas degree. So it makes sense to consider overseas study in far more depth as part of your wider and longer-term plans; you will need to look carefully at the pros and cons before you make your decision.

# The global market

As you walk around schools and colleges in other European countries, it is normal to see international opportunities on the notice boards; summer schools, study exchanges and overseas degrees are far more commonplace than in the UK. Young people in many other countries have come to expect international experiences.

This is not always the case in the UK and this causes a problem, according to a recent report into the global skills gap. Three-quarters of board- and director-level executives and CEOs think that 'we are in danger of being left behind by emerging countries unless young people learn to think more globally'. A similar proportion (74%) are 'worried that many young people's horizons are not broad enough to operate in a globalised and multicultural economy'. (The Global Skills Gap: Preparing young people for the new global economy, Think Global and British Council, December 2011.)

Picture yourself having finished university and ready to look for work. If you consider the global marketplace for jobs, then you will not only be competing against UK graduates, but against the brightest and best from across the world. And while the number of graduates from western countries is starting to plateau, countries like China and India are producing more young graduates, many of whom choose international higher education. The market is starting to get even more crowded and competitive.

Many organisations now do business or seek clients in more than one country, so job applicants with international experience, and the increased cultural awareness that brings, have added value. Some students choose study abroad as the first step towards an international career. Those graduates who have spent a summer school in the States, an exchange to Sweden as part of their first degree followed by postgraduate study in Malaysia, have a head start.

A 2011 report from the Association of Graduate Recruiters (AGR), Council for Industry and Higher Education (CIHE) and CFE (research and consultancy specialists in employment and skills) examines how global graduates can be developed. 'Students have a role to play in acquiring global competencies and choosing appropriate pathways to enable them to develop a global mindset. Experience of working outside their home country and immersion in a different culture can catapult a graduate into being considered for rewarding and challenging roles.'

The report's authors worked with multinational employers based in the UK to identify the most important qualities a global graduate will need. 'Global graduates require a blend of knowledge, competencies and corresponding attributes spanning global mindset, cultural agility and relationship management and must be able to apply them flexibly.'

Studying abroad can not only give you the opportunity to study in a new country, but also to choose a degree with an international focus while studying alongside a group of students from across the world. Consider how all these aspects can help you to develop the global mindset that will prepare you for the international job market and the global economy.

> **“** I feel I am having a much more international experience here than I ever would have had in England. I am studying in a diverse environment which is reflected in the debates and classes that we take part in. My class has such a range of nationalities that makes the lessons more dynamic, but it also has a real effect on personal development. By being in these classes you develop a more tolerant attitude and change your outlook completely on some things. **”**
>
> *Clare Higgins, The Hague University of Applied Sciences, the Netherlands*

# Competition in the UK

## Competition for university places

In 2012, nearly 190,000 students applied for university in the UK without gaining a place. For some of the most competitive courses in the UK, there are tens of applications per place. You have to be truly exceptional, and perhaps a little bit lucky, to get a place for medicine or veterinary science in the UK. Yet there are internationally recognised universities offering the same opportunities in the Caribbean and parts of Europe. Although you still need to demonstrate academic excellence and the right aptitude and attitude, the level of competition for places is not as extreme as in the UK. It is not surprising that applicants, frustrated by the limits in the UK, are looking for alternatives.

The UK operates a highly competitive system, where great importance is placed on predicted grades and high academic achievement. Competition for places is one of the reasons why entry criteria are shooting through the roof. A cap on the number of places available means that demand is currently outstripping supply, so the universities can pick and choose their candidates and ask for higher and higher requirements. The removal of this cap for some students hasn't necessarily made the situation any easier. More places are on offer to students achieving grades AAB (and ABB from 2013); this has meant that students narrowly missing these grades have started to lose out.

Other countries do things differently. Some countries will accept you provided that you have achieved three A levels (or equivalent) but are not so concerned about grades. This doesn't mean that they are less stringent in their entry processes; in some cases, they are more concerned with how you actually perform at university – if you don't achieve in your first year, they may ask you to leave.

A number of countries don't have a coordinated central application process like UCAS. On the downside, this may mean having to complete more application forms. On the positive side, it also means that you aren't limited to the number of applications you make, which can keep your options open. You can even apply through UCAS at the same time as applying to overseas universities; all the while gathering the information you need to decide which option suits you best. Some students use an international university as a back-up option to their UK plans.

## Competition for jobs

Many current students and recent graduates understand all too
clearly the effects of the upsurge in numbers in higher education
over the past decade. The increase in numbers of graduates,
exacerbated by the recent economic challenges, is creating a
crowded graduate-job market. Yet the more graduates there are,
the more pressure there is to get a degree in order to compete. A
degree has become essential yet, conversely, a degree alone is not
enough. Students are looking for ways in which to stand out, to
make themselves different and to get an edge over the competition.
Studying abroad can be a way to achieve all these things.

As Dr Jo Beall of the British Council explained in 2012: 'The
good news is that people are beginning to recognise how vital
international skills are for enhancing their career. Research last
year revealed that more UK employers look for international
awareness and experience above academic qualifications. But
the bad news is that not enough people in the UK are taking
opportunities to gain international experience. That needs to
change if the UK will successfully compete in the global economy.
Our recent research showed that while almost two-thirds of
students felt they had an international outlook, they failed to see
the potential career advantages to be gained from international
experiences.'

> **"** Global leaders need to be willing to work in
> different locations as an integral part of their
> career but many employers have difficulty recruiting
> graduates willing to travel or relocate. Employers felt that
> graduates with a global mindset would be more likely to

embrace international immersion and relish the opportunity
to work in different countries. It is essential that leaders are
positioned where they are most needed and thus able to
respond to market demands. **99**

> (Diamond, A., Walkley, L. et al., *Global Graduates*
> *into Global Leaders, www.cihe.co.uk, [Online]*
> *accessed November 2012.)*

# Financial benefits

From autumn 2012, tuition fees of up to £9,000 per year have been
charged in England; this is believed to have contributed to a 10%
drop in applications from England for 2012. Fees will continue to
be charged at these rates for students starting university in 2013
and look set to continue for the foreseeable future.

Applications from the rest of the UK, where students contribute
less towards the costs of university, fell only slightly. Welsh
students are expected to contribute £3,575 per year in 2013,
while fees in Northern Ireland (for students from Northern
Ireland) are capped at £3,575. Studying in Scotland remains
free for Scottish students, although students from the rest of
the UK studying in Scotland will pay fees of up to £9,000 per
year.

On top of the increasing fees, repayment options for student loans
are also looking less appealing. In England and Wales an interest
rate of RPI plus 3% (making a total of 6.2% at October 2012's rate)
will be charged on your loan from day one, with variable rates
charged once you graduate, depending on your earnings. The
UK is not a cheap place to live at the moment either, with costs
of food, energy bills and fuel particularly high. So, in addition to

your hefty debts from fees, you might be looking at less reasonable terms on your loan and high costs of living.

Unsurprisingly, students and parents are now wondering whether there might be a more financially attractive proposition elsewhere. There are universities in countries like Sweden, Denmark, Norway and Finland that charge no fees to UK students. Many countries charge less than England, Wales and Northern Ireland – countries like Estonia and Ireland, for example. There are countries with considerably cheaper costs of living (the Czech Republic or Malaysia, for example) and there are universities with generous scholarships and sources of student financial support (for example, the USA and the Netherlands). Graduates from some overseas universities may come home with the ideal situation of no debt (or at least smaller debt), as well as many of the other benefits introduced in this chapter.

 The difference in cost is laughable! I won't get into debt over here. **99**

*Owen McComasky, Stenden University of Applied Sciences, the Netherlands*

# Academic benefits

There can be academic benefits to studying abroad, for example, the chance to try out a number of subjects before specialising; or how about the opportunity to study new subjects or specialist options not available in the UK? Some countries are world leaders in specific subjects; Australia, for example, is known for its geology and marine biology courses, among others. Other countries offer a different perspective on familiar subjects, like veterinary medicine or history. Or perhaps you relish the opportunity to study a subject in its natural setting, Arctic studies or American literature, for example.

> **❝** I developed an interest in Middle Eastern archaeology during my undergraduate studies; this interest was further enhanced by travels in the region. Therefore the chance to specialise in this region, as well as live and learn in it, was an opportunity I didn't want to miss. **❞**
>
> *Benedict Leigh, UCL Qatar, Qatar*

Studying abroad may give you a more realistic chance of studying at a world-class university or of taking one of the competitive subjects that is becoming increasingly difficult in the UK (see Competition for university places, page 12). Outside the UK, some of the best universities in the world can be more accessible in the grades they expect and in the scholarships they offer. Different countries place different importance on entrance exams, face-to-face interviews, exam results, and hobbies and interests. You may find that what is needed by other universities across the world plays to your strengths better than what the UK asks of you.

You will have the chance to experience a different academic environment, with access to different types of campus and university facilities. Some universities offer much smaller classes than in the UK, better tutor-contact time or high-profile internships; finding out exactly what is on offer is an important part of your research.

You may even find that the styles of teaching and learning outside the UK suit you better. For example, in Australia teaching is often more informal and lecturers are approachable and accessible; in Denmark, much is made of problem-based learning, while exams are required in all subjects.

# Personal benefits

Studying abroad can be a great adventure, broadening your horizons and throwing up new challenges to be faced. It is hardly surprising that so many students come home from time overseas feeling confident, mature and independent. Understanding that there are different ways of doing things can make you more flexible. Learning to cope in an unfamiliar situation reinforces your adaptability and ability to use your initiative. Most universities arrange lots of events to let international students meet one another and get settled in, so your social skills will get some practice too.

> **"** If I had not gone abroad I may have never had the confidence to move away from home so easily, or fallen into such a fantastic job. It really does change your outlook on your own life; it helped me figure out what I wanted to do for my future career. **"**
> *Rosie Hodgart, University of South Carolina, USA*

The list of personal benefits goes on and on. Many courses delivered in English attract a wide and varied mix of international students, not just those from English-speaking countries. The chance to make friends from across the world makes you more culturally aware, but also means a wider network of contacts for future life and work.

Even if you are being taught in English, studying in a non-English-speaking country means that you will need to develop your language skills in order to be able to communicate effectively. Most institutions will offer language courses to their students. Language skills can make you more employable; Britain lags behind the rest of Europe with its foreign-language skills, so here is another way to make you stand out.

> **"** I wanted to achieve something unusual, something even more challenging. This was to learn the Dutch language fluently during my study. **"**
>
> *Rebecca Jackson, Stenden University of Applied Sciences, the Netherlands*
>
> **"** If I were to study in the UK, I would certainly improve my French and probably spend one year in France during the course. However, actually living in the country, I figured that I would be practically bilingual by the time I had my degree, even if the course I am studying is taught mainly in English. **"**
>
> *Alican Spafford, Rouen Business School, France*

Studying in another country can also give you access to lifestyle options that aren't accessible or affordable in the UK. If you fancy a sauna in your apartment building, try Finland. Or how about surfing before lectures in Australia? If you're looking for a great place to ski, parts of the USA or Canada have much to offer.

You might get the chance to work overseas too, perhaps part-time alongside your studies or as part of an internship, co-op programme or placement related to your subject. Essentially, you will get the chance to develop a global perspective or an international outlook, which is so important in today's global society.

# The employer's view

When considering overseas study as part of a longer-term plan, you need to be sure of your prospects when you return to the UK. So what kinds of competencies could you develop through overseas study that would be attractive to employers back in the UK? Here are the views of some top employers:

> ❝ Cultural dexterity is important: an ability not to impose one's own culture on another one, to be sensitive to other cultures and how to do business in different environments. There are certain ways of working with clients in the Middle East that you wouldn't adopt in Japan. ❞
>
> *PWC*

> ❝ Adaptability and self-awareness are probably the two things that we find the toughest to find . . . we want our graduates to feel they fit with our culture and hit the ground running. ❞
>
> *HSBC*

> ❝ If you have people that can integrate with local teams, or who are able to move globally and take with them their experience in a seamless way, I think that can only help the business move forward. A lot of our work is very dependent on engaging with local governments [and]

other local and national oil companies, and we need to be able
to work with them effectively. **99**

*BP*

**66** You need the mindset that says, 'The person I'm
talking to isn't like me and I need to understand
what they are like and then work with them.' It isn't only
about having the technical knowledge, it's also necessary to
understand the values, customs, cultures and behaviours
that are significant to them. **99**

*National Grid*
*(Source: Diamond, A., Walkley, L. et al., Global*
*Graduates into Global Leaders, www.cihe.co.uk,*
*[Online] accessed November 2012.)*

If you choose to study overseas, you should develop many of the
qualities that these organisations are looking for, but you will still
need to be sure that you can articulate these strengths to potential
employers.

# Why not go?

Of course, studying abroad isn't the right choice for everyone and
there are a number of reasons why you might not choose to take
this option. Some of the reasons that make international study
ideal for one person (the chance to have an adventure or take
a leap into the unknown, for example) might make it an awful
prospect for another.

You do need a certain amount of confidence to take this step. It
is a braver move than simply following the crowd and it does
have some risks. You are further from home if things go wrong,

although many students overseas talk of the support network they build up of university staff, room-mates and fellow students.

## The need for thorough preparation and research

Ideally, you need to be fully prepared to take this step. Getting a place through Clearing in the UK can be a stressful process and can lead to students feeling the pressure to accept courses or institutions for which they are not suited. Imagine how it feels when you end up in a different country. In August 2011 and again in August 2012, there was great interest in late opportunities overseas, but not always the time and space to make an informed decision. A rushed decision doesn't always end up being a negative one, but there are benefits from taking your time with this process.

> 66 The Dutch universities start earlier so I had not even enrolled, had no financial aid or plan, don't speak any Dutch and had no accommodation, so I felt very unprepared. 99
>
> *Clare Higgins, The Hague University of Applied Sciences, the Netherlands*

When considering an unfamiliar education system, you need to find out far more about the type and reputation of an institution, the way you will be taught and assessed, the qualifications you will gain, the grading system and so on; you can't assume that anything will be the same as in the UK.

## Financial reasons

One of the downsides to overseas study is the lack of UK student financial support you can access. With no loans or grants from the UK government, you will need to find some money for fees and living costs before you go. In fact, if you need to apply for a visa, you will need to provide evidence that you have the money to study. Don't forget to factor in additional costs for application fees, travel, admissions tests, visa applications or insurance, for example.

There may be some opportunities for scholarships and occasionally even grants and loans from your host country. Even if you're lucky enough to get a scholarship or financial support from the country where you study, chances are that you'll need some money to supplement this, or in case of an emergency. If you plan to work to fund your studies, don't bank on getting work right away, particularly if you don't yet speak the language.

## Language barrier

If you are studying in a country where English isn't an official language, even though your course may be taught in English, you will still need to manage away from the university. A rental agreement for accommodation or an application for a bank account, for example, will be in another language, so you will need to consider how you might cope. If most of your fellow students don't speak English as a first language, you may feel isolated in social situations.

Learning a new language is likely to be highly beneficial, but it is another commitment on top of your studies. If you are concerned about the language barrier, it is worth finding out how widely English is spoken in your chosen country and whether the institution takes many students from English-speaking countries.

## Adjusting

You will need to be prepared to make adjustments if you decide to study abroad.

## Education

Teaching and learning can be different (as you'll learn in Chapters 5 to 10). Expectations about what you should achieve in your first year can be very high, often determining whether you are allowed to stay on into the second year. The workload may be heavier than you would expect in the UK and terminology may be unfamiliar. It will be a steep learning curve, so you will need to use your initiative and seek help to avoid falling behind.

> **❝** You cannot get away with doing no work the first two years and still get a good degree. After six weeks here, we were already taking exams that would count towards our final degree average. **❞**
>
> *James Wheeler, Bocconi University, Italy*

## Lifestyle

Moving abroad means that your normal way of life will be thrown into disarray. The familiar and comforting will have disappeared, replaced by the new and strange, and the life you expect to lead at university may not always be realised. You may spend a disproportionate amount of time studying, adjusting to the new education system and working (rather than socialising). You may find that other home students from the host country are older or living at home. There will be cultural and social differences to the ways you spend your time and you will be far away from your normal support network of family and friends. In combination, these factors often lead to feelings of culture shock and homesickness. It is quite normal to feel this way, but it is an adjustment that you will need to consider.

> 66 There is a big restaurant scene in Doha, but a
> limited number of bars and they are all located in
> hotels. Much of student life when we are not working
> revolves around cultural events, socialising at the souqs, or
> going to the beach and malls. 99
>
> *Benedict Leigh, UCL Qatar, Qatar*

## Risks

Although many people love their experience of studying abroad,
it is not risk-free. You might be concerned about whether you will
get a visa, have fears about how you will manage financially and
worry about the distance from family and friends. International
study can bring flexibility, but there may be more restrictions in
the choices that you make, particularly if you need a visa. It can be
problematic to change institution or course once you start. It is not
always possible to change your reason for being in a country, from
studying to full-time work, for example, so you need to be fairly
sure of your plans before you depart.

No matter how thoroughly you plan and research, you cannot
know what you will be faced with when you come to leave
university, so you cannot assume that the opportunities of
today will still be there tomorrow. You may find that employers
do not recognise or understand your degree, even if it is
equivalent to those available in the UK. Even if you're attending
a world-ranked university, UK employers may fail to recognise
its status. Perhaps you were planning to stay on in a country,
but economic conditions made that difficult. Courses that meet
certain professional standards today might not fit the bill
tomorrow, so it is worth considering a back-up plan, where
possible.

> 66 Quite a few people fail and have to retake the first
> year. I would say it's relatively easy to get in here,
> but it's hard to stay. 99
>
> *James Wheeler, Bocconi University, Italy*

Finally, international education is big business, so there are
people out there trying to make money from bogus institutions,
low-quality provision and non-existent accommodation. Be on
your guard and use some of the tips and reputable sources of
information found in this book.

Having gathered and considered all the information that you
need, you may just get the feeling that studying abroad is not the
right option for you. If it isn't the right step right now, you don't
necessarily need to rule it out for ever. You might want to consider
alternatives to taking your full degree abroad (see page 74) or you
might choose to study or work abroad at a later stage in life.

Many of the trailblazing students who have already taken the
step of taking their full degree overseas have additional reasons
for going. Some have already spent some time abroad, have
family members who had lived overseas or have personal links
to a country before they decide to study there. This is changing;
as a degree overseas has started to become more common, more
attractive and more understood in the UK, students are now
making the move without those personal links beforehand.

If you're looking for . . .

- If you're looking for the cheapest fees, try Europe
  (Chapter 5).

- If you're looking for a similar student lifestyle to that of the UK, try Ireland (page 163), the Netherlands (page 170) and many of the US campus universities (Chapter 6).
- If you're looking for accelerated degrees or tailor-made education, try a private university (page 39).
- If you're looking for a low cost of living, try eastern Europe (Chapter 5), South Africa (page 299) or China (page 313).
- If you're looking for the best in the world, try the USA (Chapter 6).
- If you're looking for a different culture, try Qatar (page 317), Hong Kong (page 294) or Japan (page 319).
- If you're looking for no tuition fees, try the Nordic countries (Chapter 5) and parts of Germany (page 158).
- If you're looking for outdoor activities, try Canada (Chapter 7), Australia (Chapter 8) or New Zealand (Chapter 9).
- If you're looking for the opportunity to stay on after study, try Europe (page 136), Canada (page 244), Australia (page 273) or New Zealand (page 289).

## Student story
## James Wheeler, Bocconi University, Italy

James Wheeler wanted to do something different. 'I felt many of the non-vocational courses in the UK were a waste of time; three years studying something which I was never going to use again seemed pointless. I also didn't have a passion for any one subject, so I thought I may as well do something more directly useful and chose a vocational degree. Many of my peers at universities in the UK were not challenged and generally seemed bored. I had a desire to meet new people and see new parts of the world, experience another culture and learn a new language. Through doing something different, I hope to stand out to potential employers.'

It was luck rather than a specific plan that led him to Italy. 'I was working in Switzerland on my gap year and my Dad came to visit me one weekend. He said that as I wasn't keen on any of my unconditional UCAS offers (Edinburgh, Durham, Warwick and Manchester), why didn't we go and have a look at this university in Milan which he knew had a good reputation. It offered a Bachelor's degree in International Economics, Management and Finance taught in English.

'The application process was very simple and straightforward. As Bocconi is private, it doesn't have to abide by any national deadline dates, so it's much more flexible.'

James didn't get much support before he arrived in Italy. 'There was a welcome kit, but not much more than that. We did visit the university before and this gave me a better sense of the city. Finding a flat was difficult, but luckily an Italian-speaking friend helped me out a lot with contracts etc.'

He settled in well to his new life in Italy, which was lucky because the work started right away. 'It is much more rigorous academically. You cannot get away with doing no work the first two years and still get a good degree. After six weeks here, we were already taking exams that would count towards our final degree average. My friends were still on freshers' week, so the difference was stark. Quite a few people fail and have to retake the first year. I would say it's relatively easy to get in here, but it's hard to stay, whereas the top UK unis are hard to get in, but easy once you're there.

'All of the teaching is done through large lectures (130 students per class) but the professors do have office hours and are reachable by email. There are no seminars and classes aren't compulsory: a big bonus.

'There is also very little pastoral or social care here, you are very much left to sink or swim. There are much fewer societies and sports teams in comparison to UK universities, but Bocconi is trying to improve in that area.'

## James's top tips

### Accommodation
'Try to get a flat, as the residences aren't great. Originally I moved into the residences as I thought it would be like the UK where everyone goes into halls. I moved out after a month. I would recommend finding the flat in person; I have friends who found flats online and were disappointed.'

### Living costs
'Milan is an expensive city. Cheaper than London but far more expensive than most other UK university towns.'

### Lifestyle
'The lifestyle is fantastic. The student body are mainly European but have an international outlook. You have to get used to the Italian way of doing things, everything is a bit slower.'

James finds it hard to pick out just one highlight from his time in Milan. 'So many things are great but the best would have to be the people here. I have made such amazing friends. Only 30% of the students on the course are Italians, so most people are in the same boat as you, they are a fish out of water, everyone is in it together. The students are really interesting people; they all have international backgrounds and are all fascinating and ambitious. Everyone has a lot of get-up-and-go.'

*Bocconi University (www.unibocconi.eu) is a private research university of international standing in business, economics and law.*

# Hotel Management School Maastricht: Profile

Since its foundation in 1950, Hotel Management School Maastricht (HMSM) has acquired an excellent reputation, both in the Netherlands and abroad.

HMSM trains its students to be a manager or entrepreneur in the hospitality industry. Our four-year programme consists of varied theory and practical modules, two internships and the opportunity to take part in an international exchange programme. Our impressive facilities are housed in and around the medieval castle, Château Bethlehem. This teaching hotel provides you with a unique learning environment.

Maastricht is an historic city on the River Maas, where you can shop to your heart's content, have fun in the student cafés, enjoy good food and an abundance of culture.

If you intend to follow up on your study after graduating from HMSM, you do not have to leave this beautiful city. You may choose an International Business programme at Maastricht University, or one of several master's degree programmes such as a European Master's degree in Innovative Hospitality Management or a one-year MBA in Hotel and Tourism Management.

Typically, 80% of graduates from HMSM will find employment immediately upon graduation. Graduates from HMSM are able to work all over the world, in management and consultancy functions.

Would you like to study hospitality management in an inspiring, international environment with a focus on innovation? Do you want to learn the ropes from experienced professionals? Then visit one of our open days (www.hotelschoolmaastricht.nl/opendays) or go to www.hotelschoolmaastricht.nl/application for more information.

# Rotterdam Business School: Profile

Rotterdam Business School is an expert in international business and management study programmes. Founded in 1990, Rotterdam Business School has been part of Rotterdam University, University of Applied Sciences since 2002.

## Practical Experience

Education at Rotterdam Business School includes a mixture of knowledge accumulation, practical experience and personal development. All of our bachelor's programmes include periods of work experience and study or placement abroad. Periods of practical training are also incorporated into our master's programmes. This allows students to gain both experience in their field and a taste of international business even before they graduate.

Our English-taught bachelor's programmes include:

- International Business and Management Studies
- International Business and Languages
- Trade Management for Asia.

We also offer four English-taught master's programmes:

- Master in Consultancy and Entrepreneurship
- Master in Logistics Management
- Master in Finance and Accounting
- Executive MBA (part-time).

## Rotterdam

The dynamic harbour city of Rotterdam offers the perfect location to embark on an international study career. Home to the largest port in Europe, Rotterdam has global trade and transport links. A major factor of our success is staying closely attuned to the pulse of the city. We also have a vast international network of partner universities and corporate relations.

Both Rotterdam Airport (20 minutes away) and Schiphol Airport (45 minutes away) are within easy reach. There are also many options for train, bus, and ferry travel between Rotterdam and the UK.

For more information about our programmes and practical information about tuition fees and housing, please contact our Global Recruitment and Student Support team (GR&SS):

Tel: +31 (0)10 794 62 50
Email: rbs@hr.nl
Web: www.rotterdambusinessschool.nl

## Rotterdam Business School: Case study

Tim Dixon, aged 22, from Yorkshire, England is a student in the Master in Finance and Accounting programme at Rotterdam Business School.

### Why Rotterdam Business School?

While studying in England I was able to go on an Erasmus exchange to Rotterdam Business School (RBS). While at RBS I achieved good results and was challenged to perform to the best of my abilities. This was mainly due to the engaging and creative teachers. It was only natural that after such a good experience I wanted to see how else RBS could challenge me at Masters level.

### Why did you choose the Master in Finance and Accounting?

While studying at undergraduate level I found accountancy and finance to be one of the most interesting fields in business specialisation. I have been surrounded by finance and accounting my whole life due to my parents' professions, so it was a natural progression of my interests to do a master in the subject.

### What do you like about studying at Rotterdam Business School?

I like studying at RBS for numerous reasons: great teaching staff, the international classroom and studying environment. I also find the varied testing and examination methods to be a well-balanced combination of tests, essays and group work.

### How do you like Rotterdam?

Rotterdam, while being a huge port city, is able to find that balance of business and pleasure; this makes it a very liveable city. The city also has a huge amount of public space, big lakes and parks. I find myself drawn to these places at the weekend to unwind.

## Do you go back to the UK often?

I go back a few times a year for family events. It's very easy to do due to the ferry port and airports nearby.

# University College Roosevelt: Profile

University College Roosevelt (UCR) is a small-scale international liberal arts and sciences college based in Middelburg in the south-west of the Netherlands. After three years of full-time studies, students receive their Bachelor of Arts (BA) or Bachelor of Science (BSc) degree from the renowned Utrecht University.

Among the special characteristics of UCR are:

- English as the official language, both in class and on campus at large
- small-scale classes (with no more than 25 students)
- highly interactive and intensive method of instruction
- residential college with inner-city campus
- international staff and faculty.

UCR's tight-knit academic community provides an environment that encourages intellectual exchange between students and professors in a friendly and informal atmosphere. The educational philosophy is based on the idea that a student benefits most from learning more about a variety of disciplines. This means that UCR students put together their own programmes with classes offered in the four departments: academic core, arts and humanities, social sciences, and science.

Classes offered range from a wide variety of disciplines, including anthropology, antiquity, chemistry, economics, French, German, geography, history, international law, life sciences, linguistics, mathematics, music and drama, philosophy, physics, political science, psychology, rhetoric, sociology, Spanish, and many more.

The tuition fee at UCR is set by the Dutch government each year. For the year 2013–2014, students pay €2,585 in tuition fees (about £1,700). A full year of studying and living at UCR is estimated to cost €10,000 (about £8,500).

For more information, see www.ucr.nl.

# Chapter 2
# What you need to know before you go

It is normal to have concerns and to feel some anxiety about whether studying abroad is the right step for you. As we have already seen in Chapter 1, common worries concern the cost of fees and access to finance; the prospect of leaving family and friends; concerns about getting a visa; whether your qualifications will be recognised when you return home; and fear of adjusting to another country, culture or language.

This chapter aims to put your mind at rest by addressing some of the questions you may have about making the move overseas.

## Education

Don't assume that education overseas will be just like that in the UK. There are lots of questions to be asked. When does the academic year start? How long do bachelor's degrees take? How do I know if my university is genuine?

### Length of study and academic year

When you start to look at the options for overseas study, it is important to understand that many countries operate a four-year bachelor's degree and a two-year master's degree. When comparing the academic experience and the cost of fees and living, an extra year can make a big difference.

Other countries may also have differences in when their academic year begins and when you can join a course. Many European universities start in early September. Some universities offer more than one start date during the year, which can save you having to wait a full year for the next intake.

## Differences in teaching and learning

Education systems vary across the world, so you will encounter some differences when you study in another country. University in the UK requires independent study and critical thinking. In some countries (although less so in Europe and the western world) university education can be more tutor-led, following set texts. You need to know how education works in your chosen country (and institution, see Different types of institution on page 39) and how you will be taught and assessed. If you study in a country where every course is assessed by means of an exam, you need to be able to cope under exam pressure. Before you apply, you should check whether the style of education suits your style of learning. Finding out what to expect will help you prepare for any differences when you arrive. Your university will be able to tell you more.

> **"** The groups are small and you are expected to contribute, so if you don't know your stuff, it shows. It is hard to get a high grade in essays as the standards are high. However, it does mean that if you work really hard, you reap the benefits and it motivates you to do better. **"**
>
> *Teresa Perez, University of Cape Town, South Africa*

> ❝ The teaching differs hugely, the emphasis is on rote learning, a lot of information may be covered in a lesson and you are expected to put in several hours outside class time to learn and memorise what is covered in class. ❞
>
> *Lewis McCarthy, Shanghai Jiao Tong University, China*

To prepare yourself and improve your chances of success, find out as much as you can about what to expect. Read through the course information and make a start on any recommended reading before you get there. See the chapters on 'Studying in . . .' for more details.

## Different types of institution

Having local knowledge can be reassuring; in the UK, you may already understand which universities are considered to be the best, which have strong vocational backgrounds or which are seen to be weaker. It is much more difficult to make these comparisons on an international scale and where the education system is unfamiliar.

As you research your chosen countries, find out about the different types of institution and how they differ. In Finland, and in a number of other European countries, universities offer research-based education, while universities of applied science offer work-related education. In the USA, you can choose between university and community college. Reputation (but also cost and competitiveness) of the different types of institution may vary.

Although there are only a handful of private institutions with UK degree-awarding powers, it is a different case overseas. The USA has many private providers, and there are plenty to be found across the rest of the world too. Private universities offer a variety of different features; they tend to have higher fees, but often offer more generous scholarships and financial aid. They may offer a more supported or bespoke service, with accelerated programmes, low student–teacher ratio and personalised tuition and internships. Don't rule private universities out on a cost basis alone; in some cases they might end up the better-value option, because of the financial support available and the opportunities to choose a tailor-made education.

## University rankings

If you are seeking out a particular type of institution, you might like to compare potential overseas universities to those that you are familiar with in the UK. Use worldwide university rankings to get an idea of how your chosen institutions fare on the world stage and how they compare to institutions that you know from the UK. Look at which international universities choose to work in partnership with a familiar university back home; it is likely that partner institutions will share some characteristics.

Here in the UK, the national league tables are familiar, but you might not know so much about worldwide rankings. Pay attention to worldwide league tables (Times Higher Education World University Rankings, QS Top Universities, and Academic Ranking of World Universities, for example) to check out how your chosen UK university measures up to the global competition. Although British universities are well-perceived, only a handful of them regularly appear at the top of the world rankings. Many universities that we might not recognise as household names are beating UK universities hands down, for example, the National University of Singapore, University of Wisconsin-Madison and University of British Columbia are all rated more highly than University of Edinburgh and LSE in the Times Higher Education World University Rankings 2012–2013.

Try some of the following league tables:

- Times Higher Education World University Rankings
  www.timeshighereducation.co.uk/world-university-rankings
- Academic Ranking of World Universities (ARWU)
  www.arwu.org
- QS Top Universities
  www.topuniversities.com/university-rankings
- *Financial Times* Business School Rankings
  http://rankings.ft.com/businessschoolrankings/rankings

If you are going to use league tables, make sure you don't use them in isolation and that you understand what they are measuring. A league table can't tell you whether a university is the right choice for you. The methods used to rank universities mean that large, research-based, English-speaking universities tend to do best. It is worth noting that many of the universities that don't make it into the top few hundred in the world can still offer you a good-quality education that might suit your needs perfectly.

## UK equivalence

There are two aspects to consider under the equivalence of qualifications. Will your qualifications be accepted by your chosen overseas institution? And, when your studies are over, will a degree from your institution be recognised when you get back to the UK?

The International Baccalaureate and A levels tend to be well-recognised overseas and often meet the entry requirements of international universities. In some cases, they exceed the requirements. In the USA, for example, you may be able to join an associate degree course at a community college without A levels. You can find out more in Chapter 6, Studying in the USA.

Other qualifications, like Scottish Highers, or vocational qualifications, like BTEC Diplomas, may need to be verified by one of the centres of academic recognition. Overseas universities don't tend to include Highers or vocational qualifications within their published entry criteria, but you shouldn't assume that these qualifications won't be accepted. Each country has its own system of comparing international qualifications to those in the home country. Go to ENIC-NARIC (European Network of Information Centres – National Academic Recognition Information Centres in the EU) at www.enic-naric.net to find out about academic recognition in the country where you wish to study. For countries that are not listed, try their Ministry of Education.

For all of the countries listed within this book, degrees at undergraduate and postgraduate level taken at accredited universities are equivalent to the level offered in the UK; this means that you should be able to use them to access further study or graduate-level employment on your return to the UK. You will need to do further checks to ensure that your qualifications meet any professional requirements. See Professional recognition on page 43 for more explanation.

Although an honours degree is the norm in England, Wales and Northern Ireland, many countries outside the UK don't offer honours degrees as standard; they might offer an ordinary bachelor's degree instead. Where honours degrees are available, they might require additional work and the preparation of a dissertation. You will need to check whether your degree is classed as an honours degree or not, as this may have a bearing on your future plans, particularly for further study.

A number of the students featured in this book have decided to stay on in their chosen country or move to a new country for further study or work. If you decide to do the same, you may also need to check out how your qualification compares to academic standards in your new country of residence. You can do this through one of the national academic recognition information centres (NARIC); for a list of national centres, go to www.enic-naric.net. If your country isn't listed, your overseas university or the Ministry of Education in your chosen country will be able to advise further.

## Professional recognition

If you intend to practise a particular profession on your return to the UK, or intend to take further study to fulfil this aim, it is essential that your qualification is accepted, otherwise you will have wasted precious time and money.

If you know that you want to move into a particular field, you should check with the relevant professional organisations in the country where you hope to practise. So, if you want to be a doctor in the UK, you could check with the General Medical Council, while prospective architects should contact the Architects Registration Board.

The National Contact Point for Professional Qualifications in the UK (UKNCP) (www.ecctis.co.uk/uk%20ncp) aids the mobility of professionals across Europe. If you return to the UK with a professional qualification, UKNCP can advise you on regulations in your profession and outline the steps you will need to take before finding employment. They can also link you to the relevant authorities in other countries across Europe. To find professional bodies outside Europe, you should speak to your overseas university's careers service.

UK-regulated professions and contact details for the professional bodies can be found on the UKNCP website. These bodies should have clear guidelines on acceptable qualifications. Check before you go and then keep checking as you continue your studies. There is a risk that changes may be made to these guidelines while you are midway through your studies; some students have been affected in this way. Should this happen, there can be options for further study to make up any shortfall in knowledge or expertise.

## Quality and reputation

One natural concern for many students is about the quality of the education they will receive overseas. The UK has its own systems for checking quality, but how can you be sure that international universities meet the same stringent standards? When you are making decisions from a distance, how can you be sure that your university even exists, let alone that it is a genuine provider of quality education?

There is money to be made from international students, so you need to be aware of potential scams and of discrepancies between what an institution says it will offer and what it actually delivers. You want to be sure that any money you spend is going towards a good-quality education that will deliver what you expect.

Use www.enic-naric.net to find a list of recognised universities from over 50 countries, as well as information on the various education systems. You can verify that your institution is recognised with education authorities or similar government bodies in your chosen country. Bear in mind that if you need to apply for a visa, there may well be a requirement that you are attending a recognised university. You are safer and better protected within an accredited and recognised university.

Ask your university about how it is inspected or checked for quality. Most countries will have national (or regional) organisations making sure that universities meet required standards. You may be able to read their inspection reports online.

You can find further information on the quality-assurance systems for higher education at www.enic-naric.net.

Using reliable and official websites, such as those included in this book, should help you to find your way to accredited and quality-assured universities. Use common sense when trawling through information and be suspicious of some of the following points:

- a purportedly official website full of errors, adverts or broken links
- an institution offering courses at rock-bottom prices
- if entry requirements are much lower than comparable institutions
- if you are being offered the chance to gain a qualification much more quickly than normal.

## How to apply

Most countries don't have the equivalent of UCAS, a centralised admissions system, so give yourself time to fill out more than one application. You may have to apply on paper, rather than online, so allow time for the application to be delivered (and take copies, in case it gets lost in the post). Pay attention to the closing dates in Chapters 5 to 10, so you don't miss the chance to have your application considered.

Countries operating centralised applications include Denmark, Finland, the Netherlands, Sweden and (for some courses) Germany.

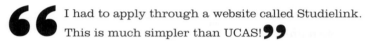

> The university application process was simple, I applied by downloading forms via their website, filled them in and emailed back. Once they had confirmed that they had space on their course, I paid some fees via a bank transfer and that was it!
>
> *Lewis McCarthy, Shanghai Jiao Tong University, China*

> I had to apply through a website called Studielink. This is much simpler than UCAS!
>
> *Rebecca Jackson, Stenden University of Applied Sciences, the Netherlands*

There may be entrance exams and additional tests that you need to sit in order to be considered for a place. These might include the Scholastic Assessment Test (SAT), Graduate Record Exam (GRE) or Graduate Australian Medical Schools Admission Test (GAMSAT). If English is your first language and you will be studying in English, you are unlikely to be tested on your English-language skills. Check with your institution, or see Chapters 5 to 10 for more details. Once a place has been offered, and where fees are payable, you may then need to pay a deposit to secure your place.

## Costs

Fees vary widely and depend on the country where you choose to study; where you are from; the type of institution you are attending; and the level of your course. Finland, Norway and Iceland are the few remaining countries that currently charge no tuition fees to students, either from home or abroad (OECD, Education at a Glance 2012). There are other countries within Europe, for example, Denmark, Sweden and parts of Germany, where you will not be charged tuition fees if you are an EU citizen. Countries like France, Spain and Italy charge low fees.

> 66 Among most EU countries, including Austria, Belgium (Flemish Community), the Czech Republic, Denmark, Estonia, Finland, France, Germany, Ireland, Italy, the Netherlands, the Slovak Republic, Spain, Sweden and the United Kingdom, international students from other EU countries are treated as domestic students with respect to tuition fee charges. This is also true in Ireland, but only if the EU student has lived in Ireland for three out of the five previous years. 99
>
> *(OECD, Education at a Glance 2012)*

You'll need to bear in mind that although, within the EU, EU nationals tend to be treated the same as domestic nationals for fees' purposes, entitlement to student financial support for living costs does not have to be included.

Further afield, some countries, like Japan, Korea and Mexico, tend to charge the same fees for domestic and international students. Most countries will charge higher fees for international students than for domestic students. This list includes Australia, Canada, New Zealand (except on advanced research programmes), the Russian Federation, Turkey and the USA (see Chapter 6 for notable differences in the US system).

Take out an International Student Identity Card (ISIC, www.isic. org) to enjoy student discounts and benefits across the world.

Fees are not the only consideration. Some countries have high fees, but extensive financial-support systems (particularly for those with academic excellence or low-income background). Other countries have high fees but a lower cost of living. Some countries with a generally lower cost of living may still have variations within pricing, perhaps high prices for accommodation, internet access or even alcohol. If you had to pay three or four months' rent to secure accommodation, as you do in some countries, how would it affect your finances? Other costs include visas, travel and costs of application. Consider all these factors when calculating the cost of study and remember that exchange-rate fluctuations can have a great impact on any cost calculations.

## Paying for your studies

One of the challenges for a student choosing to study overseas is how to fund it. The UK system of loans and grants can only be utilised in the UK. Although the terms of UK student loans are no longer as attractive as they once were, they do solve the problem of having to find the money to pay for tuition fees up front.

Any financial support when studying overseas will need to come from:

- financial support from the host country
- scholarships
- savings
- earnings.

In most cases, international students have to fund themselves. Scholarships are often highly competitive. Jobs may be hard to come by, particularly if you don't yet speak the language, and some visas may restrict or deny you the opportunity to work. If you are applying for a visa, you are likely to have to prove that you have the necessary funds; you need to consider how you will fund yourself before you apply. See page 53 for information on visas.

Even if you are staying in the EU, it is recommended to have some money saved. Mark Huntington, of A Star Future, advises young people on overseas study. 'We recommend that even those who plan to work while abroad should have at least a semester's worth of living expenses covered before they go.'

Whilst those living costs and tuition fees might not always be as high as they are in the UK, they still have to be paid for. International students often use a combination of sources to pay for their studies: savings or personal loans, income from work, and scholarships.

## Financial support from the host country

In EU countries, ask the Ministry of Education or your chosen institution about any opportunities for grants or other benefits to students. In the Netherlands and Estonia, for example, there are study allowances and grants that UK students can access. In some countries, fees may include a free or discounted travel pass or free language lessons.

## Scholarships

Scholarships are available, although competition can be fierce. You should apply early, often a year in advance, following all instructions to the letter. Bear in mind that many applicants are unsuccessful in gaining scholarships and, even if you are successful, many scholarships do not cover the full costs of study, so consider how you will cover any shortfall.

The Ministry of Education or embassy should have information about government scholarships, while your institution is the best source of information for local sources of funding. See Chapters 5 to 10 for more information. You can also search for scholarships through websites like www.scholarshipportal.eu, www.hotcoursesabroad.com/study/international-scholarships.html and www.iefa.org.

Other sources of funding include:

- US-UK Fulbright Commission: www.fulbright.org.uk
- Marie Curie scheme (EU doctoral students): www.ukro.ac.uk/mariecurie/Pages/index.aspx
- Commonwealth Scholarships: http://cscuk.dfid.gov.uk/apply/scholarships-uk-citizens
- Erasmus Mundus: www.ec.europa.eu/education/external-relation-programmes/doc72_en.htm
- The Leverhulme Trust: www.leverhulme.ac.uk/funding/funding.cfm
- UK Research Council: www.rcuk.ac.uk

## Charities and trusts

In the UK, a range of charities and trusts offer funding in various amounts. Each has their own eligibility criteria, deadlines and application procedures. You could start with the Educational Grants Services, search at www.family-action.org.uk/section.aspx?id=21211.

If you are looking for postgraduate funding, approach your university, which should have a copy of the Grants Register, a worldwide guide to postgraduate funding. If not, try your local careers service or local library.

The Association of Charitable Foundations (www.acf.org.uk/seekingfunding/index.aspx?id=70) has a useful guide to applying to charitable trusts and foundations.

## Career-development loans

If you are studying overseas because your course is not available closer to home and you intend to return to the UK or EEA to work after your studies, it may be possible to get a career-development loan. Repayments start once you complete your course, regardless of your situation. You can borrow up to £10,000 for up to two years of study, so it would be more appropriate for postgraduate students. For more information, go to www.gov.uk/career-development-loans/overview.

# Life overseas

Whether you will be 100 or 10,000 miles away from home, it is important to know that you will be supported. Finding out the basics before you go can help to ease the adjustment process. Who's going to be there to help you out? What are the essentials you need to know about moving and living overseas?

## Support available

The international office at your chosen university is likely to be your first, and probably your best, source of support throughout the process: from when and how to apply for a visa to finding the cheapest place to buy groceries. They should support you throughout the research and application process and will also be there for you once you arrive.

> **66** I emailed them non-stop with question after question and they always got back to me in a timely manner with lots of information. They told us who we were sharing rooms with and gave us the students' emails so we could make contact before arriving in the US. They arranged orientation and mixers and socials for the new study-abroad students, which was also extremely helpful and made the transition to the US much easier. **99**
>
> *Rosie Hodgart, University of South Carolina, USA*

> **66** The Sociology Department have been absolutely outstanding since I arrived. The Head of Sociology and all the lecturers are friendly, helpful, approachable and efficient. Anytime I have needed help or an extension or any sort of support, all my lecturers have been accommodating. Their doors are always open and they are always happy to talk to me. **99**
>
> *Teresa Perez, University of Cape Town, South Africa*

In addition to the support from your international office and your department, making friends with other students makes settling in a lot easier and also provides a source of much-needed support. Orientation week, welcome week, *nollning* or frosh week activities can be a great place to start meeting new friends. In the UK, we know it as freshers' week, but different countries have their own names and their own traditions.

Your university might offer special activities and events to help you meet students from across the world. Try to take the opportunity to meet domestic students as well as international students; local students will give you a different perspective on life and culture in their home country; they will also have more insight into where to go, where to shop and what not to miss. International friendships are important too and may help to ease your homesickness and culture shock, as you see other people adjusting to their new environment.

> 66 Overall the orientation week was informative and there was plenty of assistance in finishing registration. The department has an amazing student association and there are also plenty of chances to get involved in a wide range of activities and fraternities or sororities. 99
>
> *Clare Higgins, The Hague University of Applied Sciences, the Netherlands*

> 66 There are schemes set up by the university to help adjust to life, such as the buddy scheme and family scheme, as well as various trips and networking evenings. 99
>
> *Warren Mitty, Hong Kong Polytechnic University, Hong Kong*

There will normally be a team of staff to support you at university; this team might include careers advisers, counsellors and welfare officers. Support will vary from country to country and between institutions. If you have a disability, a learning difficulty or any health problems, you should discuss these with your university before you apply, to ensure that they can adequately support you.

## Getting a visa

If you are studying outside Europe, you are likely to need a visa. You can apply for a visa once you have the offer of a place. Use the services of your university to support you through this part of the process; if they recruit lots of international students, they should be experienced at easing people through. They will also understand the reasons why some people are declined, so follow their advice. If you can't get this type of support from your university, you should speak to the embassy or High Commission.

In many cases, visas are declined because of lack of correct evidence or because of insufficient finances; in other cases, if the immigration office doesn't believe that you are a genuine student and that you intend to return home afterwards. Never lie or falsify information on a visa application; if discovered, your application will be declined and future attempts to apply will be affected. Some health conditions (TB, for example) and key criminal convictions (violent offences or drugs charges, for example) can also affect your chances.

Visa applications can be complex, but it is essential to follow each step to the letter, ensuring that you provide all the evidence required.

> ❝ The application was a relatively long-winded process, but the staff in the Chinese visa centre were exceptionally helpful. Even though I had not filled in part of my form, they telephoned me and, with my permission, completed it on my behalf so it didn't need to be sent back to me again. They also processed and mailed the visa and passport back quickly. ❞
>
> *Lewis McCarthy, University of Shanghai Jiao Tong, China*
>
> ❝ To get a study permit I needed a letter from my GP to confirm I had a clean bill of health (£10), a letter referring me to a radiographer (£10), a chest X-ray (£60), a letter from the radiologist confirming that I didn't have TB (£10), Bupa International medical insurance (£150), a letter from Bupa confirming I had medical insurance, three months' payslips, three months' bank statements, a certificate from the police to confirm I had no criminal

convictions (£30), £600 (to pay for your airfare if you get deported, you get this back once you leave the country), £30 processing fee, a letter from UCT offering me a place with key information highlighted, two passport photos and a copy of your passport. I had to take the morning off work to queue up to hand in my paperwork and then again to pick up my passport with my permit in.**99**

*Teresa Perez, University of Cape Town, South Africa*

## Registering within Europe

Although the EU allows its citizens free movement, there may be some red tape to go through when you first move to another European country. In many cases, EU citizens have to register with a local government office. Normally you should do this within the first week or two of arrival. Your university will explain what you need to do.

**66** As Norway is not in the EU, they do have some checks for European citizens; however, these are minimal and it is simply a matter of registering with the relevant government departments when you arrive.**99**

*John Magee, BI Norwegian Business School, Norway*

### *EU countries*

Austria, Belgium, Bulgaria, Republic of Cyprus, Czech Republic, Denmark, Estonia, Finland, France, Germany, Greece, Hungary, Ireland, Italy, Latvia, Lithuania, Luxembourg, Malta, the Netherlands, Poland, Portugal, Romania, Slovakia, Slovenia, Spain, Sweden, UK.

## EEA countries

The EEA is made up of the all the countries in the EU plus Iceland, Liechtenstein and Norway. Although not within the EEA, Switzerland offers some rights to EEA citizens.

## Accommodation

Safe and acceptable accommodation is essential to enable you to settle in and start adjusting to life overseas. The good news is that most universities with international students do their utmost to place them in suitable housing, often giving them priority. To enhance your chances of finding accommodation, remember to:

- apply well in advance
- be realistic about the rent you are prepared to pay
- be flexible about where you are prepared to live.

Most students want good-quality, affordable accommodation in a convenient location; you may find that there is not enough to go round, so it is worth considering what you are prepared to compromise on.

### Types of student accommodation

If you're counting on university-run halls of residence, you may be surprised; some countries don't offer this option for accommodation. Some universities have campus-based halls run by private companies, while others have no accommodation at all. Alternatives on offer include temporary or short-term accommodation, rental property or home-stay with a local host family.

In Helsinki in Finland, for example, one organisation (HOAS) coordinates student accommodation across the city and

surrounding area, dealing with around 10,000 new tenancy
agreements every year. Accommodation through HOAS is available
for several years, often for the duration of your course.

> 66 Try to organise accommodation and move to
> Holland as much as six to eight weeks in advance
> of your course to organise things. The best accommodation
> will be gone if you leave it too late and you will have to pay a
> lot for a sub-standard apartment. 99
>
> *Paul Serjeant, Stenden University of Applied*
> *Sciences, the Netherlands*
>
> 66 Try to get a flat, the residences aren't great.
> Originally I moved into the residences as I thought
> it would be like the UK where everyone goes into halls. I
> moved out after a month. 99
>
> *James Wheeler, Bocconi University, Italy*

## Finding accommodation from the UK

In some university towns there is a shortage of student
accommodation, so some international students, particularly
late applicants, find themselves in the position of leaving the
UK without long-term accommodation. Arranging private
accommodation from a distance can be risky. You shouldn't pay a
deposit to a private landlord for unseen property.

Seek the advice of your university's international or
accommodation office on the safest options when finding
accommodation from the UK. They might discuss reputable short-
term options with you, perhaps bed and breakfast, a local hostel or
home-stay. Home-stay involves living with a local family; it can be
a great way to give you time to adjust and help you to learn about

life in your chosen country, as well as boosting your language skills. Securing short-term accommodation like this should then give you time to find suitable longer-term accommodation when you get there.

### Check what's included

Whichever accommodation option you choose, remember to clarify what will and won't be included in your rent (water, electricity, gas, any kind of local rates, internet) and factor in travel costs; that way you can make a more meaningful comparison between properties. Check whether you will need to buy things like cooking utensils and bedding when you get there.

## Practicalities

As you prepare to make the big move, you're going to need to know about the cheapest ways to phone home; how to open a bank account; how to navigate the area by public transport; the system for paying tax on your earnings; and much more. Talk to your university's international office or check out expat websites like Just Landed, www.justlanded.com. You can also ask questions on online message boards for prospective students, some of which are filled with information about accommodation, buying bikes and so on.

Once you arrive, you can start to use the network of friends that you make. This is where the local students, and those who've already studied there for a while, become invaluable. Most people are more than happy to help.

### Insurance: health and belongings

It is important to make sure that you and your belongings are adequately insured from the time you leave the UK until your return.

If you are studying within the EEA or Switzerland, take out a European Health Insurance Card or EHIC. It is free and easily obtainable, normally arriving within seven days of application. It entitles you to the same treatment as a resident of the host country, but doesn't cover additional costs, like ongoing treatment or returning you to the UK in the event of an accident (www.ehic.org.uk).

You will need to take out additional insurance for travel and health to cover you whilst you are away. A number of UK providers offer study-abroad insurance policies, including Endsleigh (www.endsleigh.co.uk/Travel/Pages/study-abroad-insurance.aspx) and STA Travel (www.statravel.co.uk/study-abroad-travel-insurance.htm). Alternatively, you could take out a policy in your host country. Your international office should be able to advise you further.

There may be vaccinations or preventive measures, like malaria tablets, that you need to take before you travel. Talk to your GP and see the Travel Health pages of the Foreign and Commonwealth Office (www.fco.gov.uk). You may need to demonstrate that you are fit and well in order to gain a visa; this may involve a medical examination.

> The University of Waterloo has a health-insurance policy for all students, unless you opt out of it. Lots of things are covered such as dentist visits and contact lenses. I would definitely investigate the insurance plans your university might have.
>
> *Lauren Aitchison, University of Waterloo, Canada*

> **❝** If you choose to study in Europe, make sure you have a new European Health Insurance Card (EHIC). This allows you to be reimbursed for any medical costs you encounter, such as visiting the doctor or prescribed medicine. **❞**
>
> *Alican Spafford, Rouen Business School, France*

## Personal safety

Although studying abroad is not, in itself, a dangerous activity, visiting different countries carries different risks. The Foreign and Commonwealth Office has useful information for Britons travelling and living overseas, including travel advice by country. Find out about safety and security, health issues, local laws and customs or natural disasters before you go. The Foreign and Commonwealth Office also has a useful travel checklist to follow: see www.fco.gov. uk/en/travel-and-living-abroad/staying-safe/checklist.

Follow the advice of your international office; they have a vested interest in keeping you safe and have an understanding of the risks in the local area. However, you do have to take responsibility for your own safety, much as you would if you were leaving home to study in the UK.

> **❝** Pickpocketing, having food stolen while on a train and witnessing mass brawls have all occurred in the two years I have spent in China. However, providing you are aware of risks and use some common sense you should be fine. On the whole, China is probably the country that I have felt safest in for travelling, living and walking home late at night. **❞**
>
> *Lewis McCarthy, University of Shanghai Jiao Tong, China*

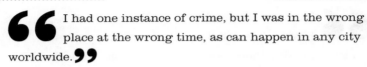

> I had one instance of crime, but I was in the wrong place at the wrong time, as can happen in any city worldwide.
>
> *Will Perkins, University of Cape Town, South Africa*

According to a 2012 British Council survey of students from over 80 countries, some of the safest places to study include Canada, USA, Germany, New Zealand and Singapore.

Top tips for staying safe include the following.

- Get to know your local area.
- Don't flash valuables and cash.
- Drink sensibly.
- Don't take unnecessary risks.
- Stay alert.
- Tell people where you are going.
- Keep in contact.

## Language and cultural issues

However much you prepare yourself and find out about what to expect, there are going to be some adjustments to make when you move abroad. Differences in language, lifestyle, culture and cuisine may bring unexpected challenges.

> 66 I knew a few people who had moments of homesickness, but as a group of international students we were there as support for anyone who felt a bit down. It took time to get used to the culture and really understand South Carolina, but it was by no means a difficult process. 99
>
> *Rosie Hodgart, University of South Carolina, USA*
>
> 66 It can be difficult to find your way around a country when you don't know the language. 99
>
> *Rebecca Jackson, Stenden University of Applied Sciences, the Netherlands*

Culture shock is a common side effect of spending time overseas, away from family, friends and the ease of your own culture. It takes time to adjust and you will need to be open-minded and flexible as you get used to the changes a new country brings.

Your university will provide orientation events to help you to adjust and make new friends. Most universities have a range of support services (student-welfare staff, counsellors, health professionals and so on) to help you if you find the adjustment process particularly challenging. If you look after yourself, by eating well, taking exercise and sleeping well, you will feel in a stronger position to tackle any challenges.

Other tips to help you deal with culture shock include the following.

- Keep in touch with family and friends back home.
- Get involved with familiar activities, like sports or cultural activities you enjoy.

- Display personal items and mementoes to make your room feel homely.
- Make an effort to meet other international students, who may be feeling like you.
- Get to know students from the host country so you can find out about your new home.

# Staying on after study

After spending three or four years in your host country, you may start to wonder whether you want to return to grey old Britain. So which countries offer the most attractive welcome for students who want to stay on? Canada, Australia and New Zealand give extra points in their immigration system to students who have studied at their universities; this can make it easier to apply to stay on for work or even permanently. In many other countries, working-visa and temporary-residence systems have been simplified for international students; you may find that you have the right to stay on and work for a period of time, for example.

Other options that can aid integration include opportunities to learn the local language, work permits and internship opportunities. See the 'Studying in . . .' chapters for more information on staying on after study.

# Returning to the UK

Coming back to the UK after your new experiences is not always as positive as you might anticipate. Reverse culture shock can be an unexpected side effect of spending time away. It can impact on the way you relate to friends and family and affect the way you adjust back to life at home. Try to remember how you managed to adjust to your new life overseas; you may well need to use these same skills to adjust to your return. Don't assume that returning home will be seamless; allow yourself time to come to terms with the changes.

You will need to consider how to highlight the benefits of your experience and how to sell yourself to potential employers (or educational establishments). Think about how you might articulate what you can now offer an employer, what you have learned and the skills you have developed. You can work with your university's careers service to prepare for this long before you leave university. Use their support to search for job vacancies and other schemes for graduates or postgraduates. Make sure that you get hold of references from teaching staff and from employers; it is much easier to do this before you leave.

There will be some loose ends to tie up before you leave, such as giving notice to your landlord, notifying your utilities' suppliers and reclaiming any deposits you have paid. Let your bank know that you are leaving and close your account; this might take a couple of weeks to finalise.

## A break in residency?

If you return to the UK having been overseas for several years, this could be considered to be a break in UK residency, which can prevent you from accessing certain services like education and benefits on your return. However, if your departure is considered to be temporary and if you maintain strong links or a base in the UK, your break may be considered a temporary absence. Advice centres, like Citizens Advice Bureau (www.citizensadvice.org.uk), will be able to advise further, as this can be a complicated subject with legal implications.

## Tax

Whether your absence is considered temporary or not will also affect the tax you will need to pay. If you leave the UK permanently and are not classed as a UK resident, then, on your return, you only pay UK tax on UK income. If you are returning after a temporary period of absence (the more likely scenario if you are only going for the purposes of study), you may have to pay UK tax on some foreign income if you bring it with you to the UK; this doesn't include income from employment but might include income from things like investments. Some countries have treaties preventing the need to pay double tax. This information can be complex and is subject to change, so you should make contact with HM Revenue and Customs at www.hmrc.gov.uk for current information.

You are also likely to be taxed by your host country on any money earned whilst overseas. To find out the rules on tax and whether you should be paying it, talk to your overseas university; they should be able to direct you to any specialist advice you need.

# Support and networking after you leave

If you want to keep in touch with your wider network of friends from university, you could join an alumni organisation. This should also keep you up to date with events and developments. Other university services may still be available to you after you leave, including careers services.

STUDYING ABROAD

## Student story
## Benedict Leigh,
## UCL Qatar, Qatar

It was a specific course and a university's reputation, rather than a desire to explore the world, which led Benedict Leigh to Qatar for his postgraduate studies. 'I developed an interest in Middle Eastern archaeology during my undergraduate studies; this interest was further enhanced by travels in the region. Therefore the chance to specialise in this region, as well as live and learn in it, was an opportunity I didn't want to miss.

'Qatar seemed like an emerging and interesting country to be in, but I came to the country because UCL's campus was located here. It is one of the world's leading institutions in the study of archaeology and offered a programme I was very interested in.'

The application process didn't throw up any difficulties for Benedict. 'It was much the same as applying to UCL in the UK, or to any other UK university. I completed the online application. The admissions team in Qatar were very helpful, friendly and informative and my many discussions with the academic staff at UCL Qatar helped confirm my decision to study there.

'I actually got to meet with UCL Qatar staff in London prior to travelling out to Doha, so I had a good idea from them of what to expect. I received the standard offer letter and information about being considered for funding, followed by a comprehensive welcome booklet which helped out with essential information. I also liaised with different members of staff about accommodation and the visa process.

'My visa was organised by UCL Qatar and was very straightforward, apart from some mandatory health checks and appointments, which all expatriates moving to Qatar must undertake after they arrive in Doha. Support upon arrival was particularly helpful, starting with a "meet and greet" at Doha airport, and followed by lots of induction activities.'

It took a little while to adjust to life overseas, but Benedict has built up a good support network. 'We've got a great group of students out here and we have created a nice community feeling so we help each other out. I haven't had any negative experiences, everything and everyone have been very positive and kind.

'The level of teaching is exceptionally strong, both challenging and very engaging. This high level of engagement and involvement is due in part to the enthusiastic lecturers and also the small class sizes, which allow the staff to personalise the course for each respective student's interest. The facilities are particularly impressive and, once UCL get fully off the ground, will rival any institutions back home.

'I would say, on the whole, the cost of study is cheaper compared to my undergraduate studies, but that is mainly due to my scholarship which covers my academic fees and includes housing. Doha can be fairly expensive for some things, particularly for transport (a car or taxis are necessary), and also because it doesn't really cater for those on a budget. In comparison to London though, the cost of living is lower, so it is certainly manageable.'

## Benedict's top tips

### *Accommodation*
'Accommodation is better than one may be accustomed to in the UK. Ample space and everything one will need to live comfortably are provided.'

### *Living costs*
'Living costs can get fairly expensive, mainly due to high transport costs around the city. And nightlife is very expensive with little attempt to tailor for a younger crowd. But other things can be done very cheaply – for example, the museums are all free and many exhibitions and events are free or cheap. Doha also hosts lots of sporting events that you can get cheap or free tickets for, and as members of Qatar Foundation we get discounts in a number of shops.'

## Student life

'There is a big restaurant scene in Doha, but a limited number of bars and they are all located in hotels. Much of student life when we are not working revolves around cultural events, socialising at the souqs, or going to the beach and malls.'

## Travel

'There is a lot of potential to travel thanks to extended holidays, placement and Qatar's location in the globe. The likes of Dubai, Jordan, Egypt, central Asia, and India are all a short flight away, and there is a decent amount of budget airlines serving the region.'

## Options for after you finish your studies

'As can be imagined on a master's course in archaeology, job possibilities tend to be dominated by academic jobs. But there is a lot of scope in Qatar as it has such a rapidly developing cultural-heritage sector. Numerous museums are opening over the next few years and they will need qualified archaeologists and conservators to work in them.'

Benedict plans to work in multiple different areas including cultural heritage and possibly make the move into international politics.

He feels his experience at UCL Qatar has given him the best of everything. 'I've been able to meet people from a range of different countries, because when you live abroad you inevitably migrate towards people who are outsiders and from different cultures. But also to engage with local people who have lived here for a long time and their ways of living. Also, because I'm at the campus of a London university that retains very strong ties to its home campus, it still feels very familiar. And this is a great part of the world to explore.'

Benedict used websites like Time out Doha (www.timeoutdoha.com) and Marhaba Qatar (www.marhaba.com.qa) to find out more about life in Qatar.

*UCL Qatar (www.ucl.ac.uk/qatar) is a partnership between University College London, Qatar Foundation and Qatar Museums Authority. UCL is the first British university to open a campus in Qatar, offering postgraduate degree programmes in the areas of Archaeology, Conservation, Cultural Heritage and Museum Studies.*

# HZ University of Applied Sciences: Profile

HZ University of Applied Sciences offers a wide range of opportunities and first-class facilities.

## A mere five-hour drive from London

HZ is located on the Dutch coast in the south-west of the Netherlands, just a five-hour drive from London.

## International university

HZ's bachelor's programmes attract students from all over the world. In addition, HZ has an extensive network of partner universities, offering students a wide range of exchange programmes.

## Ranking

Each year, HZ ranks among the top 10 Universities of Applied Sciences in the Netherlands.

## Career-oriented bachelor's programmes

Close contacts are maintained with the professional field by integrating company projects into HZ's bachelor's programmes. Moreover, during the final two years of their study, students gain practical experience by carrying out two work placements of one semester each.

HZ's international programmes are:

- International Business and Management Studies
- International Business and Languages
- Vitality and Tourism Management
- Water Management
- Civil Engineering

- Delta Management
- Chemistry
- International Maintenance Management
- Logistics Management.

## Admission requirements

To be admitted to one of HZ's bachelor's programmes, students must have passed at least two subjects at A level and four subjects at GCSE level. Depending on the chosen bachelor's programme, students may need to meet additional requirements.

For more information, please check: www.hz.nl and www.facebook.com/hzuniversity.

# HZ University of Applied Sciences: Case study

## Callum

'Studying civil engineering at HZ is hard work and challenging, but this makes it very rewarding and fun! The sub-topics that we study include structural engineering, delta, land and water, AutoCAD and GIS alongside others. Of these, my favourite is structural engineering as it comprises mechanical maths and applied physics.'

## HZ in Vlissingen

'Vlissingen is a nicely compact town where everything is easily accessible by bicycle, the beach is lovely and the cosy clubs are great for when the weather is not so good! At HZ it is very easy to talk to the lecturers if you are having problems and you will sort them out quickly. The main focus is on students and that comes through very clearly.'

## VU University Amsterdam: Profile

### VU University Amsterdam: looking further

VU University Amsterdam was founded in 1880. It started with five students and five professors – a huge difference compared to the size of the university today. Nowadays VU University is a leading international university offering a wide range of English-taught programmes at three levels: bachelor's (BA), master's (MA, MSc) and doctoral (PhD). All teaching and research takes place on our urban campus, an environment to study, explore, work, relax and meet up with friends. The campus is located in the Amsterdam Zuidas district, where science and business come together through research and education. Corporate-law students from VU University complete their master's programme at law firms located here in the Zuidas.

VU University has a very diverse student body with some 78 nationalities working and studying closely together, creating a vibrant international academic community. It is the university's belief that an environment filled with people from different backgrounds leads to new insights, focus and innovation. VU University asks and expects our students, researchers and PhD candidates to look further than their own field; to be involved; to look further than the beaten path. This is also reflected in the teaching style which is student-centred and conducted in small tutorials. Interactivity is the norm rather than the exception. In an environment of respect and dedication VU University applies itself to forging links between cultures, religions and societal trends. VU University is an open and transparent organisation strongly linked to people and society.

www.vuamsterdam.com

## HAS University of Applied Sciences: Case study

### Horticulture & Business Management

Liene (22) from Latvia: 'At HAS nobody holds your hand.'

'Living an international life is important to me, so I liked the idea of going abroad for my education to widen my chances of getting an international job. At HAS you get stimulated to be an independent thinker. The project work is really important. Nobody holds your hand, you just go for it. And that stimulates the creative and resourceful mind! All the excursions we get to make trigger your imagination. They make you realise the enormous variety of possible jobs in horticulture, possibilities you would never have thought of yourself. In my course you learn about the biological aspects of growing things but you also learn to look at what you grow as a lucrative product, as something you can put in the market, as a commercial possibility.'

### International Food & Agribusiness

Max (23) from Germany: 'This study programme is the best option out there.'

'The most important thing about HAS is that you are not just a number in the system. The school has a very relaxed atmosphere and I really feel at home here. The main reason for me to choose International Food & Agribusiness is that it's so international and because there is a lot that can be improved in the food industry. What I like most about my study programme is that our lecturers come from all kinds of different backgrounds. Some have worked for the European Union or the United Nations, others for NGOs or the private sector. It's great to learn from their experiences. I can only recommend anybody who is interested in food and sustainability to choose this study programme. I think it's the best option out there.'

# Chapter 3
# Alternative options

If you feel that a full degree overseas is not right for you, you need not necessarily rule out all of the benefits of education outside your home country. Whatever the reasons swaying you against taking a full degree abroad, there may be an alternative choice for you to consider.

## 'I don't feel ready to take my full degree overseas'

Studying for a full degree overseas is a big step, but have you considered taking part of your UK degree course overseas instead? There are a range of schemes offering you the chance to study abroad without always lengthening your degree; some of these choices even bring their own financial benefits.

> **❝** I love to travel and I have always wanted to see the world. I chose my university partly based on whether they offered study abroad or exchange opportunities as I knew that I would like to go abroad for part of my degree. I enjoy experiencing new cultures and going to new places, and studying overseas just makes it convenient. Instead of taking a gap year and travelling, I am getting to travel and study. **❞**
>
> *Angela Minvalla, exchange student at*
> *RMIT University, Australia*

As you research UK universities, look into the types of study-abroad option they offer. Perhaps you like the look of the University of Birmingham's four-year undergraduate Master of Sciences with an international year in North America, Australia or New Zealand; LLB Law with French with a year in Canada through the University of Kent; or maybe a BA in History and Tibetan at the School of Oriental and African Studies (SOAS) with a year abroad. It is important to find out whether your degree course will be lengthened by this experience and which years of study count towards your final degree classification.

More and more UK universities now have overseas campuses offering courses taught in English and mirroring some of the courses available back in the UK. These international campuses are often set up to attract international students, but an added benefit for UK students could be the chance to study for a semester or a year at the international campus. Check out which courses and in which countries you can study this way. University College London (UCL) has campuses in Qatar, Adelaide and Kazakhstan, while Leeds Metropolitan University, University of Strathclyde Business School and Lancaster University all have campuses in India. University of Wolverhampton has a campus in Mauritius, Newcastle University Medical School has an outpost in Malaysia and University of Liverpool has a base in China.

If you prefer the familiarity of a UK university name on your degree certificate, you could always opt for a full degree course at a UK overseas campus. Fees might be the same or a little lower than you'd expect at home, but the costs of living are often considerably less. See the Student story on page 66. In some cases, you might even gain a degree from the UK and from the country you will be studying in.

## What will I pay?

If you are studying overseas for part of your course, you will often continue to pay tuition fees to your university at home, rather than to your overseas university. If you choose to spend a year at certain US universities, for example, this may mean studying at a fraction of the full cost of tuition. If you are studying for a full year overseas, your UK tuition fees should be reduced. The rules vary from country to country, with a maximum of 15% charged in England and up to half fees payable in Wales. Your UK university will be able to tell you more.

> **“** Applying for the exchange was very easy and straightforward; it was all online. The staff at the International Affairs Office were quick and very useful. **”**
>
> *Warren Mitty, Hong Kong Polytechnic*
> *University (exchange), Hong Kong*

You will still be able to access the normal UK system of grants and loans, with a higher overseas rate of loan for living costs available. In some cases, you may be able to apply for a travel grant to assist with the costs of travel, medical insurance, visas and so on. There may be additional bursaries or scholarships which you can apply for. For example, the British Universities Translatlantic Exchange Association (BUTEX) offers awards to students studying in the US or Canada for at least one semester, www.butex.ac.uk.

Find out more from your UK university or from your national organisation for student finance:

- Student Finance England (www.gov.uk/student-finance/ overview)
- Student Awards Agency for Scotland (www.saas.gov.uk)

- Student Finance Wales (www.studentfinancewales.co.uk)
- Student Finance NI (www.studentfinanceni.co.uk).

> **66** As tuition in Scotland is free, the cost of tuition on
> my year abroad was covered by the Scottish
> government. Living costs proved to be far less expensive in
> the south, so the only real expense was the flights (as well as
> all the travelling I did in the US). **99**
> *Rosie Hodgart, University of South Carolina (exchange), USA*

If you are studying outside Europe, you are still likely to need a
visa in the same way as if you were taking your full degree course;
your university will be able to get you started with this process.

With these options, you can gain a degree from a familiar
university along with the benefits of international experience, but
without so many of the risks. You may get some financial support
throughout the process, with the benefit of personal support from
both institutions too. It should be reasonably straightforward to
transfer any credits achieved internationally back to the UK; your
university should have planned for this to happen.

## Erasmus

Through the European Union Erasmus scheme, you have the
opportunity to study in another European country for between
three and twelve months. This is completed as a part of your
course, so counts towards your degree.

You will receive an Erasmus grant to put towards the additional
costs of studying abroad, but you will still be expected to find your
own living costs. For 2012/2013, an Erasmus grant of €270–€370
(£216–£297) per month is available. Additional one-off funding of

€400 (£320) is also on offer in 2012/2013 for those choosing a less-visited country – Bulgaria, Croatia, Cyprus, Czech Republic, Estonia, Greece, Hungary, Latvia, Lithuania, Malta, Poland, Romania, Slovakia, Slovenia and Turkey. If you fall into the category of widening participation, there is an extra €500 (£400) available.

You will not be expected to pay fees to your host university and shouldn't have to pay more than 50% of tuition fees back home. In some cases, if you opt for a full year overseas you won't pay tuition fees at all, although this ruling varies from year to year. Some universities offer additional bursaries to students opting for an Erasmus placement.

For more information, talk to your UK university's study-abroad or international office and go to www.britishcouncil.org/erasmus-about-erasmus.htm.

The Erasmus Mundus scheme allows students to study joint programmes in multiple countries, some outside the EU, at postgraduate level. Scholarships are available. Find out more at Erasmus Mundus, http://eacea.ec.europa.eu/erasmus_mundus/programme/about_erasmus_mundus_en.php.

## English-language assistant

Once you have two years' worth of higher education under your belt, you could consider working as an English-language assistant. These opportunities are normally open to language students in the UK, giving them the chance to work in an overseas school for a year (and get paid).

You should pay reduced tuition fees to your UK institution, or sometimes no fees at all, and may qualify for the overseas rate of maintenance loan. If you choose to stay in the EU, these opportunities can attract Erasmus funding.

This option would lengthen your study by a year, but should give you some valuable experience of education and life overseas. Your university's study-abroad office should be able to tell you more. Third Year Abroad at www.thirdyearabroad.com has lots of useful information.

## Short-term study overseas

Shorter options to study overseas include summer schools and short placements. You could spend a summer learning a language or testing out international education, to see if you are ready to commit to further study abroad. Check out the costs and visa requirements well in advance of making final arrangements.

Opportunities include:

- Study China: a 17-day programme for existing undergraduate or foundation-degree students, www.studychina.org.uk
- INTO China: Chinese language summer programmes, www.intohigher.com/china
- IAESTE: summer placements for full-time HE (Higher Education) science, technology and engineering students, www.iaeste.org
- pre-university summer schools at US universities like Harvard and Stanford, www.fulbright.org.uk
- short-term exchanges in the USA, www.educationusa. info/pages/students/research-short.php#.TotkAHLhdQg.

Talk to staff at the study-abroad office at your university to find out more.

# 'I want to gain a degree from an international university without leaving the UK'

There are a couple of choices if you want to gain an international degree from within the UK: either distance learning; or choosing a UK-based overseas university.

## Distance learning

Online and distance learning is on the increase. With thousands of international universities offering degrees by distance learning, you need not set a foot out of the house to gain an international education. Of course, you will need to be disciplined and focused, and you won't gain the experience of living in another country, but you may end up with a degree from a top university at a fraction of the cost. It is worth noting that not all universities allow you to complete a full degree by distance education; they might offer blended learning, a combination of distance and face-to-face learning.

The benefits of distance learning are affordability, convenience, flexibility, choice and support (from tutors and classmates). On the other hand, you need to be truly disciplined and aware of the fact that you will lose the face-to-face interaction that you would get on campus. It can be more difficult to assess whether distance-learning providers are reliable, without a physical presence to assess them by.

### *How do I know that my distance-learning provider is genuine?*

You need to be even more thorough when researching a distance-learning provider. See page 44 for some questions to ask of potential institutions. Remember, if it sounds too good to be true, it probably is.

There may be some warning signs to look out for when checking out a distance-learning institution's website. If the organisation only provides a PO Box address, if it has a similar name to other well-respected institutions or if you can gain a higher-education qualification purely on the basis of previous experience, you might need to dig a bit deeper to ascertain whether it is genuine and accredited.

You may find it easier to be sure of the provenance of your qualifications from a traditional university that happens to offer distance-learning courses. Many traditional, accredited universities across the world, and as many as 90% in the USA (according to EducationUSA), offer distance-learning provision. If the institution claims to be accredited, double-check this with the accrediting organisation. You can find out more at the Ministry of Education of the country you hope to gain your qualification from. Check out these websites too.

- International Council for Open and Distance Education (ICDE), www.icde.org
- Study Portals (search for a distance-learning course in Europe), www.studyportals.eu
- Distance Education and Training Council (USA), www.detc.org/search_schools.php.

Free online international education is on the increase. Prestigious universities including Harvard and the Massachusetts Institute of Technology (MIT) have set up edX (www.edx.org), while Stanford, Princeton and others have set up Coursera (www.coursera.org). Both offer online and interactive learning and the chance to gain university credits with no entry requirements and currently with no fees.

Although it might be a slow process to achieve all the credits needed for a bachelor's degree, it could give you the chance to experience US-style teaching and check out your interest in particular subjects.

## UK-based overseas universities

Campuses for a number of overseas universities can be found in the UK, most commonly in London. Many of these are American universities, offering US degrees. Although these universities recruit students from all over the world, only a small percentage currently attend from within the UK. This may change, with the fees' hike in parts of the UK now making the fees at these universities appear much more reasonable.

In the case of Richmond, the American International University in London, and American InterContinental University, you can gain a dual degree from the UK and USA, while experiencing an international university and accessing the UK system of loans and grants. With undergraduate fees set at £9,000 for 2012–2013, costs are comparable to most of the top UK universities although, as these are private institutions, your maximum tuition-fee loan will be capped at £6,000.

International universities with a campus in the UK include the following.

- American InterContinental University
  www.aiuniv.edu/London
- Richmond, American International University
  www.richmond.ac.uk
- Schiller University
  www.schiller.edu/campuses/london-england

- Hult International Business School
  www.hult.edu/en/Campuses/London/About-London
- Azad University
  www.auox.org.uk
- Limkokwing University of Technology
  www.limkokwing.net/united_kingdom.

You can find out more about courses, fees and how to apply on their websites.

## Student story
## Rosie Hodgart, University of South Carolina, USA (exchange)

Rosie Hodgart has always had an interest in the US. 'Rather than wanting to study overseas, I always knew I wanted to study in the US specifically and spend a significant amount of time there. I knew that the huge benefits of studying overseas, both educationally and culturally, would change my life forever and decided I had to take a leap of faith. I also wanted a break from my home institution. In Scotland, we do four years of university rather than three and that is far too long to spend in one place.'

Rosie was studying Geography and American Studies at University of Dundee, but an exchange wasn't a compulsory part of her course. 'I had to proactively apply to study abroad in the US. I got the list of my university's exchange partners in the US and sat down and Google-mapped each institution, looking at the university and its location, as well as the university websites, to see which seemed the best fit for me. I chose the University of South Carolina because I was extremely interested in southern culture, and wanted to truly immerse myself in it. I also wanted the big-college experience with football teams, big societies etc. that is so often portrayed in films and popular culture, and it seemed the south was the place to go for that.

'As tuition in Scotland is free, the cost of tuition on my year abroad was covered by the Scottish government. Living costs proved to be far less expensive in the south, so the only real expense was the flights (as well as all the travelling I did in the US).

'Applying for a visa was a tricky process, made harder by the fact I received little support from the international office at my home university. There was a lot of paperwork, payments to make, things to send off, so it was hard to keep track. I'd heard a lot of horror stories about the visa interview as well. Although the interview itself was quick and easy, I had to wait for three to four hours before being seen. I would advise students to bring a book.

'I received plenty of support from the University of South Carolina. I emailed them non-stop with question after question and they always got back to me in a timely manner with lots of information. They told us who we were sharing rooms with and gave us the students' emails so we could make contact before arriving in the US. This was great and made me far less nervous about moving in with strangers. They arranged orientation and mixers and socials for the new study-abroad students, which was also extremely helpful and made the transition to the US much easier.

'Once I got there, I was too busy to feel homesick at any point. I knew a few people who had moments of homesickness, but as a group of international students we were there as support for anyone who felt a bit down. It took time to get used to the culture and really understand South Carolina, but it was by no means a difficult process.'

Rosie encountered some big differences in the US education system. 'The Liberal Arts system allows for a unique understanding of a breadth of courses. Rather than just Geography and American Studies courses, I was allowed to choose from any courses related to these fields. I took classes in African American Psychology, South Carolina History, Sociology, Anthropology, Geography of the Middle East etc. I looked forward to attending class each day and learned so much in my one year in the States.

'Teaching also differs hugely. Rather than the UK system focused on independent study and big final exams and essays, there was much more class-based learning, class interaction and frequent small tests and essays. It was also possible to complete extra credit assignments to boost your grade and, in some classes, attendance even counted as part of the grade.'

## Rosie's top tips

### Accommodation

'Find out if the accommodation of the university you're applying to will be shared rooms. I had to share a room with another girl which seemed extremely daunting but turned out to be great. We luckily got on very well and still keep in touch. Also be aware of whether your accommodation is catered or self-catered. The meal plans can be extremely expensive with not very nice food.'

## Food

'Be aware of regional differences in food. The south had fantastic cuisine but few organic or fresh-produce stores; mainly just massive Wal-Marts outside of the town. Make sure you try your state's famous dishes. While in the south, I sampled everything southern cuisine has to offer, from grits to gumbo.'

## Living costs

'Living costs were extremely cheap. Accommodation was cheaper for me in the US than it was in Dundee, and day-to-day costs of food, drink and meals out were cheaper. There were also many perks in going to a big college in the US, as students pay so much to go there. We had a free cinema with free popcorn every Monday night showing the latest releases; the gym (and outdoor pool) was completely free; free football tickets to the Gamecocks' matches; and free student tickets to big events like R'n'B artist, Usher, performing at the university's stadium.'

## Finding out about the USA

'I found the best sources of information to be the US-UK Fulbright website (www.fulbright.org.uk), individual university websites, Wikipedia for information on the specific town or region, and independent blogs and forums.'

## Working while studying

'I thought I might get a job second semester on campus to help support myself but I didn't have time. I travelled so frequently and was making the most of my time there that working seemed to be the furthest thing from my mind. I knew one or two people who did and it is a great way to meet more American students and earn some extra cash but make sure it doesn't hold you back from making the most of your time abroad. And don't take a job without considering how busy you will be.'

## Lifestyle and culture

'There was definitely a period of culture shock for me on arrival. The south is perhaps the least European place in the US – the politics and culture of the whole region was eye-opening. It's important to keep that in mind when choosing a university, especially in America. Each state is so different, with such different cultural beliefs. My area of study at my home university focused primarily on the US south, so I had some knowledge on what I was getting myself into, and I was eager to learn more about that region. Also for me, I wanted a place entirely different from the UK, where I could learn a whole new way of life, so it was the best decision I made.'

## *Travel*

'I travelled a lot during my year abroad. I had originally planned to go home over the Christmas holiday but had to cancel my flight and travelled with friends. Also every few weekends we would go to a different town in South Carolina or a neighbouring state. I managed to see most of the south and east coast all the way up to Pennsylvania and New York State. We also jumped on a flight over to California for a long weekend. I would recommend travelling as much as possible. Make sure you save up before going abroad so you have the opportunity to do so. Internal travel in the US is fairly cheap, especially if you book in advance, and I'd recommend having a British driving licence before going abroad, so you're able to rent cars and travel (if you're bold enough to try it on the wrong side of the road).'

Rosie's time in the US was life-changing. 'My year abroad has formed the direction I have chosen my career to take. I am so passionate about US–UK relations and educational exchange that, since returning to the UK, I have had many jobs in this field. I worked with the US-UK Fulbright Commission, then as Internship Coordinator for a company that places US students in London for internships, and I am about to begin my new role as Educational Advisor, again with Fulbright. However, if your area of interest does not lie in promoting educational exchange, your year abroad will still be extremely beneficial to any direction your career will take. It sets you apart from the crowd and will encourage employers to pick your CV out of a pile. It has provided me with a number of great opportunities that simply would not have been available to me if I had stayed in the UK. My own experience as a recent graduate has shown me that it really is difficult to get a job out of university. It is essential to have something like a year abroad to stand out and help you when you finish your studies.

'If I had not gone abroad I may have never had the confidence to move away from home so easily, or fallen into such a fantastic job. Living and studying in a completely different culture, the ability to travel within the country you're studying in, it really does change your outlook on your own life; it helped me figure out what I wanted to do for my future career.'

*University of South Carolina (www.sc.edu) is a public research university which was founded in 1801.*

# HKU: Utrecht School of the Arts: Profile

## The art of HKU: Utrecht School of the Arts (NL)

The City of Utrecht is the fourth-largest city in the Netherlands. HKU: Utrecht School of the Arts is at the heart of Utrecht's cultural and student life. With over 4,000 students, HKU is one of the largest schools of art in Europe. HKU offers bachelor's and master's programmes and research degrees in fine art, design, media, games and interaction, music, theatre and arts management.

Courage is something HKU appreciates and fosters – the courage to keep a critical eye on the content and boundaries of your own work. What HKU asks of the students is an explorative attitude, an enterprising spirit and the will to pursue their individual passion. HKU offers you the chance to discover and develop your talent.

As an HKU student, you are given the opportunity during your course to work on projects for customers in the marketplace. These may be commercial companies, non-profit organisations or cultural initiatives. That way, you learn hands-on where your strengths lie and what you can offer the world as a designer, lecturer, producer or performer. HKU produces creative professionals and entrepreneurs with initiative who know where their chances lie, both nationally and internationally. HKU works with renowned art and cultural educational institutions all over the world, so you have a wide choice of opportunities for exploring international developments in your discipline.

It's important for you to learn to present your work in a professional setting. HKU has its own Academy Theatre, concert halls and an Academy Gallery in Utrecht's city centre. Experimenting in presenting your work in these venues during your course gives you the opportunity to evolve yourself into a professional.

## University of Groningen: Profile

Founded in 1614, the University of Groningen is a leading international research university and academic community for those with a passion for knowledge. We offer over 100 English-taught degree programmes (bachelor's, master's and PhD) in virtually every field. Located in the north of the Netherlands, we utilise our rich academic history and heritage to generate innovation.

### Facts and figures

- 28,000 students
- 3,800 international students
- 89th in Times Higher Education Rankings
- 81st in *NY Times* Ranking 'What the Job Market Wants'
- 19 English-taught undergraduate degrees
- Over 90 English-taught postgraduate degrees
  - o  15 double degrees
  - o  Eight prestigious Erasmus Mundus degrees.

*Create your own information package: www.rug.nl/internationalmagazine*

### Facilities

Honours College (HC) will give talented, motivated students the chance to be challenged even more by following Honours programmes. www.rug.nl/honours

The University Library (UB) consists of one central library and seven faculty/institute libraries at various locations in Groningen, www.rug.nl/bibliotheek

NEXT – It is important to assess your employability, especially when you are about to graduate. NEXT offers courses, office hours, and workshops, www.rug.nl/next

Student Service Centre (SSC) is the student-counselling centre of the university. Our student counsellors, psychologists and trainers work together to provide an integrated package of student support, www.rug.nl/ssc

Language Centre (TC) offers a variety of language courses of different levels for staff and students of the university. As a gesture, the university will finance the basic Dutch language course, www.rug.nl/languagecentre

## Student life

As the economic and cultural capital of the region, Groningen city enjoys a bustling reputation, while retaining a safe community character. What will probably strike you most when entering Groningen is its youthful population (over half is under 35 years of age!).

- 200,000 inhabitants
- 50,000 students
- Best city of the Netherlands 2010
- Best student city of the Netherlands 2006.

www.groningenlife.eu

## Tilburg University: Profile

Understanding Society

## Tilburg University: Understanding society

### Tilburg University in a nutshell

- Founded in 1927
- Located in the Netherlands
- 13,579 students
- 1,209 international students from 85 countries
- 40 bachelor's and master's degree programmes taught entirely in English.

Choosing Tilburg University means choosing to study at one of Europe's most respected institutions. We are a specialised research university concentrating on economics, business, law, social sciences, psychology, communication and information sciences, theology and humanities.

At Tilburg University, we want to inspire you to reach your full potential and, in doing so, have a positive impact on the society around you. Our educational programmes instil a broad social awareness along with critical personal and professional skills. Being a student at Tilburg University means becoming more aware of the issues facing our rapidly globalising world and how you can contribute to the development of a fairer and more sustainable society.

Our research work aims to advance the frontiers of knowledge on issues and subjects that are of direct value to society – and are actively disseminated and applied within the community with this objective in mind.

Tilburg University has a rich student life with over 40 student organisations, a compact campus near the woods, excellent sports facilities and a large number of pubs. On a cultural level, Tilburg has cinemas, museums and concert halls. Combined with the events organised by and within the (student) community such as festivals, exhibitions and conferences, this ensures that Tilburg has something to offer everyone!

## Services for international students

- Housing support (first come, first served)
- Visa and immigration services
- Academic advisers and student counsellors
- Tilburg orientation programme for new international students
- Social integration activities
- Outstanding ICT facilities
- Free language courses (worth 12 ECTS)
- Conveniently located for public transport and air travel.

## Tilburg University: Case study

### Pawel Bespalov from the Ukraine is studying International Business Law:

'The university provides a good atmosphere for interaction between students and professors and creates an encouraging educational environment. Without doubt, being part of a truly international environment broadens your horizon. Seeing different views of people on various issues indeed develops out-of-the-box thinking.'

### Usama Tariq from Pakistan is studying International Business Administration:

'The university offers every possible facility to aid your study. The teachers are helpful and provide all the possible resources required. For guidance, classmates have always been very helpful.'

### Denitsa Encheva from Bulgaria is studying Human Resource Studies:

'For me it was very different from the experience I had in my previous university, mainly because of the constant group work, interactive lectures and new ways of teaching and learning that are used.'

### Anna Zmacinskaja from Germany is studying Strategic Management:

'I think it is great that the university organises an introduction week. This provides students with the opportunity to get to know the city and each other before the semester starts. Furthermore, I think it's great that there are academic advisers who help you throughout your studies with any kind of questions regarding your programme.'

## Meimei Dai from China is studying Economics:

'When I arrived in Tilburg, I was impressed by the green environment in and outside the university. There is a forest as a backyard! The study facilities are impressive.'

## Kalin Uzhdrin from Bulgaria is studying Social Psychology:

'I made amazing friends from all over the world. The city and the university have a lot to offer: week-long events like the Carnival or the Kermis, short trips with friends, extra-curricular training and, thanks to the many student organisations, a lot of parties and bonding activities.'

# Chapter 4

# Researching your options

There are so many questions to ask about yourself, your chosen country and your chosen university before you even apply. In the early stages, it is even hard to know what those questions should be. If you thought that narrowing down your UCAS choices to five was tricky, imagine choosing from the whole world. If that all sounds like too much hard work, consider that somewhere out there may be the perfect course for you at the perfect price; it's got to be worth a little bit of work to find it.

## Getting started

With almost the whole world to choose from, the first step should be to research the countries that you are interested in. The chapters on studying in various countries will give you an overview of the different education systems, costs and financial support, how to apply and the visa system. Each chapter will also feature the most useful and reliable websites where you can find out more. This should help you start to compare what is on offer and how it fits in with your plans.

# Where to study

This book focuses on opportunities taught in English, so the
Republic of Ireland, USA, Canada, Australia and New Zealand
are likely to have the largest choice of courses. Many other
Commonwealth countries use English, including Singapore,
Malaysia and certain Caribbean, Pacific and African nations. Find
out more at the Association of Commonwealth Universities, www.
acu.ac.uk.

Universities in many overseas countries are now actively starting
to recruit UK students in a way that was unheard of only five
years ago. Events like The Student World Fair feature university
exhibitors from all over the world, as far apart as Malaysia,
Grenada and Canada, all keen to attract UK students. You might
have seen the news stories about universities in the Netherlands,
in particular, and the increase in applications from UK students.
Although the introduction of courses taught in English was
originally aimed at international students from other countries,
many UK students are now starting to take advantage. Some
universities overseas have even started to teach all their courses in
English.

In a number of countries where English isn't widely spoken, the
government or the institutions are keen to recruit international
students so offer a high proportion of courses taught in English.
These countries include:

- the Netherlands
- Denmark
- Sweden
- Finland.

According to the OECD's Education at a Glance 2012, there will be some courses taught in English available in countries such as:

- Belgium (Flemish)
- the Czech Republic
- France
- Germany
- Hungary
- Iceland
- Japan
- Korea
- Norway
- Poland
- Portugal
- the Slovak Republic
- Switzerland
- Turkey.

The OECD tells us that very few programmes are taught in English in:

- Austria
- Belgium (French)
- Brazil
- Chile
- Greece
- Israel
- Italy
- Luxembourg
- Mexico
- the Russian Federation
- Spain.

However, it is worth noting that even these countries will feature private or international universities with a curriculum in English. Others may well be moving towards recruiting more international students, so watch this space.

# How to choose

Many people choose a country for emotional, rather than practical, reasons. Maybe you have always longed to spend time in a particular country or you've fallen in love with a place that you've visited. Perhaps your family or friends have links with an area of the world or you have a boyfriend or girlfriend who lives overseas.

In other cases, the decisions are much more measured and logical. Some have a particular type of course in mind and their decision is driven by the availability of that course. Others have a set of requirements, in terms of prestige, entry requirements or world university rankings.

Others don't even choose a specific country, but make a shortlist of institutions that meet their particular criteria. John Magee, now studying in Norway, took a very structured approach to his search for opportunities across Europe.

> **❝** Firstly, the schools had to be ranked on the *Financial Times* European Business School Rankings, so they were internationally recognisable to future employers. Secondly, the schools had to offer my desired degree, an MSc in International Business/ International Management. Thirdly, a more selfish criterion of being situated in a mountainous country that offered easy access to alpine activities. Lastly, it was preferable if the

> course offered an exchange semester, to help me secure the
> maximum amount of international experience. **99**
>
> *John Magee, BI Norwegian Business School, Norway*

In many cases, access to student financial support or scholarships
is a deciding factor.

> **66** As UK tuition fees were one of the big reasons that
> led to my decision to study abroad, I spent a lot of
> time comparing the costs of studying. My course in France is
> usually just over £6,000 a year, but I was able to win an
> academic scholarship that will reduce my fees by €1,000
> (£803) a year. Compared with the UK, I am already saving
> £12,000 over my four-year degree, which is a huge saving. **99**
>
> *Alican Spafford, Rouen Business School, France*

It is also worth considering the cost of living, how welcoming
the country is to international students (for example, how easy
it will be to get a visa and whether there are opportunities to
gain employment afterwards) and how well your degree will be
recognised when you return to the UK.

Essentially, you need to determine what matters to you and what
your priorities are. Consider some of the following factors and
weigh up how important each one is to you:

- subject availability
- length of study
- professional recognition of qualifications
- university ranking

- type of institution
- size of university
- style of teaching and assessment
- specialist options (for example, internships or specialist subjects available)
- drop-out rates
- pass rates
- destinations of ex-students
- cost of tuition fees
- cost of living
- availability of loans or grants
- availability of scholarships
- opportunities to stay on and work after completion of studies
- interest in specific countries
- opportunity to learn particular languages
- lifestyle factors
- distance from home.

## What type of university will suit you best?

Whether you see yourself as an academic aiming for postgraduate study or you want a route straight to work, you'll find a university to suit you. Many countries have polytechnics, community colleges or Universities of Applied Sciences where you'll be taught with a more vocational, work-related focus; these institutions share some characteristics with the post-1992 universities in the UK. If you are looking for a more traditional style of teaching from lecturers with a research background, try a research-based or research-intensive university. Make sure that you always find out what type of university you are applying to; it could have a big impact on what you get out of your university experience and which doors will be open to you when you finish.

Carefully considering what matters to you, much as John Magee
did, helps to focus on the essential and desirable criteria. A final
list of criteria might look something like the following.

- Essential: a city-centre, research-based university in the
  Times Higher Education Top 200, offering low cost of
  living and the possibility of a scholarship.
- Desirable: flight time of less than eight hours,
  opportunity to stay on and work.

What we describe as a course in the UK might be called a
programme or program in some countries, with course used
to refer to the modules you study as part of your degree.

## Researching the options

There is no wrong or right way to choose where you want to spend
the next few years. Just make sure that you discover the realities
of life there, not just the pictures from the glossy brochure. It
is not unusual to see universities overstating their position to
international students, so make sure that you look for a secondary
source of evidence (particularly if a university is telling you that
they are among the best in the world).

Just as in the UK, courses with the same title may be really diverse.
You should ask about course content, course structure, how you
will be assessed and so on. You might find that the course you
are looking for doesn't exist in your chosen country; there are
limited history or English literature courses taught in English
in continental Europe, for example. Courses where your learning
relates specifically to practice in a particular country don't always
travel well so they might not be available: social work or teaching,

for example. Titles may vary from country to country; whereas UK university courses often have quite broad academic titles like biology or mechanical engineering, vocational universities in other countries might use titles that are more specific and job-related. Look out for courses in econometrics, interaction design or human ageing.

Ask the universities about additional factors, such as the ratio of students to lecturers, drop-out rates, student-success rates, library services and internet access. If you have the opportunity to visit a country or campus, take it. This can be a great chance to find out more, meet the staff and ask questions. Many students talk about the feeling they get from being on a particular campus and it is hard to 'virtually' recreate this if you have very little contact with the university before making your choices.

There are other ways of finding out more. If a visit isn't possible (and let's face it, it often isn't), try visiting recruitment events in the UK. There are a number of big events that take place in the UK: the Student World Fair, USA College Day, QS World Grad School Tour, Hot Courses Global Student Fair and the Study Options Expo. At these events, you can meet representatives from universities who are actively seeking UK students. To make best use of these events, find out the exhibitors beforehand, highlight whom you want to speak to and take your list of essential questions to ask. Note down or record any responses you get, so you can consider them later.

Don't want to restrict yourself to just one country? There are a number of options where you can study in two, three or even four different countries and even gain more than one degree. Take a look at SKEMA's EAI Bachelor (www.skema.edu/international/eai-transfers) or SP Jain's Bachelor of Business Administration (www.spjain.org/BBA), for example.

## Online research

Most of the countries interested in attracting international students have their own official websites; you can find these in the 'Studying in . . .' chapters. The UK Council for International Student Affairs (UKCISA) has a list of recognised sources of information at www.ukcisa.org.uk/ukstudent/country_contacts. php. For information on European opportunities, start at www. ec.europa.eu/education/study-in-europe.

All universities looking to attract international students will have their own websites with English content. Many universities have a number of other ways to engage with their potential students via social media like Facebook, Twitter or YouTube, where you can search directly for the universities you are interested in.

Following some key organisations on Facebook or Twitter when you start your research helps to keep you up to date with new developments, events and key deadline dates. You can also attend virtual student fairs (Hobsons Virtual Student Fairs at www. hobsonsevents.com, for example) and web chats from the comfort of your own home. Other websites, like the Student Room (www. thestudentroom.co.uk), have discussions on international study. Bear in mind that information from chat rooms can be useful, but isn't always correct, so you need to double-check any facts you get from sources like this.

# Course search

The 'Studying in . . .' chapters include some of the best websites to search for courses and institutions in a specific country. If you want to search for courses before you decide on a country, try websites like Study Portals (www.studyportals.eu), EUNICAS (www. eunicas.co.uk), A Star Future (www.astarfuture.co.uk/what_to_ study.html) or Hot Courses Abroad (www.hotcoursesabroad.com).

Is the website you need opening up in another language? Look out for the Union flag or the letters EN to select the English version. If not, try a translation website like Google Translate, www.translate.google.com.

## Companies to like on Facebook

- EducationUSA
- US-UK Fulbright Commission
- The Student World
- A Star Future for Brits Studying Abroad
- Dutch Degrees
- Study in Holland
- Maastricht Students
- Study Options
- CUCAS-Study in China
- CampusFrance Paris
- New Zealand Educated
- Study in Finland
- Study in Australia
- Study in Estonia
- Study in the Czech Republic
- Study in Germany
- Study in Sweden
- Study in Norway
- Study in Denmark
- INTO China
- EUNICAS
- Hotcourses Abroad.

## Companies to follow on Twitter

- @CUCAS_CHINA
- @TheStudentWorld

- @astarfuture
- @StudyingAbroad
- @CampusFrance
- @StudyInHolland
- @StudyinNorway
- @StudyinSweden
- @EdUSAupdates
- @USUKFulbright
- @studyinde
- @EduIreland
- @StudyinDenmark
- @nzeducated
- @FutureUnlimited
- @studyinestonia
- @INTO_CHINA.

There are some great blogs and diaries out there too. Take a look at some of these:

- Third Year Abroad, The Mole Diaries: www.thirdyearabroad. com/before-you-go/the-mole-diaries.html
- Textbooks and Passports: www.textbooksandpassports.com
- Samuel Knight in Groningen: www.samstudyingabroad. tumblr.com
- Residence Abroad Blogs (University of Manchester): www.llc.manchester.ac.uk/undergraduate/residence-abroad/blogs
- Maastricht Students: www.maastricht-students.com
- The Student World Blog: www.thestudentworld.com/ news_and_blog/article/preparation_for_studying_ abroad#.UFrwCK6Dfcs.

Websites like iAgora (www.iagora.com/studies) allow international students to rate their experiences at an institution based on categories for housing, student life, academic, costs and so on. SteXX, the Student Experience Exchange (www.stexx.eu), allows students to review and rate European universities. Use sites like these to get a student perspective on your chosen institution. Perhaps you will decide to rate your experiences too, after studying overseas.

Many schools, colleges, universities and public libraries have access to Exodus, an international careers-information database. The online database features lots of useful information on studying overseas, including country profiles. Ask your UK institution for a username and password.

Students interested in postgraduate study or research should find the Prospects website useful, as it features profiles of over 50 countries (www.prospects.ac.uk/country_profiles.htm).

## Using an agent

Some applicants choose to use the service of an agent or an educational consultant to help them navigate the plethora of information out there. Many like the reassurance of working with an organisation that understands the education, application and visa system of a particular country or countries. Check whether you have to pay for the service they provide and what you will get in return. Some organisations charge no fees. It is always worth asking about the affiliations of any organisation: whether they are linked to specific universities, for example.

There are a number of organisations operating in the UK, all offering different types of support and service. Some of these are listed here.

- A Star Future: www.astarfuture.co.uk
- Study Options: www.studyoptions.com

- EUNICAS: www.eunicas.co.uk
- PFL Education: www.preparationforlife.com
- Degrees Ahead: www.degreesahead.co.uk
- Mayflower Education Consultants: www.mayflowereducation.co.uk
- M & D Europe: www.readmedicine.com
- Pass 4 Soccer Scholarships: www.pass4soccer.com.

> **"** After results day, my teacher recommended that I get in touch with A Star Future because she knew that I would be really interested in their information on clearing places at foreign universities.**"**
>
> *Clare Higgins, The Hague University of Applied Sciences, the Netherlands*

> **"** I applied through Study Options. They were fantastic and made the process so easy. They copied all of my transcripts for my A level results and sent off passport, results, organised the visa, the course, everything!**"**
>
> *Kadie O'Byrne, Murdoch University, Australia*

## Getting a different perspective

Of course, the websites listed here barely scratch the surface of the information out there. The students I spoke to share some great ways to get a different perspective.

> **❝** I did some rather intense research, checking out the university website, the city website and the online literature available. I also used more creative methods such as searching for YouTube videos of the campus and the city, listening to the local radio station online and reading the local paper online to try to get a better grip of what my future life might be like. **❞**
>
> *Simon McCabe, University of Missouri, USA*

> **❝** Other people were a really good source of information. Many other people had migrated so I could ask them about which shipping company they had used, how they had found moving and things like that. I could learn from their mistakes and take their advice to make my move easier. **❞**
>
> *Teresa Perez, University of Cape Town, South Africa*

# Finalising your choices

Let's recap the steps to finalising your choices.

- Consider your priorities.
- Write a list of essential and desirable criteria.
- Write a list of questions to ask each institution.
- Start to research in more detail.
- If you're struggling, write a pros-and-cons list.
- Narrow down your choices to a shortlist of five or six.

It is important to contact the university direct, talking to admissions staff as well as course leaders or professors. When you come to apply, this can have the additional benefit of making your name known to the recruiting staff, as well as improving your understanding of what those staff are looking for.

You should clarify the application process, documentation required and the visa requirements, as well as establishing a timescale for the process. The university should then send you the necessary paperwork or a link to the information online.

Try to apply to a number of institutions, while still considering the work required to produce a good-quality application, as well as any associated costs. Applying to a number of institutions gives you a better chance of a selection of offers to choose from.

## Student story
## Teresa Perez, University of Cape Town, South Africa

Teresa Perez's route to studying abroad ended up taking a little longer than planned. 'I had always wanted to live and work abroad, but after I did my degree and PGCE and started teaching I had a few thousand pounds of debt that I needed to pay off. So I couldn't go until I had saved some money.

'I originally thought I would work overseas and applied for jobs in a couple of places, but then my partner got a really good job offer, and wanted to stay in the UK another year. The extra 12 months of income meant that I could save up to pay for tuition fees. I started a master's course with the Open University while I worked, firstly to get my head back into studying, and secondly to confirm that this is definitely what I wanted to do. I loved it and used the essays as part of my application to University of Cape Town (UCT).

'I wanted to study overseas to experience a different culture. Especially being a sociologist, I wanted to be somewhere unfamiliar that would provide some interesting aspects of social life to study. Also, the tuition fees in the UK had just been raised, so it worked out equally expensive to stay and study in the UK, as it would to pay to study at UCT, even taking into account the extra fees for international students.

'My boyfriend is from Cape Town and after a few months of looking for jobs in Europe and Asia, he suggested going back to Cape Town. I'd been on holiday a few times when we were over visiting his family at Christmas and loved it. Sociologically and politically, South Africa is unique, and I was thrilled that I was going to have the opportunity to study there.'

Teresa's tuition fees in South Africa were comparable to her costs at the Open University in the UK. 'All in all, it will have cost me approximately £9,000 to do a taught master's over two years, including course fees, international fees and my study permits. If I had continued studying with the Open University, it would have cost approximately the same to complete my master's.'

Making her application to university turned out to be rather stressful and frustrating. 'I filled in the online application form and sent off all the required documents. A month passed and still no sign that they had arrived. I paid £50 to have them couriered to guarantee that they had arrived, then I was later informed that all the documents had to be certified copies. Finally, I found out that I could get the documents certified once I had arrived and enrolled. I applied for politics and sociology. Politics rejected me (I still don't know why) but sociology accepted me.

'So I then went about getting a study permit. I needed a letter from my GP to confirm I had a clean bill of health (£10), a letter referring me to a radiographer (£10), a chest X-ray (£60), a letter from the radiologist confirming that I didn't have TB (£10), Bupa International medical insurance (£150), a letter from Bupa confirming I had medical insurance, three months' payslips, three months' bank statements, a certificate from the police to confirm I had no criminal convictions (£30), £600 (to pay for your airfare if you get deported, you get this back once you leave the country), £30 processing fee, a letter from UCT offering me a place with key information highlighted, two passport photos and a copy of your passport. I had to take the morning off work to queue up to hand in my paperwork and then again to pick up my passport with my permit in.

'When I arrived I had to enrol and spent a long time in queues filling in more forms, but I didn't mind because I was so happy to have finally arrived and be on campus choosing my courses for the forthcoming year.

'The Sociology Department have been absolutely outstanding since I arrived. The Head of Sociology and all the lecturers are friendly, helpful, approachable and efficient. I asked about tutoring and got a part-time job teaching third-year sociology in the first semester. I absolutely loved it.

'Anytime I have needed help or an extension or any sort of support, all my lecturers have been accommodating. Their doors are always open and they are always happy to talk to me. If there is a problem then they have extra consultations and sessions. They really have bent over backwards to make sure that I have everything I need to get the work done. The academics that I see for my seminars every week are really inspiring and very well qualified. They all work so hard and are really busy, but still make the time to be available if you want to talk about anything.

'Compared to my undergraduate degree, the teaching and learning are far superior. If I haven't done my reading for the seminar, it is obvious. The groups are small and you are expected to contribute, so if you don't know your stuff, it shows. It is hard to get a high grade in essays as the standards are high. However, it does mean that if you work really hard, you reap the benefits and it motivates you to do better. The lecturers are really helpful and very fair. In my undergraduate degree I don't think any of the lecturers even knew my name. If I didn't turn up, no one noticed. Perhaps it's just because I am older and doing a master's, but there is a definite difference in expectations, and a lot of the time I have felt like I am getting individual tuition.

'One of the best things about being here has been learning in a whole new context. You learn about a completely different history from a completely different perspective. It makes you realise how many daft stereotypes there are about Africa and South Africa that are perpetuated by the western media that are utterly inaccurate.'

Teresa has adjusted well to her new home. 'Cape Town in many ways is very European. Also having Andrew and his family here made the move pretty effortless. We can go and stay with them whenever we like, they have been so welcoming.'

On the downside, she has experienced some minor incidents of crime and witnessed the levels of poverty. 'The day after we hired a car, it got broken into and the radio was stolen. There is a lot of poverty and therefore a lot of people begging. It is pretty hard to say no, especially when it's children. However, I have chosen to give my time rather than food or money, and this is what I tell people. Whenever I have refused to give money or buy people food, I have never been met with any aggression or unpleasantness, but I still feel bad that they are so desperate that they are forced to beg.'

## Teresa's top tips

### Accommodation

'I live with my boyfriend in a house. We had our stuff shipped from the UK so had to wait a few months for it to arrive so moved into a furnished house. It is OK but the landlord is unreliable. He didn't pay his share of the bills and didn't tell us, so our water was cut off. We are moving out at the end of the month!'

### Food

'Delicious. It is about the same price as the UK to eat out, but the supermarket food is more expensive. Sometimes it works out cheaper to eat out than it does to cook a healthy meal because the food is so expensive.'

### Insurance

'Health insurance is cheaper than it would be because I am on a student plan, so it's about £30 a month.'

### Living costs

'The rent is cheaper than London. We pay £500 for a two-bedroom house. It's easy to get to university and town, so no long tube journeys. Bills are cheaper too. Everything is metered so you only pay for what you use. Rent includes rates (equivalent of council tax). There is no gas and no homes have central heating so that makes bills cheaper. Electric is about £20 a month. Refuse is about £8 a month. Sewerage is about the same and water depends on how much you use. The internet is more expensive than the UK. I live on £500 a month which includes my share of the rent, bills, food, everything.'

### Working while studying

'In the first semester I worked in the Sociology Department as a course convener for third years. This just about covered my rent. This semester I got a job as a part-time researcher for the Centre for Higher Education at UCT, which, again, just about covers my rent. I could get a job in a bar or something like that, but I want to get experience that will help me get a job should I wish to do something other than teach. I also do voluntary work with SHAWCO, the student-run university NGO, so I teach children English once a week in a township. I also work with a project called the Knowledge Co-op, again at UCT, assisting the project manager.'

## Lifestyle and culture

'The pace of life is a lot slower. The weather is a lot sunnier so I am spending far more time outside than I ever did in the UK. There are lots of cultural events, for example, the documentary film festival, and there's a theatre festival on at the moment. I went to Cape Town Pride. I saw U2 at the City of Cape Town Stadium. There is always something going on and, even if there isn't, you can just sit and read a book on the beach. A lot of the time I feel like I am on holiday, even though this is where I live. Everyone is very friendly.

'I have just finished level 2 of a Xhosa language course. Not only can I speak a bit of Xhosa now, but there was also a lot of cultural insight and mixing with other Captonians, which was a bonus. My boyfriend is a surfer so I spend a lot of time on the beach, or in the winter in cafes overlooking the sea. It's a great life.'

## Travel

'We went to the Grahamstown National Arts Festival for the winter holiday, which is the equivalent of the Edinburgh Festival. I have also travelled a bit up the east coast. If you have a car, South Africa is easy to get around, and you don't have to travel far to be somewhere very tranquil and pretty.'

Teresa plans to stay on in South Africa permanently when she finishes university. 'I can either try and find a job teaching, or try and go into something else that is related to education, for example, working in the education section of an NGO. What I would really like to do is carry on studying, do a PhD and apply to become a lecturer in sociology. We will have to see how things pan out.

'Even if I was a millionaire, I would still be studying a master's at UCT. Being able to do what I have always wanted to do feels like such a privilege. It is total immersion in a different culture, while learning at the same time, it's so much better than being a tourist.'

*University of Cape Town (www.uct.ac.za) is a research-led university offering qualifications that are internationally recognised and locally applicable. It is ranked at 113 in the Times Higher Education World University Rankings 2012–2013.*

# KEA: Profile

Situated in the heart of Copenhagen, KEA – Copenhagen School of Design and Technology – offers international AP degree programmes within Computer Science, Design Technology, IT Technology, and Multimedia Design & Communications in addition to bachelor's degree programmes within Architectural Technology & Construction Management, Business Economics & IT, and Jewellery, Technology & Business. In addition, there are bachelor's study programmes in E-Concept Development, Design & Business, Software Development and Web Development. More than 4,000 full-time students are enrolled at the KEA. Approximately 1,000 of these are international students from around the world.

KEA emphasises a practical approach combined with the latest theory. This goal is achieved by designing projects that closely imitate what is happening in the profession. A mandatory period of work placement offers the students an opportunity to learn more about the professions and provides them with a platform for networking.

All study programmes are developed in close partnership with businesses to ensure that students gain insight into real-life situations and industry needs. Tuition is project-based and businesses take an active part in evaluating student skills. An internship placement (of a minimum duration of 10 weeks) is mandatory, allowing students to test their knowledge and skills in a real-world work environment.

All of KEA's programmes are subject to internal quality-assurance procedures as well as external evaluations at national and international levels to secure the academic standards. The Danish Ministry of Education approves all programmes and covers tuition fees for students from the EU countries.

The education programmes provide all students with a solid theoretical knowledge and understanding of how to apply theory to professional practice, relevant for employment in business and industry.

www.kea.dk/en

## KEA: Case study

**Roxana Larisa Dobre, a student at KEA, studying Multimedia Design & Communication.**

'Let's start by supposing it's getting dark outside and the thought occurs that I'm still in school. As peculiar as it may sound, it happens very often. It probably also means I have an important assignment to deliver by the end of the week, therefore I found myself lost in my PHP code, because I have to finish putting everything together for the website. Everyone at KEA knows that PHP is one of the most hated subjects around, because it's very moody and it always gives you errors. I guess that is what I like most about it, the fact that it is tricky to work with and not very easy to get your hands on.

'But then again, I am the coder in my group and I chose to do it. This is a natural thing for our programme, once you get to know a bit about all the subjects that you are being taught you can later pick what is of most interest for you. As a multimedia designer, you can choose to 'take care' of the design, or the programming part, or even for communication and all the promotion you have to do around your product. Of course you can do all of them, by participating actively throughout the whole process of project work, but in my opinion it's a good idea to start figuring out a field of interest suitable to your skills and your personality.

'Another great thing about KEA is a wonderful wall in the hallway. Full of posters. I love it. I mean the fact that we have so many posters, not the wall itself. You can find here a lot of events you can participate in: I see one about an HTML & CSS workshop (this means extra-help given by the tutors to the people who need help in these subjects), one for the Creativity Night (this one is such an awesome event, I love it, you can just go crazy with your ideas) and there's a third poster advertising the Friday Bar (a great way for students to relax and have some nice time at the end of a busy week), which will be held in the Chill Out – probably the most awesome place in KEA. This is where students come for a cup of coffee or tea, or to get some help for their problems from the tutors working in the Tutor Cafe. The cosy sofas and the nice music help a lot to create a nice atmosphere, in which the students feel more confident about working or socialising with their fellow students.

'To summarise, studying at KEA involves a whole lot of things: creativity, interactivity, fun, but also hard work, all to prepare the students for an adventurous trip into the jungle that the multimedia world turns into as each day goes by. I, for one, am so looking forward to the adventure!'

## Radboud University: Profile

### Research master's programme Molecular Mechanisms of Disease – Radboud University Nijmegen

*Do you want to be a scientific researcher in the domain of molecular life sciences? And expand the application of fundamental research output in disease diagnosis? Then this international two-year research master's programme is for you!*

- Challenging educational programme in a top scientific environment
- Selective programme: international and ambitious student group (max 24 students)
- Personalised supervision, small group education and teamwork
- Two six-month research internships of your choice in outstanding (international) groups
- Number 1 master in Life Sciences in the Netherlands (Keuzegids masters 2012)
- Perfect preparation to become an independent researcher

www.ru.nl/master/ncmls-mmd

Felipe Augusto Brava from Brazil says about MMD: *'The best decision I could have made'.*

'I can state with no doubt that joining the Master in Molecular Mechanisms of Disease at the Radboud University Nijmegen was the best decision I could have made. From a series of insightful and high-level lectures, to the top practical research training in state of the art facilities during the internships, passing through the opportunities to know leading scientists from around the world and discuss their work in a very personal and friendly environment, there is so much to learn that it is amazing. I believe that my master's programme represents a hallmark in my life and it will have a decisive way for my future. I want to devote my life to science and studying at the Radboud University Nijmegen has definitely opened many doors for my future career as a scientist.'

## Radboud University: Case study

### Sophie Mills, UK
*Bachelor student International Economics & Business*

'If you are willing to try something different, which is still close to home, then I would definitely recommend studying at Radboud University Nijmegen! It is easy to settle in here, and **it soon feels like home**, especially as you don't have the burden of learning a new language unless you want to: everyone here speaks English!

'The learning environment is particularly different to what I had experienced at university in the UK. We are a very small group of students, which means that **we get taught on a much more personal level**, and have the opportunity to ask questions.

'I was also surprised how **friendly people** are in general, especially to foreigners!'

### Daniela Patru, Romania
*Alumna of Master Business Administration – Strategy*

'The Master's programme itself was intensive, but there was definitely time for fun, and looking back I think that particular balance is one of the things I'll remember fondly: when you had work to do, you *worked*, and when free time was to be had you *definitely* made the most of it.

'Add to that interesting courses (with a research trip to Morocco as part of one of them), a very green campus, and the biking experience, and I can safely say that I have very fond memories of my studies here.

'I would definitely recommend this study if you're looking for a programme where the reality that strategic decisions are being made and implemented by *people*, with all their biases and foibles, is taken into account.

'And I'd say that, underneath it all, the programme teaches you critical thinking, which is a key element in any sub-field of business.'

**Bachelor's programmes in Economics and Business: www.ru.nl/ieb and www.ru.nl/iba**
**Master's programmes: www.ru.nl/masters**

## Norwegian School of Economics: Profile

NORWEGIAN SCHOOL OF ECONOMICS

NHH is an elite institution, which recruits only the best students from both within and outside Norway to its various study programmes. NHH offers three master programmes for international students within the Master of Science in Economics and Business Administration. Read more at www.nhh.no.

### Master in Energy, Natural Resources and the Environment

The goal of the Energy, Natural Resources and the Environment programme (ENE) is to educate the next generation of interdisciplinary managers in the study of energy and natural resource development and environmental impact.

### Master in International Business

The International Business programme (MIB) at NHH aims to equip students with the right mix of analytical and practical skills for a career within multinational companies, international organisations or smaller firms whose activities involve a substantial degree of international business.

### Master in Marketing and Brand Management

The Marketing and Brand Management (MBM) programme is aimed at students that want to lead and make decisions in the marketing department of a company, including positions such as brand manager, marketing analyst or head of marketing.

### Active student life

The NHH Student Union (NHHS) is the most active student organisation in Norway. The school encourages students to start new groups that cater to the multifaceted and varied interests of students; such as the telemark ski club, finance group, student choir and the entrepreneur organisation.

## The difference is Bergen and Norway

Bergen is a very charming city with a relaxed atmosphere and vibrant student life. It is located within the magnificent landscapes of Norway and proves to be a very special place to live, study and work.

## Admission

We accept applications from November for the following fall semester. Deadline for receipt of applications: 15 February.

## Further practical information

As a student at NHH you are also guaranteed accommodation in student housing and granted work permission.

## Norwegian School of Economics: Case study

'The teaching at NHH is based on the most up-to-date and timely case studies, which gives me the feeling of being part of the contemporary world energy business.'
*Maria Korotkova, Russia*

'The professors and guest lecturers share with us their valuable experiences, which is better than textbook-based discussions.'
*Sarah Raquipiso, Philippines*

'At NHH I received a world-class education; a solid grounding in economics and exposure to specialised subjects such as oil and gas. My time at NHH and in CEMS allowed me to build a diverse international network of friends and colleagues. I find NHH students to be people who are very competent in their subjects, analytically superb, but also with a keen sense of initiative.'
*Isikan Aysev, Turkey*

'I did my master thesis in collaboration with Chanel, about how women use and perceive luxury cosmetics. My present job at Chanel covers tasks as PR, growth strategy, marketing and distribution management. Being able to leverage the skills I obtained at NHH, while being constantly challenged, make my job at Chanel truly exciting.'
*Melissa Malka, Norway*

'Bergen's beautiful sceneries and atmosphere makes an ordinary day exciting. Simply exploring the city, hiking the surrounding mountains, or enjoying the night life makes my day feel adventurous.'
*Anna Sariceva, Latvia*

'NHH is truly global, both in terms of the course subject matter as well as the student body. Accordingly, students at NHH have well-rounded international perspectives.'
*Emma Micklem, South Africa*

# The Hague University of Applied Sciences: Profile

The Netherlands has two main types of higher education institutions – research universities and universities of applied sciences. The Hague University of Applied Sciences (THU) is a university of applied sciences with a professionally focused, hands-on approach mixing theory and practice. We will prepare you for the challenges ahead in your specific career. We believe that it is important to tap into the professional world to give our students real life experiences. Our international bachelor's and master's programmes are constantly updated to reflect developments and changes in the working world. Our programmes will encourage you to think independently and explore other people's perspectives, through cross-cultural debate and teamwork.

The Hague University of Applied Sciences has more than 22,000 students and 1,800 staff members who come from over 145 different countries. THU has over 300 partner institutions, all over the globe. The university welcomes exchange students and lecturers from different countries and cultures through the Socrates programme.

We offer nine full-time bachelor's programmes with an international focus:

- European Studies
- Industrial Design Engineering
- International Business and Management Studies
- International Communication Management
- International Financial Management & Control (starts 2012)
- Law
- Process and Food Technology
- Public Management
- Safety and Security Management Studies

For more information please visit our website: www.thehagueuniversity.com

## The Hague University of Applied Sciences: Case study

### Philip Rolfe, 27 (Dagenham, UK)

'Unlike many young people, I had no intention of just grasping the first opportunity that presented itself. It actually took me six years before discovering that what I really wanted to do was in the public management sphere. Public Management at THU has everything that interests me: history, science, philosophy, you name it. It certainly keeps you on your toes. The text books create an excellent foundation, and I'm enjoying the lectures which are both absorbing and full of energy.

'The basis we are now receiving gives us lenses through which we can see and compare politics in its various guises in different countries. It's a brilliant programme, really rich and the start of something that's going to be very interesting for me. Another advantage of this programme is that it allows you to work in the commercial sector as well as for the government. With an in-depth knowledge of policy-making processes I could even play an intermediary role, reconciling the interests of business and government, from either side.

'Different nationalities bring so much more to the table. When we're discussing global politics, for example, the input of people from far-flung places is of great value and it forces you to consider aspects you wouldn't otherwise have thought of. By comparison, studying in a single-nationality environment would be a lot duller.

'The university campus is very well designed, smooth running, everything is easy to find, there's plenty to do, it has great facilities and the people are really helpful. And being located right next to the railway station means it's also easy to reach.'

# Chapter 5
## Studying in Europe

UK students are lucky to have such a diverse range of countries right on their doorstep. Flights to some European cities can be as cheap or as quick as a train journey within the UK. European study brings the benefit of cultural and language differences, without having to travel too far.

One myth about studying in Europe is the need to have brilliant language skills. Increasingly, European universities are offering entire courses in English. Of course, living in a different country will also enable you to immerse yourself in the language, thereby developing new language skills as a bonus. Some universities will offer you the chance to take language lessons alongside your studies.

This chapter focuses on EU (European Union) or EEA (European Economic Area) countries where UK students are charged the same fees as those for home students. The countries featured offer a range of courses available in English. The European countries that aren't listed in this chapter will still have opportunities for study in English (most European countries do) but you may find that some are more limited, perhaps restricted to private or international institutions.

In the Times Higher Education World University Rankings
2012–2013, a listing of the top 200 universities in the world,
you will find universities from many European countries
– Switzerland, France, Germany, Ireland, Sweden, Finland,
the Netherlands, Belgium, Denmark and Austria are all
represented.

# Compatibility in the education system

Although there are differences in the education systems across
Europe, a system known as the Bologna process has helped to
make higher education more compatible and comparable across
much of the continent. With transparent, mutually recognised
systems and a clear credit framework, studying across Europe is
now much simpler.

The Bologna process covers the European Higher Education Area
(EHEA), an area much wider than the EU or EEA. It includes
some countries applying for EU membership (Croatia, Montenegro
and Turkey, for example) and some post-Soviet states (Armenia,
Ukraine and Azerbaijan, for example).

The process of studying for an entire degree abroad is sometimes
known as 'diploma mobility'.

Bachelor's degrees, master's degrees and doctorates in these
countries are all comparable in level. The European Credit
Transfer System (ECTS) is used to measure workload and allows
comparison between degrees in different countries. This makes
it fairly straightforward to study a first degree in one European
country and a postgraduate degree in another; some students even
move part-way through their studies. Credit can be awarded for

academic study, relevant placements and research, as long as they are part of the programme of study. Sixty credits equate to one full-time academic year. You may see bachelor's degrees of 180 or 240 credits, for example.

Another benefit of the coordinated system is the diploma supplement, a detailed transcript used across Europe and the EHEA which outlines any studies you complete and gives full details of the level, content and status of your achievements. It is particularly helpful if you intend to work or study in another country as it provides a recognisable context to any attainments.

The coordination of quality-assurance standards means that higher education across all these countries has to meet minimum requirements. It is important to note that this doesn't remove the need for thorough research into what you will receive at your European university. You will find a range of different types of opportunity on offer. Just as in the UK, universities across Europe vary in their prestige, research, teaching and facilities. Ensuring that you find a good match to your needs is a key part of the research that you undertake.

It is important to note that most bachelor's degrees outside the UK are not classed as honours degrees as standard; extra study is normally required to gain an honours degree.

# Finding a course and institution

A Star Future (www.astarfuture.co.uk/what_to_study.html) and EUNICAS (www.eunicas.co.uk) feature course listings specifically for undergraduate courses taught in English. Another option is to use the Study Portal websites, www.bachelorsportal.eu, www.mastersportal.eu and www.phdportal.eu, but make sure that you select English as the language of instruction. You can use PLOTEUS (Portal on Learning Opportunities throughout the European Space) at www.ec.europa.eu/ploteus/home-en.htm. Try the advanced search on GES Database (www.study-info.eu/index. htm). EURAXESS has a database of research opportunities across Europe (www.ec.europa.eu/euraxess).

Different websites often bring up a different range of courses, so it is worth searching more than one website. Although these websites are a good starting point, the information on application deadlines and fees can sometimes be incorrect, so you should turn to the institutions for the latest information; you will be able to clarify any details with them.

ENIC-NARIC (European Network of Information Centres – National Academic Recognition Information Centres) has information on the education system of 54 countries, within Europe and beyond. The website also lists higher-education institutions for each country, so you can be sure that your chosen institution is recognised (www.enic-naric.net).

# Entry requirements

Entry requirements vary between countries and between institutions. Similarly, competition for places varies as well. Most European countries do not have such a competitive system as we have in the UK, where the cap on numbers means some students won't gain a place, even when they have the academic ability to cope with the course. Many European countries ask that you have completed A-level study, without asking for specific grades; they are often more concerned with your performance at university than beforehand, so some students will lose their place after the first year if they cannot cope with the academic demands.

Certain courses in some countries are subject to selective recruitment; look out for the terms *numerus clausus* or *numerus fixus*, which might indicate a competitive system for restricted places. Your nationality should not prevent you from accessing education in any EU country, although you will need to ensure that you meet any entry requirements.

### What is your UK qualification equivalent to?

Unless you have taken an internationally recognised qualification, like the International Baccalaureate, it is possible that your UK qualifications will need to be compared to the qualifications in the country where you wish to study. A levels tend to be understood overseas, but many other UK qualifications will require further evaluation. Each country has its own system for ensuring the adequate comparison of academic qualifications. Your chosen institution will be able to advise you further on any information that they require, so it is best to speak to them initially. You may later need to contact the ENIC-NARIC organisation in your host country for formal comparison of your qualifications (www.enic-naric.net). There will be a fee for this service.

# Applying

Each European country has its own system and timescale for application. In some countries this is centralised, a bit like UCAS, but in other cases you have to apply individually to each university. The country guides will give you an idea of the different systems and deadline dates for application.

# Registering your stay

Although UK students studying in the EU or the EEA will not require a visa, you will need to register your stay if you are going to be in the country for longer than three months. In most

countries, you simply need to take your passport to a police station
or immigration department. It is advisable to do this early; in some
cases it must be done in the first week of your stay. Some countries
charge a small fee for this service. Your university's international
office will be able to tell you more.

# Costs and help with finances

For course fees, UK nationals studying at public universities in
other EU countries are treated in the same way as home students
from that particular country. That means that they pay the same
fees as those for home students. Tuition-fee loans may also be
available to EU students, in the countries where they are offered to
home students. There is no requirement to offer maintenance grants
and loans to EU students, although some countries choose to do so.
Your university should be able to tell you more about the possibility
of a loan or grant and any conditions you might need to meet.

The Netherlands is one of the few countries offering grants and
loans to EU students, although you will need to be in work to
access the grants. Loans are also available, but you will need to be
under the age of 30. For more details, see the country profile for
the Netherlands on page 170.

There are public and private universities across the EU and
EEA. Public universities are more likely to have a standardised
system of tuition fees. In France, for example, courses at public
universities tend to cost the same, regardless of subject or
institution. In other countries, different courses or universities can
charge varying amounts. Private institutions will charge a broader
range of fees, often based on what they believe the market (i.e. the
student) is prepared to pay. On the other hand, private institutions
may well have additional opportunities for scholarships and
favourable financial support, so it is worth investigating further.

# Cultural differences

Although you may be familiar with some of the European countries on the UK's doorstep, there will still be cultural differences to come to terms with. Different countries and their inhabitants have their own distinctive characteristics that you will need to get used to if you are to adjust properly. Although the language barrier may not impact on your ability to study (when courses are taught in English), it can add to your isolation outside the university environment. Taking advantage of language classes can be an important factor when trying to settle in.

In some countries, many students stay in their local area and part-time study is common, while elsewhere students traditionally go to university when they are older; all this will impact on your university experience, so it is important to look into this before you decide on your venue for study.

> **❝** There are much fewer societies and sports teams in comparison to UK universities, but Bocconi is trying to improve in that area. **❞**
>
> *James Wheeler, Bocconi University, Italy*

> **❝** The culture and lifestyle here in the Netherlands are excellent! Everyone is friendly and you can expect strangers to say hello to you as they walk past. The pub culture is excellent. Apart from the weird and potentially awful style of music some of the pubs might play, you've got the chance to really enjoy yourself. **❞**
>
> *Owen McComasky, Stenden University of Applied Sciences, the Netherlands*

Talk to your university's international office or try to make contact with other UK students in preparation for the cultural differences you will face.

# Working while studying

The opportunities to work will vary from country to country, often based on the number of local job opportunities for those with skills in English. In some countries, your opportunities will be limited so, to be on the safe side, you should plan your finances with the expectation that you will not find work.

If you need to work to get access to student grants and loans, as in the Netherlands, it may be worth moving to your new country a little earlier to begin the search. Alternatively, you can search for job opportunities through the European Job Mobility Portal (EURES) at www.ec.europa.eu/eures/home.jsp?lang=en. Your university may also have job shops advertising student-job vacancies.

If you hope to work in Europe, either during or after your studies, it may be useful to prepare a Europass CV, which comprises a standard CV template used widely across Europe; it should make your educational background and work experience more easily understood. Find out more at www.europass.cedefop.europa.eu.

> ❝ The advice I was given by my mentor at Stenden was: 'Don't get a job straight away. If possible, lean on your parents for financial support, at least at the start.' He told me this because he knew how much work the course would be for us. Boy, was he right! ❞
>
> *Owen McComasky, Stenden University of*
> *Applied Sciences, the Netherlands*

> **❝** It is not as difficult to find part-time work as you might think. Although working in bars or restaurants allows you to meet many different people, tutoring is a much better use of your time. **❞**
>
> *Alican Spafford, Rouen Business School, France*

## Staying on after study

As a free mover in Europe, staying on after study should not be restricted by legislation, although it may be limited by local opportunities. Competence in the local language, economic issues and local job opportunities may determine whether you choose to stay on for further study or work. Even if they don't remain in their university town or country, most students talk about the realisation that there is a whole world of opportunities out there for them.

> **❝** I'd like to travel the world. I don't want to be fixed. I want to see the world and make a difference. I won't be going back to the UK, that's for sure. Being abroad has caught on like a bug. **❞**
>
> *Rebecca Jackson, Stenden University of Applied Sciences, the Netherlands*

## Country-specific information

### Note

A number of European countries are very limited in the undergraduate courses they offer taught in English at public institutions. The list includes Austria, Belgium, France, Iceland, Italy, Spain and Norway. However, private providers and international universities in these countries do offer a range of undergraduate degrees taught in English; they will be more expensive than the public institutions, but might still end up being cheaper than the UK options due to a more generous package of scholarships or financial support.

## Belgium

There are 341 UK students enrolled in higher education in Belgium, according to OECD, Education at a Glance 2012.

### Higher education in Belgium

The Flemish and French communities each have their own education system. Most higher-education opportunities in Belgium require Flemish- or French-language skills, but there are some courses taught in English. These are more often at postgraduate level, with quite limited options for undergraduate study.

### Applying

Applications need to be in quite early with most September-start courses showing deadlines of mid-September the previous academic year. Apply directly to your chosen university.

### Costs

Tuition is free, although there are registration fees which can be up to €837 (£672) per year. See the You could study . . . section below for examples. The cost of living in Belgium is comparable to that in Denmark and Ireland, which makes it slightly more expensive than the UK. It is ranked at number 7 out of 90 countries on the Numbeo 2012 Cost of Living Index at www.numbeo.com.

Four of Belgium's universities can be found in the Times Higher Education World University Rankings Top 200 for 2012–2013.

## You could study . . .

### BA Philosophy
Katholieke Universiteit Leuven
Three years
Apply by 1 June
Annual fees €578 (£464)
Monthly living costs €654 (£525)

### MSc Chemicals and Materials Engineering
University of Liège
Two years
Apply by 31 August
Annual fees €835 (£670)
Monthly living costs €850 (£682)

### PhD Architecture and Interior Architecture
Hasselt University
Four years
No application deadline date
Annual fees €270 (£217)
Monthly living costs €610–€770 (£489–£618)

## Useful websites
www.highereducation.be (Flemish community)
www.studyinbelgium.be (French community)

### Also worth considering . . .

Luxembourg could provide an alternative venue to Belgium, although any opportunities taught in English are likely to require additional skills in French, German or Luxembourgish. The only university is the University of Luxembourg (www. en.uni.lu), although there are a couple of international campuses there too. Find out more at ENIC-NARIC's Luxembourg page, www.enic-naric.net/index.aspx?c=Luxembourg.

## Cyprus

Cypriots understand the value of international education. Every year, tens of thousands of students leave Cyprus to study overseas, while around 10,000 students make the opposite journey to undertake their higher education on the island.

### *Higher education in Cyprus*

Higher education in Cyprus is based at universities and non-universities, both public and private. Some institutions offer courses taught in English, although there appear to be more opportunities in the private institutions. There is a separate system in place in Turkish Northern Cyprus, where universities primarily offer courses taught in English; these institutions are not recognised by the Republic of Cyprus; you will be expected to make a direct application and applicants may be required to sit entrance exams.

Bachelor's degrees tend to take four years, with master's degrees taking from one year and doctorates from three years.

### *Costs*

In the public institutions, you can expect tuition fees of around €3,400 (£2,728) per year for bachelor's degrees, €5,000 (£4,012) for master's degrees, followed by €4,000 (£3,210) for doctoral degrees. EU undergraduate students at public universities should get their fees paid by the state.

Cyprus came 25th out of 90 countries in a 2012 cost-of-living ranking; living there should be cheaper than living in the UK (see www.numbeo.com).

## *You could study . . .*

### BA Hospitality Management
College of Tourism and Hotel Management, Cyprus (private)
40 months
Apply by September
Annual fees €5,900 (£4,733)
Monthly living costs €500 (£401)

### MA Byzantine Studies
University of Cyprus
Two years
Apply by 30 March
Annual fees €5125 (£4,112)
Monthly living costs €700 (£562)

### PhD International Law and European Law
University of Cyprus
36 months
Apply by 15 April
Annual fees €1250 (£1,003)
Monthly living costs €700 (£562)

## *Useful websites*
www.highereducation.ac.cy/en
www.kktcenf.org/en

---

### *Also worth considering . . .*

If you're looking for higher education on another island,
then how about Malta? Find out more at the ENIC-
NARIC country page for Malta, www.enic-naric.net/index.
aspx?c=malta. Malta only has one university; the website for
the University of Malta is at www.um.edu.mt.

## Czech Republic

The Czech Republic has a long tradition of higher education and is home to the oldest university in central Europe. It offers a range of courses in English, and low living costs. According to OECD, Education at a Glance 2012, 412 UK students are already studying in the Czech Republic.

### *Higher education in the Czech Republic*

Courses in the Czech Republic are based at public universities and private colleges, some of which are international. They run a two-semester system, with courses starting in September or February.

Undergraduate studies tend to take three to four years, with master's degrees taking two to three years, and doctorates from three years.

There are opportunities to study for competitive courses like medicine, dentistry and veterinary science in the Czech Republic and in other countries in eastern Europe.

### *Applying*

Applications are made directly to your chosen university, before a deadline often in late February or March. Additional requirements might include academic transcripts and certificates, a letter of motivation, an admissions test and interview. Your university's international office will advise further on all aspects of the application process.

You can search for courses through the database on Higher Education Studies at www.naric.cz/HigherDB/index.php?Sezn=S1, as well as through PLOTEUS and the Study Portals listed on pages 130–131.

## *Costs*

Although courses taught in Czech are free, you will be charged
tuition fees for courses taught in English. The universities set
their own tuition fees for such courses and there is no maximum
limit. Fees usually start at around €2,000 (£1,605) but can be as
much as €15,000 (£12,000) for a degree in medicine or dentistry.
Scholarships may be available; you can find out more at the
Ministry of Education, Youth and Sports (www.msmt.cz) or from
your university.

For its cost of living in 2012, the Czech Republic is ranked 56 out
of 90 countries according to Numbeo (www.numbeo.com), which is
considerably lower than western Europe and the Nordic countries.
Study in the Czech Republic (www.studyin.cz) suggests allowing
for living costs of around US$350–US$750 (£220–£473) per month.

## *You could study . . .*

### BSc Applied Informatics in Transport
University of Pardubice
Three years
Apply by 28 February
Annual fees €1,500 (£1,203)
Monthly living costs CZK6,000 (£188)

### BA (Hons) Graphic Design
Prague College (degree awarded by University of Teesside)
Three years
Apply by 1 May (September start) or 1 October (May start)
Annual fees CZK108,000 (£3,390)
Monthly living costs CZK8,500 (£267)

### MSc Mathematics
Charles University, Prague
Two years

Apply by 28 February

Annual fees €6,000 (£4,814)

Monthly living costs CZK8,500 (£267)

*Useful websites*

www.studyin.cz

---

*Also worth considering . . .*

If you're interested in opportunities in eastern Europe, have you considered Bulgaria, Hungary, Poland, Romania, Slovakia or Slovenia? Find out more at:

- ENIC-NARIC country page for Bulgaria, www.enic-naric.net/index.aspx?c=Bulgaria
- Study Hungary, www.studyhungary.hu
- Study in Poland, www.studyinpoland.pl
- ENIC-NARIC country page for Romania, www.enic-naric.net/index.aspx?c=Romania
- Study in Slovakia, www.studyin.sk
- Slovenia, www.slovenia.si/en/study.

---

# Denmark

According to annual figures from OECD Education at a Glance 2012, 548 UK students have already made the move to study in Denmark. You will find that education in Denmark centres on problem-based learning, developing your ability to present creative solutions to complex problems. The country has a strong tradition of public universities and, best of all, there are no tuition fees. At PhD level, there are even fully funded, salaried opportunities in English.

## *Higher education in Denmark*

Denmark offers over 500 higher-education programmes taught in English. You can study at research universities (universitet) at undergraduate and postgraduate level; it takes at least three years to complete a bachelor's degree, two years for a master's, and three or four for a doctorate. Programmes at university colleges (professionshøjskole) are more professional in nature, leading to three-year to four-year professional undergraduate degrees in areas like engineering, teaching or business. Academies of professional higher education (erhvervsakademier) offer degrees in partnership with universities and two-year academy professional degrees (AP); an AP can be topped up to a professional bachelor's degree with further study.

The academic year runs from September to June, with the possibility of February intake too. Some courses are competitive and have additional requirements beyond the completion of A-level-standard qualifications.

All courses in Denmark are assessed by oral or written exams.

## *Applying*

At undergraduate level, applications can be made through the Danish Co-ordinated Application System (KOT) at www.optagelse. dk/vejledninger/english/index.html. Danish students can apply online but UK students will need to send their forms by post. You can choose up to eight courses and can opt for a quota 1 or quota 2 application; the option you choose depends on the qualification you are applying with – your chosen university will advise you as to which one is most suitable. The application deadline is mid-March for undergraduate courses starting in August and September.

Students applying through KOT also have the option to be put on standby: this means being added to a waiting list if you are not admitted initially. If you get a standby offer, you may be contacted about a place as late as two weeks into the semester; if you get a standby offer that doesn't become a study place, you will be guaranteed a place for the following year.

Direct application is required at postgraduate level, with deadlines varying; your chosen university will be able to advise you further.

## Costs

Danish students are eligible for State Educational Support (SU) in the form of a grant of DKK5,662 (£609) per month and access to loans. In some cases, under Danish rules or under EU law, students from other countries may qualify, particularly if you are classed as a worker in Denmark. For further explanation, see the Ministry of Education website, www.su.dk/English/Sider/foreign. aspx. Some scholarships may be available. See Study in Denmark (www.studyindenmark.dk) for details.

Denmark is an expensive country to live in. It comes in at number six in the cost-of-living rankings 2012 (www.numbeo.com), but with no fees and with wages of around €12 (£9.60) per hour for students, it is still possible to have a reasonable standard of living. Students with no Danish language can find jobs in English-speaking bars and cafés, for example.

Aarhus University (ranked 116), University of Copenhagen (130) and the Technical University of Denmark (149) are all in the Times Higher Education World University Rankings Top 200 for 2012–2013. All three institutions have moved up the rankings since last year. UK universities with comparable rankings are University of Nottingham (120), University of Southampton (130) and University of Exeter (153).

## You could study . . .

### BSc Economics and Business Administration
Aarhus University
Three years
Apply by 15 March
Tuition fees €0
Monthly living costs DKK5,000 (£538)

### BA Retail Design: Fashion and Furniture
VIA University College, Central Jutland
Four years
Apply by 15 March
Tuition fees €0
Monthly living costs DKK5,000 (£538)

### MSc Sustainable Energy
Technical University of Denmark, campuses across Denmark
Two years
Direct application by 9 March for September start
Tuition fees €0
Monthly living costs DKK5,250–DKK7,480 (£565–£805)

### Useful websites
www.studyindenmark.dk
www.en.iu.dk/education-in-denmark

## Estonia
Estonia offers good value for money and a vibrant student life. As many as 90% of international students say that Estonia is a good place to study (International Student Barometer™ 2011) but, so far, there aren't many UK students based there.

## *Higher education in Estonia*

The country is keen to attract international students and is expanding its courses taught in English; it currently offers more than 100 recognised degrees taught in English. These programmes are accredited and are available at the following institutions:

- Estonian Academy of Arts: www.artun.ee
- Estonian Academy of Music and Theatre: www. studyinestonia.ee/study/institutions/international-degree-programmes/estonian-academy-of-music-and-theatre
- Estonian University of Life Sciences: www.emu.ee
- Tallinn University: www.tlu.ee
- Tallinn University of Technology: www.ttu.ee/en
- University of Tartu: www.ut.ee
- Estonian Business School: www.ebs.ee.

Other higher-education institutions may offer alternative options taught in English, including modules for exchange students or short courses.

Education in Estonia takes place in public universities, private universities and professional higher-education institutions. The academic year starts in September and is divided into two semesters. Generally, you would be looking at a three-year academic bachelor's degree, a one-year to two-year master's qualification, and a three-year to four-year doctorate. Programmes in medicine, dentistry, pharmacy, veterinary science, architecture and civil engineering take five to six years.

All courses include exams which take place at the end of each semester. Grades are standardised, ranging from A (or 5) to E (or 1). Grade F (or 0) means that the assessment has not been passed.

## Applying

Applications should be made direct to your chosen institution. Deadline dates are set by the individual institutions and range from May to August for courses starting in September. Some doctorates are open to applications all year round.

## Costs

According to Study in Estonia, fees range from €1,023 to €7,350 (£820 to £5,898) per year. Medicine, law, business administration, and social sciences are often more expensive. PhD students should not have to pay fees.

Estonia is one of the few countries offering some form of financial support to EU students, although this looks likely to change in 2013–2014.

The Ministry of Education and Research has indicated that EU students studying at bachelor's and master's level can also be considered for study allowances in Estonia: 'Students can apply for study allowances, but only if they are enrolled to full-time studies in Estonia. The allowance is €55.93 (£45) per month. Allowance is built up on merit, so a student cannot apply for a study allowance in the first semester.' Doctoral students with a state-funded study place have the right to receive an allowance of €383.47 (£308) per month.

Some scholarships are available, primarily for postgraduate study; ask your university for more information.

Livings costs in Estonia are reasonable. You should allow a minimum of €160–€225 (£128–£180) per month for living costs, excluding accommodation. Expect to pay from €96 (£77) per month for a room in a dormitory and up to €450 (£360) for a private flat. Estonia is ranked at number 48 out of 90 countries on the cost-of-living rankings for 2012; this is considerably lower than the UK and much of western Europe.

## *You could study . . .*

**Bachelor of International Law**
Tallinn University of Technology, Tallinn
Three years
Direct application by 1 July
Annual fees €2,580 (£2,070)
Monthly living costs €500 (£400)

**MA Software Engineering**
University of Tartu
Two years
Direct application by 16 April
Annual fees €3,200 (£2,568)
Monthly living costs €500 (£400)

**PhD Sociology**
University of Tartu
Four years
Direct application by 1 June
Annual fees €0
Monthly living costs €500 (£400)

## *Useful websites*
www.studyinestonia.ee

---

*Also worth considering . . .*

If you're interested in opportunities in the Baltic states, have you considered Latvia and Lithuania? Find out more at Study in Latvia, www.studyinlatvia.lv and Study in Lithuania, www.lietuva.lt/en/education_sience/study_lithuania and the Lithuanian Centre for Quality Assessment in Higher Education, www.skvc.lt/en/content.asp?id=235.

---

# Finland

Finland is considered to be a safe and forward-looking nation with a high-quality education system. Temperatures can range from +30°C to –20°C and the sun never sets in parts of the country in June and early July. The academic year runs from August to the end of May; it is split into two semesters, August to December, and January to May. Most students start in August, with limited opportunities to join in January.

The latest figures from OECD Education at a Glance 2012 show us that 187 UK students were studying in Finland at the last count.

## Higher education in Finland

Higher education in Finland takes places in research-based universities or vocationally focused polytechnics (or Universities of Applied Sciences). In the universities, few programmes are taught in English at undergraduate level, although master's and doctoral degrees are more widely available. It is the opposite in the polytechnics, where there are plenty of programmes taught in English at undergraduate level, with a smaller number of UAS master's programmes. (Doctoral qualifications are not available in the polytechnics, only in the universities.) To access a UAS master's programme, you will need to have had three years of relevant experience, in addition to any academic requirements. To

search for programmes, go to the Study in Finland database at
www.studyinfinland.fi/study_options/study_programmes_database.

The degrees vary in length as follows:

- bachelor's degree: three years (university); three-and-
  a-half to four years (polytechnic/university of applied
  sciences)
- master's degree: two years (university); one-and-a-half to
  two years (polytechnic/university of applied sciences)
- doctoral degree: three to four years (university); not
  available at polytechnic/university of applied sciences.

## Applying

Applications tend to be online, although the application process
and timescale are split between the universities and polytechnics.

At universities, undergraduate applications are direct.
Applications to master's programmes can be made direct or
via www.universityadmissions.fi; ask your university which
way to proceed. In most cases, you should apply for bachelor's
and master's degrees between November and January. Doctoral
programmes require direct application; the application timescale
varies between institutions: some accept applications at any time,
while others have specific timescales in which to apply. Speak
to the international office or the relevant faculty at your chosen
university.

At polytechnics, undergraduate applications should be made in
January or February via www.admissions.fi. For a UAS master's
degree, you should apply direct to the polytechnic at the time
they specify; you can find out more on your chosen institution's
website.

Undergraduate admissions procedures normally require an entrance test. This tends to be a written test, but may be an audition or portfolio for certain art, drama or music programmes. Most university tests are taken in Finland, but some polytechnic entrance tests can be taken outside the country. Make sure that you prepare fully, following any instructions provided by the institution.

> **❝** If you get your school grades and meet the admissions criteria, they put you through to the entrance exam, which includes an English exam. The next step is a group aptitude test and then an interview. This definitely ensures that all the students are serious about studying at this university. **❞**
>
> *Fiona Higgins, HAAGA-HELIA, University of Applied Sciences, Finland*

## Costs

Higher education in Finland is free to EU students at all levels of higher education. There is no entitlement to grants or loans.

Overall, Finland is very slightly less expensive than the UK, coming 14th (to the UK's 13th) in the cost-of-living rankings for 2012 (www.numbeo.com). It comes in lower than Norway, Denmark, Ireland and Australia. The average monthly living costs are between €700 and €900 (£562 and £722); expect to pay more in Helsinki than in smaller towns and cities. Student housing is reasonably priced; your university will support you in finding accommodation. As an EU citizen, you have the right to work in Finland, although language issues and a fairly heavy workload at university mean that this is unlikely.

> ❝ The housing is very cheap (cheaper than the UK)
> and relatively decent. The only thing that costs a
> lot is the food and the alcohol, but as long as you are aware
> of money, then it should work out! ❞
>
> *Fiona Higgins, HAAGA-HELIA,*
> *University of Applied Sciences, Finland*

Most scholarships are for doctoral study or research, although
institutions may have limited scholarships for students on other
levels of study. Speak to your institution about this possibility. For
more details, see the 'Scholarships' section at Study in Finland,
www.studyinfinland.fi/tuition_and_scholarships/other_possibilities.

## You could study . . .

### BEng Chemical Engineering
Saimaa University of Applied Sciences, Lappeenranta and Imatra
Four years
Apply by 14 February
Tuition fees €0
Monthly living costs €700–€900 (£562–£722)

### MA Russian and European Studies
University of Tampere
Two years
Apply by 15 February
Tuition fees €0
Monthly living costs €700–€900 (£562–£722)

### PhD in Economics
Hanken School of Economics, Helsinki
Four years

Apply by 8 April for autumn start, 30 September for spring start

Tuition fees €0

Monthly living costs €700–€900 (£562–£722)

## Useful websites

www.studyinfinland.fi

---

### Also worth considering . . .

If you're interested in the Nordic countries, perhaps you would be interested in studying in Iceland. To find out more, go to Study in Iceland at www.studyiniceland.is and the ENIC-NARIC country page for Iceland at www.enic-naric.net/index.aspx?c=Iceland.

---

# France

France is the UK's closest continental neighbour, offering good-quality education with a strong international reputation. It attracts 6.3% of all international students at university level, but has limited English-medium options at undergraduate level in its public universities. According to OECD Education at a Glance 2012, 2,704 UK students are studying in France.

France has seven universities in the Times Higher Education World University Rankings Top 200 Universities 2012–2013.

## Higher education in France

Higher education takes place in universities, grandes écoles and institutes of technology. The grandes écoles focus on science, engineering and business courses. They are the most prestigious and selective institutions. They charge higher fees and require a competitive exam for entry, which students may spend two years working towards (after achieving A-level-standard qualifications).

There may be some opportunities for the best international students at these institutions, perhaps after initial study at another university. You are advised to contact them to discuss their requirements, but you are likely to need proficiency in the French language.

The academic year starts in September or October and ends in May or June, much as in the UK.

> **" **The class size is around 30–40 students, and there is an emphasis on group work. Furthermore, the professors are always willing to help students individually, and often give up their spare time in order to ensure that each student is on the same level. **"**
>
> *Alican Spafford, Rouen Business School, France*

## *Applying*

Applications for courses taught in English should be made through the international office of your chosen institution. There is a centralised application process known as APB or Admission post-bac for courses taught in French. You can normally make direct applications from around November. Application deadline dates vary between spring and summer, but you should apply as early as you are able. Some institutions have a rolling programme of application and recruitment, which goes on throughout the year.

In addition to your application form and application fee, you may need to include some of the following documents:

- academic transcript
- certificates

- personal statement, to include motivation for studying and future career goals
- letters of recommendation (normally two)
- research proposal (for postgraduate research)
- copy of passport.

The master's degree you choose depends on your future plans; choose a professional master's degree as a route to employment, and a research master's degree as a route to a doctorate.

## Costs

France invests in education; it spends an average €10,000 (£8,024) per student per year. One result of this is the low price for degrees from public universities, which are generally under €500 (£400) per year for most undergraduate and postgraduate study. Fees at public universities are set by law, while private institutions are more expensive, ranging from €3,000 to €10,000 (£2,407 to £8,023) or more per year.

The fees listed below are those set for 2012–2013.

- Bachelor's degree or licence: three years, annual tuition fees of €181 (£145).
- Master's degree: two years, annual tuition fees of €250 (£200).
- Doctoral degree or doctorate: three years, annual tuition fees of €380 (£305).

France is a fairly expensive place to live, ranked number 16 of 90 countries in the cost-of-living index (www.numbeo.com), but that still makes it slightly cheaper than the UK. CNOUS, the National Centre for University and Student Welfare, suggests that students would need around €600 (£481) per month for living costs. Costs in Paris are considerably higher. You'll find lots of useful information on student costs, and student life in general at www.cnous.fr.

Grants may be available to some international students through the French Ministry of Foreign and European Affairs. Entente Cordiale scholarships are awarded for postgraduate-level study. Information on these and other scholarships can be found at CampusBourses (www.campusfrance.org/fria/bourse), while CNOUS (www.cnous.fr) has more information on the system of grants and loans. Note that application deadlines for funding may fall earlier than course application deadlines.

If you are looking for work, the nearest CROUS centre will offer a temporary-student-employment service, although any vacancies are in high demand. Search on the CNOUS site for your regional CROUS office (www.cnous.fr/_vie_59.htm).

## *You could study . . .*

### BA in Arts
College Universitaire de Sciences Po, Reims (private)
Apply by 2 May
Three years
Annual fees €9,300 (£7,462)
Monthly living costs €700 (£562)

### Master's degree in Marine Physics
Université de Bretagne Occidentale, Brest
Apply by 30 June
Two years
Annual fees €462 (£370)
Monthly living costs approximately €600 (£481)

**PhD Neutronics**

National Institute of Nuclear Sciences and Engineering (INSTN), Gif-sur-Yvette

Apply by 11 March

Three years

Annual fees €0

Monthly living costs not provided, thesis allowances available

## Useful websites

www.campusfrance.org/en

# Germany

Germany offers a world-class education with reasonably low tuition fees in a country with the largest economy in Europe. Almost 2,000 UK students already study there (OECD Education at a Glance 2012).

## Higher education in Germany

In Germany, higher education is run by each of the 16 states, rather than by one central Ministry of Education. You can choose between universities, universities of applied sciences and specialist colleges of art, film or music. Universities offer the more academic options up to doctoral level, with universities of applied sciences taking a more practical approach, but only to master's level. Colleges of art, film and music offer creative or design-based courses and often have additional entry requirements to determine artistic skill or musical aptitude.

What is *numerus clausus*? This phrase relates to courses that have far more applications than there are places (medicine, dentistry, veterinary medicine and pharmacology, for example); some courses have a nationwide *numerus clausus*, while other courses may be restricted only at a particular university. If your chosen course is classed as *numerus clausus*, pay careful attention to any additional entry requirements and check how they will decide who will gain a place.

Most institutions are publicly funded, with a smaller number financed by the Church or privately funded. Most German students study at the public institutions; they are cheaper and the standard of education is comparable. At HochschulKompass (www.hochschulkompass.de) you can search for institutions by the way they are funded or by the category of institution.

The academic year officially begins in September, although classes don't start until October. *Wintersemester* teaching runs until mid-February, while *Sommersemester* commences in April and ends in late July.

If you want to study in Germany, you'll need a *Hochschulzugangsberechtigung* or university entrance qualification. You can check whether your qualifications are comparable at the German Academic Exchange Service (DAAD) online admission database www.daad.de.

> Some German universities prefer students to have studied maths at A level, even for courses without mathematical content.

## Applying

Application processes vary between different universities and even between different courses at the same institution. Some will opt for a central application service, like those listed below, while others require direct application. The best advice is to check with the international office at your university.

Over 100 universities are members of uni-assist (www.uni-assist.de/index_en.html), the university-application service for international students, most often used when applicants have qualifications from outside Germany.

Applications for competitive options like medicine, dentistry, veterinary medicine and pharmacy tend to be made through the Foundation for Higher Education Admission at www. hochschulstart.de. You may need to translate this website through a service like Google Translate (www.translate.google.co.uk) as it isn't available in English.

Regardless of the system you use, you may be charged a fee for processing and you may need to provide additional information or evidence, including:

- certificates of qualifications achieved (your university will tell you how to get an authenticated copy)
- CV
- essay
- academic reference
- educational transcript
- SAT or ACT (American College Test) scores (see College Board for further details, www.sat.collegeboard.org/ register/sat-international-dates)
- research proposal.

Most application processes are open between October and June or July (for an autumn start), although you should check individual deadline dates and apply in good time.

## Costs

Only two of the 16 states in Germany charge undergraduate tuition fees of up to €500 (£400) per semester (or €1,000 (£800) per year):

- Bavaria
- Lower Saxony.

The remaining 14 states do not charge tuition fees.

In addition to any fees, higher-education institutions across the country charge semester contributions; this covers certain administration charges and should entitle you to student discounts and free public transport. The cost varies between institutions; you should budget for around €200 (£160) per semester.

Fees at postgraduate level range from around €650 (£522) to a few thousand euros per semester. It is important to note that fees at private universities and colleges will be considerably higher, in some cases as much as €20,000 (£16,046) per year.

Living costs vary depending on where you study. Rent and bills start at around €200 (£160) in Chemnitz and Dresden, and up to €350 (£280) in Hamburg and Munich. Students in Germany live on an average of €770 (£618) per month, according to information provided by DAAD. Germany is ranked number 26 of 90 countries on a 2012 cost-of-living ranking (www.numbeo.com), so living there should be not only cheaper than the UK, but also cheaper than New Zealand, Cyprus, Canada and Singapore.

Any scholarships are unlikely to cover all costs. Scholarships are limited; this is particularly the case for undergraduate study. Search on the DAAD Scholarship Database and ask your university about their opportunities, www.daad.de/deutschland/stipendium/datenbank/en/12359-scholarship-database.

## You could study . . .

### BA Aviation Management
Worms University of Applied Sciences
Three years

Direct application by 15 July
Tuition fees €0
Monthly living costs €670 (£538)

## MSc Cartography

Technical University of Munich (with semesters spent at TU
Vienna and TU Dresden)
Two years
Direct application by 31 May
Tuition fees €500 (£400) per semester in Munich
Monthly living costs €830 (£666) in Munich

## PhD Economics

Graduate School of Economics and Social Sciences, University of
Mannheim
Up to five years
Direct application by 15 April (early application by 15 January)
Tuition fees €0, plus grants awarded
Monthly living costs €600–€700 (£481–£562)

## Useful websites

www.study-in.de/en

### Also worth considering . . .

Alternatives to Germany might include Austria,
Liechtenstein or Switzerland. Discover education in Austria
at OeAD (Austrian Agency for International Mobility),
www.oead.at/welcome_to_austria/education_research/EN. You
can research opportunities in Liechtenstein through ENIC-
NARIC, www.enic-naric.net/index.aspx?c=Liechtenstein. Find
out more about higher education in Switzerland at www.
swissuniversity.ch or the Rectors' Conference of the Swiss
Universities at www.crus.ch/information-programme/
study-in-switzerland.html?L=2.

## Republic of Ireland

The Republic of Ireland is close to home and English-speaking, with a higher-education system that has much in common with the UK system. It is therefore a popular choice among UK students, with 3,880 UK students based there at the last count (OECD Education at a Glance 2012).

### *Higher education in Republic of Ireland*

Degrees can be awarded by universities and by a number of institutes of technology. Other higher-education institutions exist, where qualifications are awarded through HETAC, the Higher Education and Training Awards Council (www.hetac.ie). A number of the higher-education institutions in Ireland are private. For a list, see the Education in Ireland website, www.educationinireland.com/en/Where-can-I-study-/View-all-Private-Higher-Education-Institutions.

For general information on education in Ireland, go to the Irish Council for International Students website, www.icosirl.ie.

Trinity College Dublin tops the two Irish universities on the Times Higher Education World University Rankings Top 200 2012–2013. It is ranked number 110 (just above the universities of Nottingham and Warwick). University College Dublin also features, at number 187, and falls just below Newcastle University and the University of East Anglia.

The qualifications on offer differ slightly from those in England, Wales and Northern Ireland in that a three-year ordinary degree is available, as well as a three-year or four-year honours degree (Scotland offers a similar choice). The grading system (first, upper second, lower second and so on) echoes the UK. Taught and research master's degrees should take one to two years, with doctorates taking a minimum of three years' research.

You can search for undergraduate and postgraduate courses through the Qualifax Course Finder (www.qualifax.ie). Postgraduate options can be found through Postgrad Ireland (www.postgradireland.com).

## Entry requirements

The A-level requirements for most degrees can make Irish universities a challenge to enter. This contrasts with many other European countries where the completion of A-level-standard qualifications is sufficient and specific grades aren't always necessary. Irish universities tend to be looking for academic subjects that echo those taken at school in Ireland. If you are applying with different qualifications, you should speak to the university's international office or admissions office in advance; they may need to evaluate your qualifications before you apply.

Most degree-level programmes ask for three Cs at A level, or equivalent, as a minimum requirement. For the more competitive courses, like medicine, they ask for particularly high grades. In the scoring system for A levels, grade A* at A level is worth 150 points, and grade E is worth 40. (For full details, see the Central Applications Office website at www.cao.ie/index. php?page=scoring&s=gce.)

At universities and associated colleges, your best four A levels (or three, plus an AS in a different subject) will be considered up to a maximum of 600 points. Some institutions will consider different combinations of A-level and AS-level grades, so may be accessible for those without four A levels.

## Entry to medicine

For entry to medicine, applicants must have at least 480 points (which can be obtained from four Bs at A level, for example), plus any minimum requirements from their university. Both exam results and HPAT scores will be considered when offering a place. See Undergraduate Entry to Medicine brochure for more details, (www.cao.ie/downloads/documents/UGMedEntry2013.pdf).

> The Health Professions Admission Test (HPAT, www.hpat-ireland.acer.edu.au) is required for undergraduate entry to medicine, while the Graduate Medical School Admissions Test (GAMSAT, www.gamsat.acer.edu.au/gamsat-ireland) is needed for applications to postgraduate medicine. Application dates are often early and examination dates may be restricted to a single day.

## Applying

While the academic year is in line with the UK, running from September to June, the application system has its differences. Undergraduate applications are based on actual grades (and an admissions test, in some cases) and little else, so offers aren't made until results come out.

You can apply online or on paper from 5 November through the Central Applications Office (CAO) at www.cao.ie. Applications should be made by 1 February or earlier, particularly for restricted-entry courses, although there is a late closing date for other courses of 1 May. In most cases, there is no need for references or a personal statement. A fee is charged for processing.

## Postgraduate applications

Postgraduate applications can be made direct to your chosen university, often via the international office. Some institutions use the Postgraduate Applications Centre (PAC) at www.pac.ie. Closing dates vary, even within a single institution. In most cases, a minimum of a 2:2 grade in an undergraduate honours degree is required for a master's degree.

In addition to the application form and fee, you may need to include an academic transcript, references, a CV, a research proposal (where relevant) and a statement of interest, explaining your motivation, commitment and what you hope to achieve.

Postgraduate research at Trinity College Dublin can be applied for at any time. Each programme of taught postgraduate study has an individual deadline; many programmes require applications by 30 June, but you should check for your chosen course.

## Costs

UK students on their first full-time undergraduate degree should not have to pay tuition fees. However, you will be required to pay a student contribution or registration fee of a maximum €2,250 (£1,805) in 2012/2013.

According to Postgrad Ireland, you can expect postgraduate fees of over €4,000 (£3,210) for research degrees, with taught programmes ranging from under €4,000 (£3,210) to as much as €29,500 (£23,676) for an MBA.

At number eight out of 90 countries on a 2012 cost-of-living ranking, Ireland is a little more expensive than the UK (see www. numbeo.com for more details). In the Republic of Ireland, Dublin is the most expensive place to live. Education in Ireland estimates that, on average, a student can expect to spend between €7,500 and €12,000 (£6,021 and £9,633) per year; of course, this will depend on where you live and the lifestyle you choose.

## You could study . . .

### BArch in Architecture
University of Limerick
Five years
Apply through CAO by 1 February

**166**

€2,250 (£1,805) registration fee

Living costs of up to €10,500 (£8,429) for one academic year

**MA Human Resource Management**

University College Cork

Two years

Apply by 31 August

Annual fees €5,000 (£4,014)

Monthly living costs €1,145–€1,495 (£919–£1,200)

**PhD Philosophy**

University College Dublin

Three years

No application deadline date

Annual fees €5,400 (£4,335)

Monthly living costs €1,285 (£1,032)

## *Useful websites*

www.educationireland.ie

## Italy

Very few public universities in Italy teach their courses in English. Even so, the latest figures show us that 183 UK students are studying in the country (OECD Education at a Glance 2012).

## *Higher education in Italy*

The majority of universities in Italy are state-funded, although there is a range of alternative provision including non-state universities, universities for foreigners (focusing on Italian language, literature and culture), specialist postgraduate schools, and telematic (or distance learning) universities. Most programmes are taught in Italian; English-medium opportunities in Italy are most often found at private universities and colleges. Although the options for a full degree may be limited, Italy remains a popular destination for students on Erasmus exchanges.

> **❝** All the teaching is done through large lectures (130 students per class) but the professors do have office hours and are reachable by email. There are no seminars and classes aren't compulsory: a big bonus. **❞**
>
> *James Wheeler, Bocconi University, Italy*

The academic year runs from September or October until July. The qualifications on offer are a three-year *laurea* which is the Italian bachelor's degree, the two-year *laurea specialistica* which is comparable to a master's degree, while the *dottore magistrale* is comparable to a doctorate. Much of the assessment in Italian higher education is exam-based.

> The Politecnico di Milano recently announced plans to deliver most of its degree courses and all of its postgraduate courses in English from 2014.

## Applying

Provided that you meet the general entry requirements for higher education in the UK and have completed 12 years of education, you can be considered for undergraduate study in Italy. If you have a bachelor's degree, you can be considered for a master's degree, and if you have a master's degree, you can consider applying for a doctorate. You should apply direct to individual institutions, which may set their own additional entry requirements. You can discuss the process and timescale with your university's international office before you apply.

## Costs

Fees are set by the individual institutions. You should expect to pay up to €1,000 (£803) per year for undergraduate study in the public institutions and more with the private providers, although these might still end up costing less than many of the courses in the UK.

Postgraduate fees start at around €800 (£640) per year. For living costs, Italy comes out a little cheaper than the UK. It is ranked 22nd (to the UK's 13th) in the cost-of-living rankings for 2012 at www. numbeo.com.

## You could study . . .

### *Laurea* (Bachelor's) degree in Electronic Engineering

Politecnico di Torino, Turin

Three years

Apply by 31 July

Annual fees €1,780 (£1,429)

Monthly living costs €600–€800 (£482–£642)

### Master's degree in Economics and Political Science

University of Milan, Milan

Two years

Apply between April and September (competitive application)

Annual fees €2,755 (£2,211)

Monthly living costs of up to €1,000 (£803)

### PhD Science and Management of Climate Change

Ca' Foscari University of Venice

Three years

Apply by 11 April

Annual fees €1,120 (£899)

Monthly living costs from €700 (£562)

## Useful websites

www.study-in-italy.it

### *Also worth considering . . .*

If you want an alternative to Italy, you might have wondered about Greece, although few international students choose Greece for their studies. You can find out more at the Greek Ministry of Education (www.minedu.gov.gr).

## The Netherlands

Interest in the Netherlands as a study venue has been growing steadily, with its cheaper fees and hundreds of programmes taught entirely in English. Dutch universities are keen to attract international students and have been actively recruiting in the UK by visiting schools and attending education fairs. According to the latest figures, some 860 UK students are studying in the Netherlands, with the universities also reporting an increase in applications.

The Netherlands has an impressive 12 universities in the Times Higher Education World University Rankings 2012–2013 Top 200.

### *Higher education in the Netherlands*

The style of teaching in the Netherlands is interactive and student-centred, with a focus on problem-based learning. The academic year runs from early September to late June.

You can opt to study at a research-based university (WO) or a University of Applied Sciences (HBO), which offers more vocational options. An academic or research-oriented bachelor's degree (WO) takes three years, while the applied alternative (HBO) would take four years, with the chance of a work placement and often a study-abroad opportunity. Associate degrees take two years, with the option to move on to an applied bachelor's degree.

> **"** We're taught in a classroom. There are no lectures. The classes are very practical and laid back. I find the teaching style very personal as there are only up to 30 people in a class. We're really aided and guided. **"**
>
> *Rebecca Jackson, Stenden University*
> *of Applied Sciences, the Netherlands*

At master's level, you again have the choice of either a research-based degree (WO) or the applied route (HBO), both of which take one to two years. In contrast, doctorates are only available through the research universities (WO).

To find a course, you can browse the NUFFIC database at http://ispacsearch.nuffic.nl or use Study in Holland's database at www.studyinholland.co.uk/what_to_study.html.

## Applying

In most cases, two or three A levels, or equivalent, should be sufficient to meet the requirements for most bachelor's degrees. If you studied an alternative qualification, you should discuss it with your chosen university. At postgraduate level, you will need a bachelor's degree to progress to a master's. It is likely that any offer you receive will require you to pass your courses, rather than achieve specific grades. Although getting a place at university may seem easier than in the UK, the university will need you to prove your capability in the first year. Students who can't cope academically will be asked to leave the course.

In some popular subjects like medicine or law, places may be restricted through a scheme known as *numerus fixus*. For these courses, the allocation of places is decided through a slightly complicated lottery system, which can vary according to the requirements of the university; talk to your chosen institution to gain an understanding of how to give yourself the best chance of success.

## Studielink

You can apply to public institutions at undergraduate and postgraduate level through Studielink (http://info.studielink.nl/en/studenten/Pages/Default.aspx) from 1 October onwards. You can choose up to four options, including one *numerus fixus* course. Requirements for supporting documentation vary, but could include:

- certificates
- academic transcript
- personal statement or letter of motivation indicating why you are applying
- copy of passport
- CV
- two letters of recommendation
- research proposal (where relevant).

For some postgraduate study, an admissions test like GRE (www.ets. org/gre) or GMAT (www.mba.com) will be needed. In all cases, your institution will be able to tell you whether they require application through Studielink and any supporting information they need.

Most courses have an application deadline of 1 June, although *numerus fixus* courses require an earlier application. You can find a helpful guide to Studielink at the Study in Holland website, www.studyinholland.co.uk/studielink.html. Some courses will require a direct application instead.

The application process at university colleges differs, in that it requires an earlier application that should be made direct; another key difference is that students are invited to an interview.

> 66 I had to write a personal statement and an essay. I was out of Europe when I applied so they did the interview over Skype. They were also fine with me scanning and emailing a lot of the documents, which was a huge help. 99
>
> *Shanna Hanbury, Amsterdam University College,*
> *the Netherlands*

## *Costs*

In the public universities, you can expect annual fees starting at around €1,835 (£1,473) for 2013–2014 at undergraduate level, and something similar at postgraduate level. This can be paid upfront or through an instalment system. Fees at university colleges are usually higher.

Undergraduate students under the age of 30 who work for at least 32 hours per month should be entitled to a basic grant of around €260 (£209) per month in 2012 with the possibility of topping this up further with a supplementary means-tested grant. Preparations are being made to increase the 32-hour requirement to 56 hours per month. Access to grants at postgraduate level varies. EU undergraduate and postgraduate students can take out a student loan for tuition fees from the Netherlands. You can find out more about loans and grants at DUO-IB-Groep (Department of Education), www.ib-groep.nl/International_visitors/EU_EEA_ students/Grant_for_tuition_or_course_fees.asp.

Scholarships are also available. You can search for a scholarship through NUFFIC's Grantfinder at www.studyinholland.nl/ scholarships/grantfinder.

At number nine out of 90 countries on the 2012 Numbeo (www. numbeo.com) cost-of-living ranking, the Netherlands is not cheap; it is comparable in living expenses to the UK or Ireland.

> 66 I pay €289 (£232) a month for a shared space in student accommodation, with bills included. It's not a lot of space, but it's reasonable and nice. You don't spend any money on transportation because you bike everywhere. Food is very expensive here, definitely more than in the UK. I usually spend about €20 (£16) at the supermarket for a well-rounded shopping list, but if I go to the Turkish shops it's cheaper, around €10 (£8). 99
>
> *Shanna Hanbury, Amsterdam University College, the Netherlands*

## *You could study . . .*

### Bachelor of Fashion Technology
Amsterdam Fashion Institute, Amsterdam University of Applied Sciences
Four years
Apply by 1 April
Annual fees €1,835 (£1,473)
Monthly living costs €900–€1,200 (£722–£963)

### MSc in Mathematics
Radboud University Nijmegen
Two years
Apply by 1 May
Annual fees €1,771 (£1,422) in 2012–2013
Annual living costs of up to €10,000 (£8,028)

### PhD in Development Studies
International Institute of Social Studies (ISS), Erasmus University, Rotterdam
Four years

Apply by 1 September for January start

Annual fees €32,000 (£25,688), although fellowships are available

Monthly living costs €900 (£722)

## Useful websites

www.studyinholland.nl

## Norway

With around 14,000 students from overseas, approximately 340 students from the UK and no fees at public universities, how about studying in Norway? It offers many postgraduate courses in English, although only a handful at bachelor's-degree level. Norway has high costs but one of the best standards of living in the world; it has been ranked top by the UN for the past four years. It can be cold, but you will discover a great outdoor lifestyle.

> **❝** Within the first month of arriving here, I'd been on fishing trips, hiking trips, whizzing around in a little rib boat on the Saltstraumen, swimming in some of the most beautiful lakes which are a 15-minute walk from the university, and even met the Norwegian Prime Minister. It's been quite something! **❞**
>
> *Megan Doxford, University of Nordland, Norway*

## Higher education in Norway

Higher education takes place at universities, specialised university institutions, university colleges or national colleges of the arts. Universities have a research focus, while university colleges focus on professional studies. It is possible to gain a master's degree and sometimes even a doctorate at a university college. Most higher-education institutions in Norway are state-funded, although there are some private university colleges. In Norway, you would generally study a three-year bachelor's degree, a two-year master's, and a three-year doctorate. The academic year runs from mid-August to mid-June.

It is common for students in Norway to take time out to work or travel before university, so they may be a little older.

You can search for study opportunities through Study in Norway at www.studyinnorway.no.

## *Applying*

According to the GSU list (the list of minimum requirements for admission to Norwegian higher education), you will need five subjects in total, including two A levels (or one A level and two AS levels); you could make up the other two or three subjects from GCSEs. Students from Scotland will need to pass five Highers. Some subjects will have additional requirements. You can find the GSU list at the Norwegian Agency for Quality Assurance in HE (NOKUT) website, www.nokut.no. Successful completion of a bachelor's degree is needed to progress to master's level.

You should apply direct to your chosen institution sometime between October and March for courses starting in August. Application deadlines vary, but your institution will be able to advise on specific deadline dates, as well as any supplementary information needed. This could include:

- academic transcript
- copies of certificates, for qualifications already gained
- CV
- research proposal, where necessary.

> 66 The application process was very simple and
> relatively hassle-free. Everything was done online
> and they only required a few documents such as my
> undergraduate transcripts, my CV and some essays I was
> required to write to apply for a scholarship. A GMAT score
> was also required. 99
>
> *John Magee, BI Norwegian Business School, Norway*

## Costs

Whether you are studying at undergraduate level or for a master's degree or a PhD, you are unlikely to have to pay fees at a state-funded university or university college. There is a small semester fee of NOK300–NOK600 (£33–£65), which gives you a student-discount card along with membership of student-welfare associations, access to campus health services, sports facilities and so on. Private institutions charge fees, although these should still be lower than those charged by universities in the UK, perhaps with the exception of some MBAs.

There are some scholarships available for study in Norway. See the Study in Norway website for details.

Living costs in Norway are high; in fact, it ranks number one out of 90 countries in a 2012 cost-of-living index, see www.numbeo. com. You should expect to have at the very least NOK8,900 (£971) per month for living expenses.

> **❝** The price of living is very high, so the Norwegian government requests you have ample funds for the year ahead. You have to have NOK90,000 (£9,823) in a Norwegian bank account in order to be accepted. This is the amount of money needed to survive a year at university out here. It is possible to get work, which helps an awful lot financially, especially as the minimum wage is a lot higher than in the UK. **❞**
>
> *Megan Doxford, University of Nordland, Norway*

## *You could study . . .*

### BA Acting
Ostfold University College, Halden
Three years
Apply by 1 March
Tuition fees NOK0
Monthly living expenses NOK8,000 (£873)

### MSc Telemedicine and e-Health
University of Tromsø
Two years
Apply by 1 December
Tuition fees NOK0
Monthly living expenses NOK8,290 (£905)

### PhD Aquaculture
University of Nordland
Three years
Apply by 1 April
Tuition fees NOK0
Annual living expenses NOK92,500 (£10,097)

## *Useful websites*

www.studyinnorway.no

## Spain

Although the option to study in Spain on an exchange programme is a popular one for UK students, with over 1,000 university students based there according to latest figures, opportunities for a full degree are limited. Most options at public institutions are taught in Spanish. This looks set to change as the Spanish government is keen to recruit more international students. There are already opportunities in private institutions, which make up around a third of the higher-education institutions in Spain.

### *Higher education in Spain*

The website, www.universidad.es, is developing a searchable database of courses. You can also find information through the Ministry of Education at www.educacion.es.

Undergraduate degrees take from three years, master's degrees last one or two years, while doctorates take from two years. Some of the private universities offer accelerated programmes to reduce the length of study.

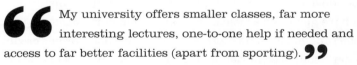

My university offers smaller classes, far more interesting lectures, one-to-one help if needed and access to far better facilities (apart from sporting). 

*Eleanor Spooner, IE University, Spain*

### *Applying*

As long as you have the general qualifications to access HE in the UK, you should meet the general requirements for HE in Spain. Talk direct to your chosen university about their application procedures. You may need to apply through UNED at www.uned.es for

evaluation of your qualifications. (Note: you may need to translate
this page using a service like Google Translate.)

Completion of a bachelor's degree in the UK or the European
Higher Education Area will satisfy the general requirements of
a master's degree. Sixty ECTS credits are required to progress to
research at doctoral level.

> **❝** The university application process explored your
> whole range of interest and motivations. It was
> personal and comprehensive, wanting to derive the best
> aspects from their applicants. **❞**
>
> *Esme Alexander, IE University, Spain*

## *Costs*

A bachelor's degree or *grado* at a public university cost between
€535 and €1,280 (£430 and £1,028) per year in 2011/2012. Cuts in
public spending have led to an announced increase in tuition fees.
An average increase of €500 (£400) per student is expected.

At private universities, fees start at around €5,000 (£4,014), but
can be considerably higher than this, although these institutions
often have generous schemes of financial support. Master's
(*máster*) and doctoral (*doctorado*) degrees are paid for per credit;
a master's course comprising 60 ECTS credits may cost between
€995 and €1,920 (£799 and £1,542). Private institutions set their
own fees, but these must still fall within government limits.

Scholarships are available and can be found through the
Universidad website at www.universidad.es/information_and_
resources/scholarships. You can also ask the international office of
your chosen university.

# ALGOMA
## university

experience.algomau.ca

SMALL UNIVERSITY
# BIG EDUCATION

## A Community of Students Learning Together.

Algoma University is committed to placing you first. Our professors encourage interaction, discussion & independent thought in small classroom settings. At Algoma University you get the support, guidance & mentoring you need to succeed. Here is your chance to make new friends from every corner of the world!

- Internationally recognized degrees
- A welcoming & diverse campus
- Competitive international fees
- Undergraduate degree & certificate programs
- Never more than 65 students in a class
- A true Canadian experience in the heart of the Great Lakes in Sault Ste. Marie, Ontario

Contact us!  international@algomau.ca

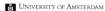

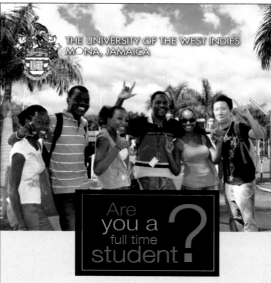

# THE UNIVERSITY OF THE WEST INDIES
## MONA, JAMAICA

Inspiring Excellence, Producing Leaders

## WHY NOT STUDY AT THE UNIVERSITY OF THE WEST INDIES, MONA?

The University of the West Indies (UWI) is an innovative, internationally competitive, contemporary university deeply rooted in the Caribbean and committed to offering quality higher education. It is the largest tertiary level institution in the English-speaking Caribbean with campuses at Mona and Montego Bay in Jamaica, St. Augustine in Trinidad and Tobago, Cave Hill in Barbados and its Open Campus. While its programmes are international in scope, The UWI has a unique Caribbean focus. This strong emphasis on Caribbean issues makes The UWI the ideal educational institution for local and international students with an interest in Caribbean society.

## THE UWI MONA CAMPUS

Nestled at the foot of the Blue Mountain Range, the picturesque Mona Campus in Jamaica is the oldest of the University's four campuses and you can choose from five faculties: Humanities & Education, Law, Medical Sciences, Science & Technology and Social Sciences. Our undergraduate degree programmes are normally three years, on a two semester system, beginning in August and ending in May. Postgraduate diplomas and higher degree programmes are offered through a number of Institutes and Centres of Excellence affiliated with the University. Special group and summer programmes in Caribbean Cultural Studies are also available during the winter, spring and summer breaks.

## SPORTS

Hone your skills or discover your talent in Track and Field, Cricket, Football, Basketball, Hockey, Rugby, Volleyball, Table Tennis, Tennis and Swimming at the Mona Bowl for Sporting Excellence, site of the UWI-Usain Bolt Regupol Track. Our athletes are a competitive force at every level: one of our athletes won a medal in the 110m hurdles at the 2012 London Olympics.

## ENTRY REQUIREMENTS

For further information, contact our
Senior Assistant Registrar (International Students),
at iso@uwimona.edu.jm or
visit our website www.mona.uwi.edu

# THE UNIVERSITY OF THE WEST INDIES
## MONA, JAMAICA

Inspiring Excellence, Producing Leaders

## CASE study

**ELKE POLZER**,
Third year student
of English and
American studies at
Chemnitz University
of Technology in
Germany

Elke came to The University of the West Indies, (UWI) Mona in September 2012, having registered to pursue a degree in English and American Social and Cultural Studies at her home university in Germany. The opportunity to study at The UWI, Mona was for her a perfect opportunity. " (It) fits not only perfectly into my regular Bachelor program at my home university, but offers me the opportunity to improve and develop my skills in the field of Linguistics , with a special focus on Caribbean Dialectology, Culture, Philosophy and Language Education", she says.

"The experience provides me with a unique opportunity to look beyond my own cultural horizon, to evolve my organizational skills and my productive work habits.

Another reason why I chose The UWI, Mona is to broaden my horizons. I am very interested in current research and projects, like the Caribbean "Wikiproject" and the ongoing debate about English vs. Jamaican Patois and the possibility that Jamaican Creole might become a second official language in Jamaica, which should be used as a tool to teach children who have it as their first language."

Elke maintains: "At The UWI, Mona, I have the opportunity to interact with persons doing research in areas including cultural studies, Language Education and Literature. I gain the best access to the basics and fundamentals for my thesis and research, which will concern Applied Linguistics with a special focus on sociolinguistics and Jamaican Creole." She adds: "I was really surprised that Mona Campus possesses an extensive and worldwide interacting library system. The Information Technology infrastructure is modern and expanding rapidly. I was overwhelmed by how well-equipped the Campus is with multimedia classrooms and lecture rooms."

Elke is one of approximately 400 international students studying at the UWI, Mona Campus. Students from Belgium, Botswana, Burma, Canada, China, Denmark, France, Germany, Guadeloupe, Japan, Nigeria, Norway, Puerto Rico, Sweden, the United Kingdom, and the United States of America as well as from all 15 countries in the English-speaking Caribbean are enrolled at Mona.

# LOOKING FURTHER INTO VU UNIVERSITY AMSTERDAM

12 FACULTIES

OVER 70 PROGRAMMES TAUGHT IN ENGLISH

OVER 24.000 STUDENTS

OUTSTANDING EDUCATION AND RESEARCH

14 INTERDISCIPLINARY RESEARCH INSTITUTES

150 RESEARCH PROGRAMMES

CAMPUS UNIVERSITY IN AMSTERDAM

WWW.VUAMSTERDAM.COM

VU UNIVERSITY AMSTERDAM

LOOKING FURTHER

Shaping a New World,
Making a Difference

Tilburg, the Netherlands

www.tilburguniversity.edu

Understanding Society

**AP PROGRAMMES**
/ AP IN COMPUTER SCIENCE
/ AP IN DESIGN TECHNOLOGIST
/ AP IN IT TECHNOLOGY
/ AP IN MULTIMEDIA DESIGN AND
COMMUNICATION

**BA PROGRAMMES**
/ BA OF ARCHITECTURAL TECHNOLOGY
AND CONSTRUCTION MANAGEMENT
/ BA IN ECONOMICS AND IT
/ BA IN JEWELLERY, TECHNOLOGY AND
BUSINESS

**BA – TOP–UP PROGRAMMES**
/ BA IN E-CONCEPT DEVELOPMENT
/ BA IN DESIGN & BUSINESS
/ BA IN SOFTWARE DEVELOPMENT
/ BA IN WEB DEVELOPMENT

*Free education for EU citizens

**kea**
COPENHAGEN SCHOOL OF
DESIGN AND TECHNOLOGY

MY TOUCH
EXPLORING NEW
FRONTIERS

UTWENTE.NL/ATLAS

gh potential students with an interest in technology and
ciety shape their future at ATLAS University College.
LAS offers the first Liberal Arts & Sciences programme
the Netherlands strongly focused on new technology.
you are an honours student with the talent and
mbition to develop a depth of knowledge in multiple fields
study, this selective and intensive Bachelor of Science
ogramme might be right for you. Driven by the technology
the future you will work alongside other multifaceted
inkers on integrating social, technical, behavioural and
sign perspectives to create a meaningful impact on
ciety. Become part of this fully English-taught BSc
ogramme and take on the challenges of the future.
e you ready to explore new frontiers?

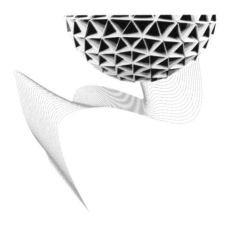

LAS. Lift the world.

**UNIVERSITY OF TWENTE.**
HIGH TECH HUMAN TOUCH

**www.niie.edu.vn**

# INTERNATIONAL PATHWAYS TO CAREER SUCCESS

NTT Institute of International Education (NIIE) is a member of Nguyen Tat Thanh University, an university with the student population of more than 20,000, which locates in Ho Chi Minh City. NIIE is specialised in providing international education in Vietnam with a wide range of programmes.

Studying at NIIE, you are truly immersed in an international environment with students coming from European and Asian countries. You will be part of a vibrant city centre campus and community with rich culture and heritage. With our emphasis on developing professional and entrepreneurial skills, our graduates are able to approach problems with creative, practical solutions and take up leadership roles

Life at NIIE is exciting with many extra-curricular activities such as fashion show, football tournament, etc. You can also join a variety of student clubs organized by NTTU student union such as martial arts club, dancing club etc. The people at NIIE are friendly and we do our best to make students feel at home.

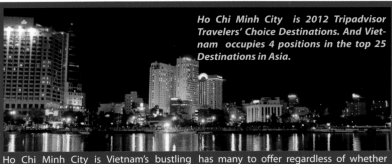

*Ho Chi Minh City is 2012 Tripadvisor Travelers' Choice Destinations. And Vietnam occupies 4 positions in the top 25 Destinations in Asia.*

Ho Chi Minh City is Vietnam's bustling largest city which sets the cultural and economic pace for the country. Formerly known as Saigon in the so-called "Vietnam war", visitors of the city will only see the signs of the war in the attractions like Re-unification Palace and the War Remnants Museum. Being chosen as 2012 Tripadvisor Travelers' Choice top destination, the city has many to offer regardless of whether you are a casual traveler or a long-term stayer. Tantalising tastes of foods, dizzying maneuver of motorbikes, timeless wander between ancient pagodas and sleek skyscrapers, endless music in exotic nightclubs make it more a place to 'be' than a place to 'see'.

# A Leader In International Education

Founded as an independent School of Medicine in 1976, St. George's University has evolved into a leader in international education, drawing students and faculty from 140 countries to the island of Grenada, in the West Indies. Students attending St. George's enjoy the benefits of a thriving multicultural environment on the True Blue campus, offering all the amenities and technologically advanced facilities of a world-class institution.

## Academic Accolades

The University is often acknowledged as the best private school in the Caribbean region and its approvals and accreditations rival those of the elite institutions in the world. In 2011, the American Veterinary Medical Association's Council on Education granted full accreditation to St. George's School of Veterinary Medicine, the highest standard of achievement for veterinary medical education in the United States. In 2010, the US Council on Education for Public Health accredited St. George's Public Health programme — making it one of only five non-US institutions to receive this coveted approval.

## Successful Alumni

The University's doctor of veterinary medicine graduates have demonstrated impressive pass rates on the Royal College of Veterinary Surgeons Statutory Licensing Examination, and last year had a 100% pass rate. St. George's doctor of medicine graduates have practised in 45 countries, including the UK and a number of former Commonwealth countries. In 2011, St. George's University's US and Canadian medical students achieved a 96% first-time pass rate on the USMLE. The first-time pass rate for the School's entire student body, hailing from 34 countries, was 95%.

## Degree Programmes

This University provides many degree options to international students including programmes in medicine and veterinary medicine, master's level degrees in public health, business, and research and sciences, and bachelor's degrees in the life sciences, business management information systems information technology, medical sciences psychology, and liberal studies. Joint degrees in public health, science, and business are available to medical and veterinary medicine candidates.

## Stunning Campus

The University's $250+ million state-of-the-art campus has been described as one of most beautiful academic environments in the world. Academic residential, student life, and student support buildings are among 65-plus buildings spread across the stunning multilevel campus, and include restaurants, a small animal clinic and large animal resource facility, and the Windward Islands Research and Education Foundation Research Institute.

Information on the University is available on www.sgu.edu and through YouTube, Facebook and Twitter at StGeorgesU

St. George's University
THINK BEYOND
Grenada, West Indies

**WHERE WE STAND**
OUR INTERNATIONAL TRAINING PUTS MORE
DOCTORS IN US HEALTH CARE THAN 2/3RDS
OF US MEDICAL SCHOOLS

LAUNCHING YOUR CAREER WITH A RARE
COMBINATION OF CLINICAL AND CULTURAL SKILLS
**WILL MAKE YOU
STAND OUT**

©2013 St. George's University

# St. George's University Alum Swims English Channel, Raises Funds for Animal Foundation

St. George's University's School of Veterinary Medicine graduate Brittany King doesn't shy away from challenges. She's run five marathons, completed an Ironman and climbed Mount Kilimanjaro, all while navigating her way through veterinary school. However, this past September, Brittany attempted her most intense physical test yet — swimming the English Channel.

Only 1,400 individuals have successfully swum the English Channel's 22-mile stretch. "I have never done one single activity for that amount of time," Dr. King explained. "If the tide's wrong, you can be washed six miles south and swim much more than 22 miles. There are so many variable factors — it's the hardest thing I've ever done."

Dr. King's English Channel swim was a fundraising effort for the Banfield Charitable Trust organization's Laps of Love, which allows for the treatment of pets whose owners are unable to finance their care. Dr. King has practised with Banfield Pet Hospital in Texas since graduating from St. George's in 2010. She speaks glowingly about her stint at St. George's University, ranging from its caliber of education and its motivated faculty, to the off-campus experience and student activities.

"St. George's is the best thing that ever happened to me," Dr. King explained. "The professors are incredible and so supportive, and it doesn't matter what your dreams are — the University supports them. I went to Grenada and learned what's important – what to value and what not to value. St. George's changed my soul and I'm more motivated with everything in life."

All of Dr. King's hard work and training paid off when on September 4, 2012, she completed her swim across the English Channel in 13 hours and 48 minutes. She says it was an immense challenge, but believes that being able to provide for animals was the motivation she needed to complete the journey and join an exclusive group of athletes.

"I've loved the career path I've been on from the moment I started at St. George's," Dr. King said. "I love veterinary medicine and I love that the animals we treat give so much love to their owners. I love being able to give back to them."

## About St. George's University

St. George's University is a dynamic centre of higher education with a global network of scientific collaborators in education, medicine, research, and science. Nearly Over 6,000 students from over 14,097 countries attend St. George's and are taught by 2,300 faculty members recruited from across the world. Over 12,000 graduates of the University enjoy successful careers in medicine, veterinary medicine, public health, science, and business worldwide.

Information on the University is available on www.sgu.edu and through YouTube, Facebook and Twitter at StGeorges

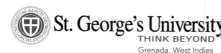

St. George's University
THINK BEYOND
Grenada, West Indies

## THE HAGUE
### UNIVERSITY OF APPLIED SCIENCES

**SUPPOSE YOU...**

... study in the international city of **peace and justice**

## International Bachelor Studies

- European Studies
- Industrial Design Engineering
- International Business and Management Studies
- International Communication Management
- International Financial Management and Control
- Law
- Process and Food Technology
- Public Management
- Safety and Security Management Studies

www.thehagueuniversity.nl

## International Master Studies

- Master in Accounting and Control
- Master of Business Administration
- Master in International Communication Management

H/ THE HAGUE UNIVERSITY OF APPLIED SCIENCES MAKES YOU THINK

# Going abroad and want to learn the language?

Teach® Yourself

**Trust Teach Yourself, the preferred language learning brand for over 70 years**

## Grasp the basics

Get Talking and Keep Talking courses give you:
- the skills and confidence to speak a language in just 10 days through common scenarios
- culture and travel advice

Available separately or in a pack.

## Become a confident speaker

Available in over 60 languages!

Complete courses use the new Discovery Method to ensure you:
- master all four skills (reading, listening, writing and speaking) going from beginner to intermediate speaker in one course
- communicate confidently and comfortably

*Succeed with the NEW DISCOVERY METHOD
Learn faster, remember more

## Learn on the go with Complete Apps

With over 50 hours of learning, Complete language apps have:
- four levels, taking you from beginner to intermediate
- **interactive** exercises including record-and-compare and fill-in-the-gaps
- **free** reference section with a talking dictionary and grammar help

Search 'Teach Yourself'

# £2 OFF*

## ALL STUDENT ESSENTIALS

These practical and jargon-free guides show students how to easily master essential study skills in just one hour, covering every key area, from developing critical thinking and essay writing to revision and exam know-how.

STUDENT ESSENTIALS

IN 1 HOUR

ESSAY WRITING

Sophie Fuggle

STUDENT ESSENTIALS

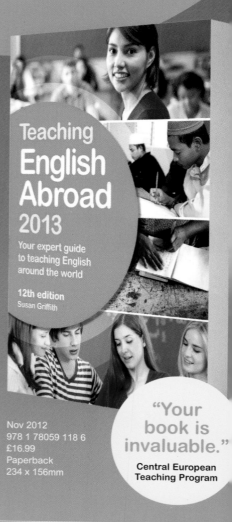

Living costs are lower than in a number of the European countries mentioned in this chapter. Spain is ranked number 36 out of 90 countries in a cost-of-living survey for 2012 (see www.numbeo. com), comparing favourably to the UK at number 13. Prices in the major cities can be much higher.

## *You could study . . .*

### **Bachelor's degree in Aerospace Engineering**
Leganes campus, University Carlos III de Madrid
Four years
Apply by 13 July
Annual fees €1,608 (£1,291)
Monthly living costs from €500 (£400)

### **MA Political Science**
Universitat Autònoma de Barcelona
12 months
Apply between January and August
Annual fees €2,700 (£2,168)
Monthly living costs €700–€1,000 (£562–£803)

### **PhD Translation and Intercultural Studies**
University Rovira I Virgili, Tarragona
Three years
Apply between 15 September and 10 October
Annual fees €400 (£321)
Monthly living costs €600 (£482)

## *Useful websites*
www.universidad.es/en

***Also worth considering* . . .**

Interested in studying in Portugal? Nearly all courses are in Portuguese, but you can find out more at DGES (General Directorate for Higher Education) at www.dges.mctes.pt/DGES/pt.

## Sweden

As many as 30,000 international students currently choose Sweden for their studies and nearly 600 of them are from the UK. With a strong focus on innovation and a forward-thinking, student-centred academic environment, Swedish higher education has much to offer.

Five Swedish institutions are in the Times Higher Education World University Rankings Top 200 2012–2013.

### Higher education in Sweden

The academic year runs from late August to early June and is divided into two semesters. Three-year bachelor's degrees or *kandidatexamen* are the norm. A master's degree or *masterexamen* will take one to two years, while doctoral research or *doktorsexamen* takes at least four years.

Higher education takes place in universities and university colleges, with universities the only institutions with the automatic right to issue doctoral degrees. Local collaboration is widespread, so many institutions offer options reflecting the needs of local industries and businesses.

You can search for study options at Study in Sweden, www.studyinsweden.se/Course-search.

The name of the institution will not always reveal whether it is a university or university college; most university colleges will call themselves universities, while some universities are called *högskola* (or university college) in Swedish. Degrees awarded by both types of institution are equivalent to one another.

## Applying

Any qualification that gives you access to HE in the UK should do the same for undergraduate studies in Sweden. Individual institutions then set their own procedures for selecting applicants; this might include grades, assessment of samples of work, interviews, admissions tests or work experience. Your institution's international office will be able to advise further about any special requirements.

For bachelor's and master's degrees, applications are made online through University Admissions at www.universityadmissions.se. Deadlines are generally mid-January for August start and mid-August for any courses starting in spring. At doctoral level, applications are made direct to the institution and often to the specific department, accompanied by copies of certificates, academic transcripts and letters of recommendation. Check any deadline dates with your academic department.

## Costs

In most cases, university courses in Sweden are free of tuition charges, although student-union-membership fees are payable at SEK50–350 (£4.65–£33) per semester. A range of scholarships are available at Study in Sweden (www.studyinsweden.se/Scholarships). Ask your institution about any scholarships that they administer.

An average monthly budget for a student is around SEK7,070 (£657). Sweden is ranked number 11 out of 90 countries in

Numbeo's 2012 cost-of-living table at www.numbeo.com, which makes it cheaper than the Netherlands, Denmark and Australia, but a bit more expensive than the UK.

## You could study . . .

### Bachelor's degree in Software Engineering and Management
University of Gothenburg
Three years
Apply via www.universityadmissions.se by 15 January
Tuition fees SEK0
Monthly living costs SEK9,000 (£836)

### MA/MSc in Global Health
Karolinska Institute, Stockholm
12 months
Apply via www.universityadmissions.se by 16 January
Tuition fees SEK0
Monthly living costs SEK8,000 (£743)

## Useful websites
www.studyinsweden.se

# Pros and cons of study in Europe

Pros

- Relatively close to home.
- Often cheaper for tuition fees than much of the UK.
- No visa restrictions.
- Able to work and to stay on after study.

Cons

- Language issues.
- Some countries have high costs of living.
- Pressure to do well in first year to remain on the course.

## Student story
## Alican Spafford, Rouen Business School, France

The increase in tuition fees got Alican Spafford thinking about studying abroad. 'The recent rise in fees was a major factor in my decision to study abroad. Considering other countries offered the same degree that I wanted at a much lower cost, studying overseas seemed to be the obvious conclusion. Why would I waste time learning about international culture, when the opportunity is there to experience it directly? It is an opportunity that students in the UK all too often overlook, in my opinion, to their disadvantage. As a student seeking a career in business, I was aware that international experience would be an excellent asset to have. It takes no more than a quick internet search to realise that the best UK universities are just a small proportion of the best across the world. In this modern age, new possibilities have arisen in the field of education and, for me, studying abroad was a chance that I had to take.

'I had always been interested in the French language and planned to choose a degree that would integrate the subject into my course. I was therefore looking at UK courses such as International Management with French, French and International Business etc. France was therefore the first country that I considered in my international search.

'Being in a different country from the institution you want to study at means that there is only so much information that you can gather in order to compare those that interest you. I found a wide selection of universities that offered the course I wanted. I sent many emails asking about qualification language requirements. I needed to be sure that by going abroad I was increasing my career prospects rather than damaging them, so I spent a great amount of time looking at many different business-school ranking tables. This eventually allowed me to draw up a list of about six or seven European institutions offering a course that I wanted to do, with fees and living costs suited to my budget. In the end, I chose BSc in International Business at Rouen Business School thanks to the great career prospects that it offered and its excellent international reputation, which finally outweighed the lower tuition fees of business schools in Holland or Scandinavia.

'As UK tuition fees were one of the big reasons that led to my decision to study abroad, I spent a lot of time comparing the costs of studying. My course in France is usually just over £6,000 a year, but I was able to win an academic scholarship that will reduce my fees by €1,000 (£803) a year. In comparison with similar European courses, this is one of the more expensive. Yet compared with the UK, I am already saving £12,000 over my four-year degree, which is a huge saving. If I wanted to pay even less, I could have chosen to pay less than £1,500 a year in Holland, or gone to study in Sweden, Finland or Denmark, where there are no tuition fees.

'The cost of living also tends to be much better suited to a student's budget abroad than in the UK. I discovered that the average cost of living in European countries is almost always lower than in the UK, even in fairly expensive European cities. I pay £160 a month for my accommodation that is less than a 10-minute walk away from Rouen Business School, and will be reimbursed about half of this by a subsidy available to all students, regardless of nationality. Student accommodation in the UK would cost me around ten times more than the rent I pay here in France.

'The application process for the BSc programme at Rouen Business School was very simple and I was aided along the way through a very helpful recruitment team. The application was completely online through the school's own website, where I had to create an account and complete my profile as an applicant. I uploaded my CV and personal statement, answered a short questionnaire about myself, and was soon contacted with the offer of an interview by videoconference. A couple of weeks after the interview, I received a confirmation and registered officially to the course, again online.

'As students studying abroad are not eligible for the UK student loan, I had to discover ways to help finance my course. The Recruitment Department at Rouen Business School was extremely helpful in providing me with the information I needed with regards to financing, and even contacted other people on my behalf. They also suggested that I apply for a scholarship, which I had not previously thought of, and thanks to this I have made a saving of €4,000 (£3,212).

'During my first week at Rouen Business School I met with the Director of the Programme a few times, who ensured that I felt very welcome and answered any questions that I had. I also met with the recruitment team that I spoke with during the application process.

'From my experience of universities in the UK, the majority of courses offered are taught through lectures, with minimal personal contact and tutoring with professors. At Rouen Business School, classes have a much better atmosphere. The class size is around 30–40 students, and there is an emphasis on group work. Furthermore, the professors are always willing to help students individually, and often give up their spare time in order to ensure that each student is on the same level.'

Alican has had no problems making the move to France. 'I've had almost no need to adjust as the culture is very similar to Britain. In the north of France, even the weather's the same so it's as if I'm home.'

## Alican's top tips

### Accommodation
'Don't apply to a university without guaranteed residence unless you have family or friends in the area who are willing to help you find independent accommodation, as this is very difficult to arrange from abroad.'

### Food
'Cooking and preparing your own food bought from the supermarket is a lot cheaper than buying meals from the canteen or restaurants. You can find some great bargains in supermarkets if you look hard enough.'

### Insurance
'If you choose to study in Europe, make sure you have a new European Health Insurance Card (EHIC). This allows you to be reimbursed for any medical costs you encounter, such as visiting the doctor or prescribed medicine.'

### Living costs
'Make sure you find out about student discounts and voucher cards that can be claimed for free. This can help save money on books, transport and leisure activities.'

## Financial support

'Ask the institution what kind of financial support they might offer and if you may apply for a scholarship. It's always worth asking.'

## Working while studying

'For UK students going abroad to study, it is not as difficult to find part-time work as you might think. Although working in bars or restaurants allows you to meet many different people, tutoring is a much better use of your time. Many websites exist that allow people to advertise English-language tutoring, and often people will just want someone British to practise with, so teaching experience isn't even necessary.'

## Student life

'If you are worried that you would be missing out on UK student life, you don't need to be. Student lifestyles are very similar and there is always something for everyone. Nonetheless, the atmosphere in your university town should be considered when you make a choice. Whether you want a city with a big nightlife and lots going on, or a quiet village in the forest, take a look at reviews on the internet to make sure the university you choose is best suited to you.

'The best thing about studying abroad is meeting different people and experiencing cultures that you wouldn't necessarily have had the opportunity to discover before. It's an adventure that allows you to become more cultured and open to new ideas, and develops you into a culturally aware individual with a strong personality.'

Alican used some of the following websites to help research his options:

- Student Cash Point, www.studentcashpoint.co.uk
- FT Business School Ranking, http://rankings.ft.com/businessschoolrankings
- Campus France, www.campusfrance.org
- L'Etudiant, www.letudiant.fr.

*Rouen Business School (www.rouenbs.fr) was ranked number 51 in the FT European Business Schools Ranking 2011 and is rated 19th on the FT's Masters in Management Ranking 2012. It is considered to be amongst the top business schools in France.*

## Jacobs University Bremen: Profile

## Jacobs University Bremen

Jacobs University Bremen is Germany's premier, private, international, English-language university, where 1,300 students from over 100 nations worldwide represent 75% of the student body.

The campus is a vital, multicultural community united in the exciting and challenging work of shaping Jacobs University's mission: our goal is to prepare the leaders of tomorrow to responsibly meet global challenges.

In a suburban setting the 34-hectare green campus houses state-of-the-art laboratories, classroom facilities, a modern library and research centre, a cinema, theatre, café, Interfaith House, and a new sports centre, including playing fields and a fitness centre, ensuring that there is always something interesting to do. All undergraduate students live in single rooms in residential colleges for all three years of their degree.

Jacobs University awards bachelor's, master's, and doctoral degrees in the natural sciences, engineering, the humanities and social sciences. The focus on studying across different disciplines allows students to declare their major at the beginning of the second year. They will be involved in hands-on research opportunities starting in the first year of study. The challenging three-year undergraduate programme will be complemented with a mandatory internship.

With a student–faculty ratio of 10:1, Jacobs offers excellent individual attention. The constant inter-cultural exchange helps to develop global perspectives. Thus, students are uniquely well equipped for a career in an international area. Within three months of finishing their degree, 90% of each graduating class successfully enter the workforce or a graduate school. Harvard, Yale, London School of Economics, Cambridge, and Oxford all have been destinations of Jacobs' graduates wishing to continue their education.

Jacobs University is one of the top-ranked universities in Germany according to the annual CHE rankings published in *Die Zeit*.

Inspired? Then find out more about Jacobs University on www.jacobs-university.de.

## Jacobs University Bremen: Case study

### Sarah Islam from Bangladesh, Electrical and Computer Engineering (Class of '12)

**At Jacobs, students come from 110 countries. What is your background?**

My schooling started in England where I was for a year. Then I came back to Bangladesh where I was born and studied through to 10th grade. I then went to America for a year as an exchange student.

**How did you hear about Jacobs University?**

The son of my father's friend attended Jacobs and praised it a lot (but warned me about the weather!). I chose Jacobs because of its reputation and high academic standing coupled with the unique international setting. No other university I looked at had this diversity. The scholarships offered by Jacobs are also substantial.

**Why did you choose your major?**

I chose Electrical and Computer Engineering because I want to work in the power sector of Bangladesh which needs development.

**What do you like best about the campus?**

The campus is small enough that you can go anywhere in 10 minutes. The number of students is limited so even though it is not a huge area, there is a lot of space. It is 'quaint'. The colleges are very friendly places!

**In the residential colleges you share a double-suite with Denise from Germany. What was your best experience of living together?**

I enjoyed just about everything. The random Saturday afternoon talks or going on YouTube together; those moments make the experience special. There is always a friend in the next room; that is a great feeling.

**What are the advantages of college life?**
The main advantage would be having a support system 24/7. Also, there is
no fitting in to deal with here. Everyone is different, coming from different
countries and cultures. It is just being yourself and enjoying the different and
fun people.

# HAN University of Applied Sciences: Profile

Inspiring environment. Innovative and skilled professional staff. International student body. At HAN University of Applied Sciences, we make it our business to offer higher education of an outstanding quality to students across the globe.

HAN University of Applied Sciences is one of the largest providers of education in the Netherlands, with more than 30,000 students and almost 2,500 staff members spread over two campuses. HAN excels at putting theory into practice in an international context throughout all four years of undergraduate study. Spread over the cities of Arnhem and Nijmegen close to the German border, HAN has modern buildings, state-of-the art multimedia centres, world-class laboratories and wireless internet access.

The HAN bachelor's degree delivers its graduates high-powered credentials and marketable skills upon entering the global career market. It is our goal to prepare each of our students to meet the unique challenges found in today's working world. At HAN we ensure that our lectures and projects leave room for personal attention and student development.

An interactive and student-centred teaching style gives students the needed guidance as well as the freedom to develop professionally. Students attend lectures in the Netherlands, do their work placement abroad, study at partner universities anywhere in the world and do their graduation assignment for an international company.

Classes are held only in English and in small groups of maximum of 30 students, facilitating individual contact with teachers and fellow students. Joining the international student body means merging education with social networks. In the dynamic HAN community students are at the heart of a multitude of activities: city trips, parties, thematic weeks and so on.

International bachelor's degrees:

- Automotive Engineering
- Business Management Studies (HRQM)
- Communication
- Finance and Control
- International Business and Management Studies
- Life Sciences
- Logistics Management (Economics).

More information about course content and admission requirements can be found on www.han.nl/international/english.

# HAN University of Applied Sciences: Case study

HAN offers a great learning environment: the atmosphere is relaxed, open and friendly – teachers know your name and if you're really struggling with something, they often make time after class to help you and answer questions. Class size is small, which allows for a more personalised learning experience. Within your class you'll again be separated into smaller groups for many assignments and projects. The focus is on gaining practical and strategic knowledge about business as a whole and your specific field.

Jana Light is a third-year Bachelor of Communication student from Britain, currently doing her internship at Greenpeace, New Zealand.

'My favourite thing about the university has to be the international environment. In my year alone there are students from Holland, Germany, China, Japan, Vietnam, Malaysia, Indonesia, Russia, Ukraine, Bulgaria, Columbia, the Caribbean, Mexico, Brazil, Ghana – you name it, we've got it. While at first it's somewhat difficult to come to grips with the different cultures and their habits, it's an integral part of your learning experience, and it's one I'm certainly glad to have had.

'Along with assembling all these different cultures in one classroom, the bachelor's degrees feature a year abroad, in two countries of your choice. During your third year you spend half a year as an exchange student at one of the 90-plus partner universities, and the other half you spend at a company and country of your choice, doing an internship. Then, if you want to, you can spend your final semester also abroad, doing your final internship and graduation assignment. Who needs a gap year if you can have the equivalent count towards your study?

'This international experience will certainly make you appear more attractive to future employers, especially now that the world is connected on a whole new level through social media. I'm not worried about the economy: there will always be jobs in business, and my study at HAN so far has taught me a lot about myself and my skills – and how to use them correctly.'

**196**

# Amsterdam University College: Profile

Do you have broad interests? Do you enjoy discussion and debate? Do you like to be challenged? Do you feel at home in an international environment? Then you're warmly invited to join the international AUC student community!

Amsterdam University College (AUC) – a joint institute of the University of Amsterdam and VU University Amsterdam – offers a top-quality, selective, English-taught, international, liberal arts and sciences bachelor's programme that crosses the boundaries of languages, cultures and academic disciplines. Discussions start from 'big questions' in science and society and lead to in-depth study in a wide range of disciplines. You can major in the sciences, social sciences or humanities. AUC is located at Amsterdam Science Park and enrols up to 50% science majors.

As a residential and selective honours college, AUC attracts students from all over the world who study and live together on our brand-new campus. As an AUC student you form part of an engaging academic and social community, which is supported by small class size, a residential campus and a strong international setting, with 50% of the students having an international background.

Would you like to know more? Visit the AUC website: **www.auc.nl**

## Amsterdam University College: Case study

### Nick Tennies, Class of 2014
**A healthy environment**

'As I was considering what my next step in life would be and had decided that I wanted to continue my academic career, I knew one thing for certain: I wanted a new city and culture more focused on humanity and the greater good. Amsterdam is where I ended up and I couldn't be more pleased. AUC itself incorporates many of the things I love about its setting here in Amsterdam: diversity, international opportunities, and a general sense of social consciousness.

'AUC's core philosophies encourage multifaceted problem-solving skills that incorporate a wide variety of disciplines and perspectives. As a science major focused on energy, climate, and sustainability, I believe that this approach is absolutely necessary in facing global issues such as climate change, pollution, and overpopulation.

'AUC's diverse undergraduate education will help me to expand my horizons for furthering my education in a master's programme and open me up to other passions that I would not have discovered otherwise.'

# Utrecht University: Profile

## Welcome to Utrecht University

Founded in 1636 and located in the heart of the Netherlands, Utrecht University is one of Europe's leading institutions for teaching and research. The university is engaged in high-quality and innovative research and collaborates with universities and research centres all over the world. Utrecht University provides an interdisciplinary environment and offers its students a personalised educational experience.

## What we offer

Utrecht University offers four English-taught bachelor's and 80 English-taught master's degree programmes. You become part of an academic environment where committed teaching staff share their knowledge with ambitious students. A master's degree from our university gives you an edge if you want to do a PhD at Utrecht or get into another world-class university.

## What we expect

As a student at Utrecht University, you become a member of our academic community. We expect you to be critical, to voice your opinion and to take part in academic discussions. You are also expected to conduct research.

## Our academic staff

You will be taught by dedicated experts – top researchers or professionals who also hold influential positions outside of the university. Utrecht University academics want to get to know their students and build a relationship with them.

## International environment

Each year, more than 2,000 international students come to Utrecht University to take part in its excellent English-language programmes and courses.

They follow their ambition – just like Utrecht University. We are proud to offer you a curriculum with an international perspective that educates and prepares you for an increasingly globalised world.

## Master's programmes

Our one-year and two-year English-taught master's degree programmes enable you to specialise in a specific area of interest to you. The programmes are designed to prepare you for a professional or research career.

## Entry requirements

Individual programme entry requirements may differ. Please check www. uu.nl/internationalstudents.

# Chapter 6
## Studying in the USA

The USA is an increasingly attractive destination for UK students; in the academic year 2010/2011, a record 8,947 UK students went to the USA. Over 4,000 opted for undergraduate-level study, nearly 2,500 for postgraduate education, with the rest on non-degree programmes or post-study work schemes.

More and more students seem to want to discover the appeal of the American higher-education system: a system with a choice of over 4,500 universities and a broader, more flexible approach to university studies. Quality of education in the USA is unsurpassed; around one third of the 200 universities featured in the Times Higher Education World University Rankings 2012–2013 are from the USA. Some students are turning down places at the leading universities in the UK to take advantage of the breadth and quality of education on offer stateside.

> The academic year in the USA runs from mid-August or early September to late May or early June.

## The education system

In the States, the terms 'university' and 'college' are generally used interchangeably. However, community colleges are different; they can only offer two-year associate degrees, rather than four-year bachelor's degrees.

## Choosing where to study

When deciding where to apply, you need to consider which type of institution is right for you.

- Public universities are funded by the state and tend to have more students and lower fees. International students will end up paying more than state residents.
- Private universities tend to be campus-based, with better facilities and fewer students. They are funded by private donations, grants and tuition fees. Fees are higher, but the same fees are charged for all. More scholarships tend to be available.
- Community colleges offer associate degrees over two years (see page 204), with the possibility of transferring to a university to top up to a full bachelor's degree. They are often cheaper and less competitive.

The Ivy League is made up of eight prestigious private universities and colleges in the north-east of the USA. It started out as a sports league, rather than any kind of elite group or ranking system. For this reason, many top universities from across the country are not in the Ivy League, including Berkeley, which is a public university, and Stanford, which is on the west coast.

Keep an eye out for the public Ivy League which includes the universities of Michigan and California; these institutions offer a quality education without such extortionate fees.

American degrees offer a much wider choice of subjects to study than you would expect in the UK. They are made up of a range of types of courses.

- Core (or general education), providing the compulsory foundation for university study. Students will often be required to select from a broad range of courses including sciences, history, maths, English composition and literature and so on.
- Major courses, your main subject area; choose from options like English, engineering or history.
- Minor courses, taken in a secondary subject or allowing you to specialise within your main subject area. You could minor in a foreign language or consider adding a computer-science minor to a maths major.
- Academic track, a group of courses focused on a specific topic within a major; a student majoring in computer science could select a track in computer systems, for example.

Some universities offer co-operative education programmes, made up of paid work experience, rather like a sandwich course in the UK. In other cases, unpaid internships may offer degree credit.

## Finding a course

You can use College Board (undergraduate), www.collegeboard. org, or College Navigator (undergraduate and postgraduate), www.nces.ed.gov/collegenavigator, to search for courses at public, private or community colleges. EducationUSA features a list of other college or course search sites on its '5 steps to study' web page, www.educationusa.info/5_steps_to_study.

## Transfers

It is possible to transfer between universities. Transfers would normally take place after freshman year (Year 1), but (since you need a minimum of two years at a university to graduate) any later than sophomore year (Year 2) could prove tricky.

> The Sutton Trust runs a US Summer School Programme to encourage talented young people from low-income backgrounds to consider university in the USA. You can find out more at www.suttontrust.com/summer-schools/us-summer-school.

### *Associate degrees*

Associate degrees like Associate of Arts (AA) or Associate of Science (AS) are two-year programmes of general studies along with foundation courses in a chosen subject (a major or field of concentration). The qualifications often relate to vocational areas like hospitality management or health sciences. The programme might include core and concentration courses, electives, practical work, fieldwork and supervised study.

They are broadly equivalent to the first year of UK undergraduate study. After completion, students may wish to transfer to a US bachelor's degree by completing an additional two years of study.

Students who are only applying with GCSE qualifications could apply for an associate degree. Certain vocational qualifications might be accepted by community colleges, but not by the more competitive universities.

## American college year names

Year 1   Freshman Year
Year 2   Sophomore Year
Year 3   Junior Year
Year 4   Senior Year.

### *Bachelor's degrees*

Bachelor's degrees generally take four years to complete, although there are some five-year courses in architecture, sciences and engineering. A US bachelor's degree is comparable in level to a British bachelor's degree. Unlike in the UK, where you choose your subject before you apply, you can apply for an undecided major, and decide on your chosen subject at the end of sophomore (or second) year. This has more in common with the Scottish system of education than with the rest of the UK. Much of the first year, and some of the second year, is spent on a range of introductory courses. Some of this core curriculum will relate to subjects you may wish to make your main subject choice (or major). For example, if you are considering majoring in psychology, you might opt for maths and quantitative reasoning, and social and behavioural sciences as your core subjects.

> ❝ I have had one-to-one support from the international student adviser who was fantastic in setting up my schedule and what I was going to study. ❞
> *Stuart Bramley, Scottsdale Community College, USA*

Entry requirements vary, but most would require a minimum of five GCSEs or Standard Grades at C or above, including maths and English. You would need to show that you are completing advanced-level study; the universities will be able to check your attainment from your academic transcript and any admissions tests you sit. Competitive universities will be looking for three A levels or equivalent. Less competitive universities may consider vocational qualifications, like a BTEC level 3 Extended Diploma, a vocational course broadly equivalent to three A levels. For more information on applying, see the following section.

### Honours degrees

Gaining an honours degree in the USA tends to indicate that the student has defended an undergraduate thesis (or piece of original research) known in the UK as a dissertation. Confusingly, a degree with honours can also mean that someone has achieved with particular academic merit, although this is more usually known in the USA as *Cum laude* (with honour), *Magna cum laude* (with great honour) or *Summa cum laude* (with highest honour).

### Graduate school

What we know as postgraduate education in the UK is described as graduate education or grad school in the USA. Master's degrees and PhDs gained in the USA are comparable to British master's degrees and PhDs. Certain subjects that you could start at undergraduate level in the UK can only be taken at graduate level in the USA; these include medicine and law. Pre-med and pre-law programmes are available at undergraduate level, although these programmes aren't a mandatory requirement for medical or law school.

# Applying

The application process for undergraduate and postgraduate courses has some similarities to the UK system, although there is no admissions service like UCAS to coordinate applications. For the most part, applications are made direct to the chosen institution, although some universities use the Common Application for undergraduate programmes; see page 208 for more information.

As part of the application process, you will be required to send detailed academic records and official course information for qualifications you have completed. You may be required to submit your academic documents to an organisation that can convert your qualifications to a comparable level of study in the USA. Your university will give you further details of which organisation to use or, for a list of approved agencies, try the National Association of Credential Evaluation Services (NACES), www.naces.org.

## Undergraduate applications

The timescale for applications is similar to that of UCAS, although there is a separate system if you are applying for a sports scholarship.

After Christmas in your first year at sixth form or college (Y13 in Northern Ireland or S5 in Scotland), you will need to start researching degree programmes and universities. It is suggested that you narrow down your choice to between three and seven universities, due to the time and costs involved.

Most applications comprise:

- application form
- fee (around $50 to $100 (£32–£63) per university)
- admissions test scores
- a few essays (of around 500 to 750 words)
- transcript (details of your academic performance)
- two or three recommendations

- financial statement
- possibility of an interview.

You will be applying to the university as a whole, so admissions staff will decide your fate, rather than academic staff from your chosen department. They will be looking at more than just success at A level; GCSEs, AS levels, your passion for learning, your love for your subject (if you have decided on a major), your extra-curricular activities and you as a person will all be considered.

> Although you can apply for an undecided major, you will normally apply to a particular school within the university, for example, the School of Arts, School of Engineering or School of Management.

## Application forms

From 1 August, the Common Application becomes available at www.commonapp.org. This is used by around 450 universities, although each university involved still retains its own deadlines, administration fees and requirements. All other universities require direct applications, so you may have a number of forms to complete. Even if you're not using the Common Application, most applications are similar, so you will not have to start completely from scratch with each one. There tend to be more sections to complete and more space available than on the UCAS application, so it can result in quite a lot of work. You will be able to copy and paste information, as long as you remember to amend and target it each time.

Universities tend to offer separate deadlines for early-decision and early-action applications, often sometime in November. The benefit of applying early is that you are being considered before the majority of applicants and competing with fewer students, so you might have a better chance of an offer. On the downside, you'll need to sit any admissions tests early. Most institutions offer either early decision or early action; some offer neither.

The main difference between the two is that early decision is binding, whereas early action gives you the comfort of knowing you have an offer, but with no strings attached. You can only apply to one university as early decision and you are committing yourself to that university if they offer you a place. This demonstration of commitment can have its benefits for consideration by the university and for scholarships. You might choose early decision if you have your heart set on one specific university, but it could be risky if the amount of scholarship or financial aid you are offered will play a part in deciding where you study.

Regular admissions deadlines come a little later, often in December or January. Check individual institutions for full details.

### Undergraduate admissions tests

You will need to check whether an admissions test will be necessary. Many universities will be looking for both good grades and strong admissions-test scores; this is particularly so if you are applying for academic merit-based scholarships (see Help with finances on page 219). Where an admissions test is required, the amount of importance placed upon the test scores varies between universities.

Most universities ask for the American College Test (ACT) or the Scholastic Assessment Test (SAT) for undergraduate-level study; both tests are designed to assess academic potential. If the university accepts both, you will be able to choose which test to sit. Although the tests are both well-recognised and essentially achieve the same objective, the tests themselves are different and you may find that one will suit you more than the other. The SAT originally set out to measure aptitude, while the ACT was achievement-based, although both have changed since their inception.

The ACT includes more questions, so you end up with less time per question; it includes English, reading, science and higher maths. It comprises a single test, which may be more convenient, but is only available in limited locations across the UK. For the more competitive universities, you are likely to have to complete a supplementary 30-minute writing section (in addition to the nearly three-hour-long ACT test). It costs around $60 (£38), plus $15 (£9) for the written section.

The SAT comprises a reasoning test of nearly four hours, plus two or three subject tests for the more competitive universities. The test is widely available in the UK, but both tests are taken on different dates. It costs around $80 (£50) for the reasoning test, $54 (£34) for the first subject test and $12 (£8) for subsequent basic subject tests.

It is essential to be prepared for these tests. Take a look at www.fulbright.org.uk/study-in-the-usa/undergraduate-study/ admissions-tests/preparing-for-the-sat-act and www.collegeboard. org to help you prepare.

Sitting a test in early autumn of year 13 in England and Wales, Y14 in Northern Ireland or S6 in Scotland, is ideal, as it gives you time to resit, if necessary. Some candidates choose to take their first test as early as the previous spring. Candidates need to register sometime between spring and mid-September. It is worth registering early as places can quickly fill up. You can register and find a testing centre through the ACT website, www.act.org, and the SAT website, www.sat.collegeboard.org.

## *Essays*

Essays are likely to be based on your response to specific questions set by the university; make sure that you answer the questions fully and directly. They may want to find out about your skills and personality traits; why you want to study at this university; what are your goals; and what inspires you. Although you might choose to write on a subject related to your area of interest, you do not normally have to do so. The Fulbright Commission (www. fulbright.org.uk/study-in-the-usa/undergraduate-study/applying/ essays) has examples, video tips and useful handouts on this subject.

Sample questions for the Common Application essay (University of Virginia).

- Discuss some issue of personal, local, national or international concern and its importance to you.
- Indicate a person who has had a significant influence on you and describe that influence.
- Describe a character in fiction, a historical figure or a creative work that has had an influence on you, and explain that influence.

## *Transcripts*

The transcript should include predicted grades from your current qualifications, but also your progress from year 10 (Y11 in Northern Ireland or S3 in Scotland) onwards. It could include GCSE or Standard Grades, details of any exams taken since then (AS levels and so on), results of mock exams or other internal assessments and any academic honours achieved. Where relevant, ask your school or college to include explanations for any anomalies in your academic record. Qualifications may also need to be explained and details of the institution incorporated.

The format of the transcript is generally chronological. It should be around a page in length and produced on official headed paper. You will need to work with your school or college to help them prepare this, directing them to sample transcripts, such as those on the Fulbright Commission website (www.fulbright.org.uk).

On the application form, you'll be asked for your GPA. The Grade Point Average cannot be officially converted from UK qualifications, so you should leave this section blank.

## Recommendations

You will need to arrange two or three letters of reference or recommendations from staff who know you well; follow your chosen university's guidelines on whom to ask. The restrained and often modest tone taken in a UCAS reference might not be enough for a US university. Recommendations from US schools tend to be far more detailed and far more positive, so you will need to prepare your referee to really sell you. Refer potential referees to the Fulbright Commission website for tips and sample letters, www. fulbright.org.uk/study-in-the-usa/undergraduate-study/applying/ reference-letters.

The EducationUSA website (www.educationusa.info) explains why you might choose to waive your right to see a copy of the recommendation:

> **66** A recommendation form may include a waiver where you can relinquish your right to see what is written about you. If this option is offered, most admissions officers prefer you to waive your right so that recommenders may feel more comfortable when writing their evaluations. Admissions officers usually interpret waived recommendations as more honest. **99**

## Financial statement

How will you fund your studies in the USA? Your university will want to know, so you will need to complete any requests for evidence. You can use the evidence again when applying for a visa. You will need to show that you can at least cover the first year's costs, maybe even the costs for the length of the whole course. If you need financial assistance, you should include how much will be required. In most cases, a 'need-blind' admissions system means that your application will not be affected by this evidence.

## Interview

These days, the internet and Skype are typically used for interviewing. You may be surprised to find yourself being interviewed by an ex-student. Alternatively, the interview may be with a member of admissions staff. They may come to the UK or may ask you to go to the States, in which case you could enquire about help with travel expenses.

You could be asked why you have chosen this university, how you will contribute and why you intend to study in the USA. They will want to know about your subject interests, whether you have any ideas about your major or what your strengths and weaknesses are.

To prepare, you should look over the research you did when choosing this university. You can read over the essays you sent and look at how you can expand upon what was written. You should prepare questions to ask of the interviewer, but make sure that any questions aren't already answered in the university's prospectus or website.

## Offers

Early-action applicants get an answer in December or January, while regular applicants hear later in the spring. The response could be one of three options: accepted, wait list, or not accepted.

Those accepted can choose to accept, decline or defer. (Deferring is rare, so you should always check the process with your university. Even if your university agrees, any offers for funding might not also be deferred.) A deposit of around $500 (£315) will secure your place.

If you are placed on a wait list, there is still a possibility that you will be offered a place; follow any instructions you receive about the wait-list process and keep your fingers crossed.

Your offer won't be conditional, but it is still important to work hard and do well. You may gain university credit or advanced standing from good UK qualifications.

## Applying for graduate school

As with undergraduate admissions, students apply direct to their chosen universities. The Fulbright Commission suggests restricting applications to between four and six institutions.

The details of deadline dates, entry requirements and application fees will vary, although most will require some of the following:

- application form
- fee (around $50 to $100 (£32–£63) per university)
- admissions test scores
- a few essays (of around 500 to 750 words)
- research statement
- transcript (details of your academic performance)
- two or three recommendations
- possibility of an interview.

Each application may be different but, rather like a job application, you should be able to adapt the information you provide, rather than starting from scratch each time.

Most universities will be looking for at least a 2:2 from UK undergraduate study, with the more competitive universities looking for considerably more. They will be looking at your all-round offer, not just academic achievements, but also the way you demonstrate a good understanding of your chosen university and how this matches you as an individual. US universities are also keen to know about your involvement in extra-curricular activities. Contact the universities direct to discuss their requirements.

Much of the information in the previous section on applying for undergraduate study will also apply to postgraduate applications (see page 206). Notable differences include the research statement and the different admissions tests.

## Research statement

The research statement allows you to outline your areas of interest, specialism and plans for how and why you intend to complete your research. Here are some of the key points that you need to consider when writing a research statement.

- Sum up your current plans for research, understanding that they may well change as you refine your ideas or as other developments occur.
- Relate your plans to your chosen university department and professors.
- Demonstrate your intellectual skills, but without alienating the admissions staff who may be considering your application.

## Graduate admissions tests

Most postgraduate options require an admissions test and there are a number of different tests to consider:

- Dental Admissions Test (DAT), www.ada.org/dat.aspx
- Graduate Management Admissions Test (GMAT), www. mba.com
- Graduate Record Exam (GRE), www.ets.org/gre
- Law School Admissions Test (LSAT), www.lsac.org
- Medical College Admission Test (MCAT), www.aamc.org/ students/applying/mcat.

The cost of these tests can be quite substantial, with DAT costing $360 (£227) and MCAT $355 (£224). Some tests are available across the country, with others restricted to London, and the DAT currently only being tested in the USA.

How the tests are used also varies, with some tests being a central factor in a successful application, while other tests are considered along with a variety of different aspects. In some cases, looking at how your scores compare to last year's averages can help to indicate your chances of success.

Preparation is vital, as the system tends to rely quite heavily on multiple-choice testing. Remember that you will be competing with US students who are used to this style of testing, so you need to know what to expect. See the individual test websites for sample papers or use the Fulbright Commission's 'Preparing for Admission Exams' page at www.fulbright.org.uk/study-in-the-usa/ postgraduate-study/admissions-tests/preparation.

## You could study . . .

**Associate degree in Computer and Information Sciences**
Baton Rouge Community College, Louisiana
Two years
Apply by 18 August (financial aid applications by 15 April)

Annual fees $6,643 (£4,190)

Annual living costs $8,642 (£5,450)

**Bachelor's degree in English Language and Literature**

University of Virginia (public)

Four years

Apply by 1 January (early-action application by 1 November)

Annual fees $37,336 (£23,546), merit scholarships are available

Annual living costs $9,419 (£5,940)

**Master's degree in Evolutionary Biology**

Rice University, Houston, Texas (private)

Two years

Apply by 1 January

Annual fees $37,292 (£23,520), financial aid available for
international students

Annual living costs $10,750 (£6,780)

# Visas

If you plan to study in the USA and you aren't a US citizen or a
permanent resident in the USA, you will need a visa. Find out
about the rules and the procedures at Embassy of the US, London
(http://london.usembassy.gov).

You should apply for your visa at a US embassy or US consulate
before you leave the UK. There are two visa categories, F-1
Student Visa and J-1 Exchange Visitor Visa; F-1 is for students
undertaking a full-time programme in the USA, while J-1 is for
those on study-abroad programmes or exchanges. Your university
will tell you which one to apply for. There are differences in
restrictions on these two visas: whether you can work, for example
(see page 222).

> **❝** After you receive your visa you will need it upon entry to the USA and then again for opening accounts etc. After this you should store it carefully. Be aware of things that may impact on it, for example, if you decide to travel or get a job. **❞**
>
> *Simon McCabe, University of Missouri, USA*

Once you have been offered a place at a university and provided evidence as to how you will fund the first year of your studies, your institution will prepare a Form I-20 (F-1 visa) or Form DS-2019 (J-1 visa); you will need this to apply for your visa. The university will also send instructions as to how to apply. The process will involve a visa interview at the US Embassy in London or the US Consulate in Belfast, as well as completion of an online SEVIS I-901 form (requiring a $180 (£114) fee for J-1 or $200 (£126) fee for F-1) and an online visa application or MRV (requiring a $160 (£100) fee).

If your application is successful, you will normally be admitted for the duration of your student status. You should check any visa restrictions and follow them to the letter, as breach of these conditions is an offence.

## Costs and help with finances

Tuition fees in the USA can be considerably higher than across the rest of the world. However, weigh this up against a strong tradition of financial aid and things might not always be as expensive as first anticipated. One third of international undergraduate students in the USA have a scholarship as their main source of funding, while two-thirds of undergraduate students receive some form of financial support.

## Costs

According to the College Board (www.collegeboard.org), the following average annual tuition fees are reported for 2012/2013:

- four-year, public institutions (out-of-state students): $21,706 (£13,688)
- four-year, private institutions: $29,056 (£18,326).

Fees for out-of-state students at two-year community college should be around $8,000 (£5,046) per year.

> If you are looking at ways to make US education more affordable, you could consider taking a year or two at a community college before transferring to a university.

You should allow in the region of $10,000 (£6,307) per year for accommodation, food, books and materials, travel and so on. Costs vary widely depending on where you live and the type of lifestyle you lead. Universities will provide an idea of local living costs on their websites.

The USA comes in at number 33 of 90 countries on a cost-of-living ranking from Numbeo (www.numbeo.com). This suggests that its living costs are more reasonable than the UK, Canada, Australia, New Zealand and much of northern Europe.

### Help with finances

Research carried out by EducationUSA reveals that in 2010/2011 more than 1,000 universities supported their international students in the following ways: some awarded amounts of over $10,000 (£6,307); some offered options costing under $20,000 (£12,616) per year (including fees, accommodation, travel etc);

while others brought costs below $20,000 (£12,616) with financial aid or scholarships.

While you cannot access the UK student loans and grants for overseas study, there may be some alternative options available. You should be researching universities and investigating funding concurrently, since your choice of university will impact on your options for certain scholarships or financial aid. Start early and consider that support will often be pulled from a number of sources:

- scholarships from universities
- scholarships from external bodies
- sports scholarships
- savings or personal loans from the UK
- financial aid.

Much of the additional funding you may be applying for comes direct from US universities. Scholarships are allocated based on a range of criteria: merit, achievements, financial need, talents or personal background (country of origin, gender or ethnicity). Use the admissions or financial-aid pages on the university's website to find out which institutions offer scholarships to UK students. Keep in mind that, even if you are lucky enough to get a scholarship, it is unlikely to cover all your costs.

The amount of financial aid varies between colleges. For example, if you have the brains to get into Harvard and your family income is under $65,000 (£41,003) per year, then you would not have to pay anything. The threshold is $75,000 (£47,312) at MIT (Massachusetts Institute of Technology). Further financial aid is awarded on a sliding scale for family income over these amounts up to around $150,000 (£94,623).

You might be able to speed up your studies, and thereby reduce some of your costs, by taking additional courses each semester or gaining credit over the summer break.

Sports scholarships are a highly competitive option and you will need to start the process even earlier than for a mainstream application. Applicants must meet and maintain academic standards, while also having the sporting talent to participate at varsity (inter-university) level. Scholarships are awarded for a range of sports, with opportunities for UK students in soccer, golf, athletics or swimming, for example.

Certain sporting associations will require scores over a particular level on SATs or ACTs. You can make contact with university coaches direct or use the services of an agent, who will often charge a fee. Both EducationUSA and the Fulbright Commission have handouts on their websites taking you through each option.

There are a range of external bodies that offer scholarships, each with their own specifications and deadlines. Try this web page for more details of organisations you might want to contact: www.fulbright.org.uk/study-in-the-usa/undergraduate-study/funding/external-funding-bodies.

The following websites will help you get started on your search for funding:

- www.educationusa.info
- www.edupass.org/finaid/databases.phtml
- www.iefa.org
- www.internationalscholarships.com.

# Cultural differences

If you have watched enough Hollywood films, you may feel that you already know the USA. You may have heard of Thanksgiving and Spring Break and you probably have some ideas about campus life. Therefore you might not expect to experience culture shock when leaving for this western, English-speaking country. Although the changes won't necessarily be too extreme, it may still take a little while to adjust and feelings of homesickness and uncertainty are normal.

Meeting new people and making friends are important to help you start to feel at home. It may be tempting to stick with other international students, but if you want to get to know the real America, you will need to meet some Americans. As a nation, they are much more open than the Brits, so introduce yourself to hall mates and classmates or get involved with activities.

Drinking is less of a way of life than in the UK. The legal age is 21 and many university events, and even whole campuses, are dry.

# Working while studying

It may be possible for you to work while you are studying in the USA, but it is essential to follow the rules to the letter. Remember that breaking employment law could lead to deportation. The information here should provide some of the basic details to get you started. For the latest rules and regulations, talk to the university's international office. You should check with them before taking on any work or voluntary commitments.

Full-time students on a Student Visa (F-1) can work 20 hours per week on campus. If you're on an Exchange Visitor Visa (J-1), you may request permission from your international office to work 20 hours per week on campus, but this is not guaranteed. You must have all appropriate paperwork, including SEVIS I-20, passport and Social Security Card – speak to your university for more information. Campus jobs might include library, cafeteria or office work. It makes sense to wait until you have had time to adjust to your new country before you start looking for work.

> **❝** I thought I might get a job second semester on campus to help support myself but I didn't have time. I travelled so frequently and was making the most of my time there that working seemed to be the furthest thing from my mind. I knew one or two people who did and it is a great way to meet more American students and earn some extra cash but make sure it doesn't hold you back from making the most of your time abroad. And don't take a job without considering how busy you will be. **❞**
>
> *Rosie Hodgart, University of South Carolina, USA*

Paid, off-campus employment is possible on a J-1 visa through Curricular Practical Training (CPT), but it must be an integral part of your degree curriculum. If you are interested in CPT, look out for courses where an internship or practicum (practical work in a particular field) is required. Technical courses, like engineering, or vocational courses, like special education, might require this type of experience.

On a J-1 visa, you may be able to gain work experience during your studies in the USA and to work for up to one year on an Optional Practical Training (OPT) scheme; it is possible to do this during your studies, although most students opt to do it afterwards. The work is paid and at a professional level but must be related to your field of studies as listed on your SEVIS I-20. You will also need permission from the US Citizen and Immigration Services. If you have an F-1 visa, you could request permission for a period of Academic Training.

# Staying on after study

Once your course has finished, unless you have further study or
Optional Practical Training lined up, it will be time to return to the
UK. You normally get 30 ( if you have a J-1 visa) or 60 (if you have
a F-1 visa) days' grace at the end of your studies, which you could
spend tying up your affairs or seeing some of this vast country.
If you have any queries about when you should leave, try your
university's international office.

Occasionally, some students get job offers which mean that they
can stay on and eventually apply for a green card, giving the
right of permanent residence. Alternatively, if close family are
permanent residents of the USA, they may be able to sponsor
you to stay on permanently. Don't go to the States banking on
the chance to stay; these opportunities are the exception, rather
than the rule. You can find out more at the website for the US
Citizenship and Immigration Services, www.uscis.gov.

# Pros and cons of study in the USA

Pros

- Some of the most highly rated universities in the world.
- More international students choose the USA than
  anywhere else.
- Opportunities for financial aid or scholarships for
  international students.
- Great facilities and campuses.
- English-speaking country.

Cons

- Few opportunities to stay on permanently.
- High university tuition fees.

## Student story
## Simon McCabe, University of
## Missouri, USA

After completing his first degree and a master's degree in the UK, Simon McCabe started looking for a position as a teaching or research assistant or for a place on a PhD. After applying for over 50 positions with no success, he started to look further afield to Europe and the USA. He ended up gaining a place on a PhD in Social Psychology at University of Missouri in the USA.

'I didn't pick the country so much as the country picked me. I could not afford to fund a PhD out of my own pocket so the financial support and waivers I have received are a necessity to me. I found that a lot of the universities I was applying to in the UK did not offer the financial support that I could find in the USA.'

Money wasn't the only factor for Simon; academic expertise played a large part too. 'I'm researching in an area called terror-management theory and there are more researchers, professors and articles existing in the USA than there are in the UK.

'I was interested in learning about American culture and spending some time abroad to experience more of the world. I believe that the combination of academic progression and cultural exploration can enhance the experience of graduate school.'

Simon realised that good research is key when deciding where to study. 'I applied to five universities in the USA and reached the interview stage of two of those. I made my choice based on my impression of my potential advisers and their publication record, as well as information attained from their current graduate students. I did some rather intense research, checking out the university website, the city website and the online literature available. I also used more creative methods such as searching for YouTube videos of the campus and the city, listening to the local radio station online and reading the local paper online to try to get a better grip of what my future life might be like.'

# STUDYING ABROAD

The university application process required a lot of work. 'Applying to a US university is not the same as applying to a UK university. I spent a whole year preparing my application, as recommended by the Fulbright Commission. I found out I would need to take the GRE (requiring a trip to London)*, three letters of recommendation and a personal statement, alongside some sample work. When you multiply that to accommodate the five universities I wanted to apply to, it mounts up and time disappeared fast.'

Simon did more than just complete the applications; he started to build up a relationship with his potential department. 'I honestly think that the most important part of my application wasn't in any of these materials requested by the university. I was emailing back and forth with potential advisers over a period of eight months and feel that this dialogue can greatly swing favour in your direction if you can put forward some ideas and get a handle on what the department is looking for in its applicants.'

After gaining an offer of a place, the next big hurdle is to get a visa. 'Applying for a visa is tedious, anxiety-inducing and confusing, at first. You will need to travel to London and wait for hours at the US Embassy with hundreds of other people. You will need to take part in an interview (which in my case was extremely brief, but I have read horror stories online of problematic utterances leading to further probing). The online website will cause you a headache but if you approach it as just a hurdle to jump, you can dismiss a lot of the worry. After you receive your visa you will need it upon entry to the USA and then again for opening accounts etc. After this you should store it carefully. Be aware of things that may impact on it, for example, if you decide to travel or get a job.'

Simon had plenty of help from his university before he travelled to Missouri. 'The international centre had me sign up to their mailing list early and sent regular updates on things I should expect and interviews with previous international students with tips and suggestions for places to get furniture, to eat and seek help if required. If your university does have an international centre, check out the website to get some really helpful info.'

The support has continued since his arrival. 'The university does a great job of providing students with all that they need, be they international or not. This includes support for filing taxes and opportunities for employment.'

In spite of all his research and the support available, Simon did face some difficulties adjusting and he has had some negative experiences. 'My girlfriend came here after two months of my arrival with the plan for her to stay. Unfortunately, due to US laws this was impossible. After one month of talking to lawyers and exhausting other resources, she returned to England and we ended our relationship. This was a particularly hard first semester for me and may have contributed to some adjustment issues.'

He hasn't yet decided what he will do or where he will go after he finishes his studies. 'At the moment I am not sure what country I will end up in, it depends on life events – if a parent gets ill and requires care or if I meet a love interest here – all those things that you can't predict. But I will hopefully be getting a tenure track job as an assistant professor.'

For Simon the best thing about studying overseas has been his personal experiences. 'I like that when I walk out of my office at the end of the day, when the books are back on the shelf and the computer has whirred down to shut off, that I continue learning and experiencing new people, places and culture. For me it's about seeing the world and I think that the personal experiences you have are as important as the academic experience you attain at any institute.'

## Simon's top tips

### Accommodation

'Look early for accommodation! I had 20 sheets of A4 paper on my wall with the name, online rating, price, distance to campus, distance to bus stop, distance to the mall and pool/gym/laundry/utilities listed. I then closed out the options that were unsuitable and I have a great place. Whilst others have moved into new places, I do not think I will move in my remaining four years. Apartment Finder (www.apartmentfinder.com) is your friend.'

### Food

'Just try the food. If you don't like it, you don't have to have it again. Remember to tip. Cook stuff from your own country to feed to American friends, they will love you.'

## Insurance

'Get insurance. Although I have had no problems yet, I would dread it and kick myself if something broke, was stolen or damaged which I could not afford to replace.'

## Living costs

'Budget: keep an eye on your accounts and do a monthly forecast. Be aware you may not be able to take out credit cards or loans immediately on arrival, as you need to build a credit rating.

'Usually the head of department will have a list of available opportunities for financial support and scholarships. Get in touch with them and, even if they don't, they can point you in the right direction. Otherwise Google, Google, Google.'

## Working

'I wouldn't recommend working while studying if you can help it (during a graduate course). Summer, winter and spring break may give you some more free time than usual but it can damage your academic productivity. Even 20 hours a week will nibble into important school-oriented pursuits.'

## Culture shock

'Adapting to the lifestyle and culture has been difficult for me. I have been here for one year and sometimes feel alienated from US culture. The US government have made available a PDF on one of their websites for tackling this psychological issue and recognise the challenges of incoming students from other countries. (Lots of university websites have this information, along with YouTube clips on dealing with culture shock.) You would think that being from the UK and going to the USA wouldn't be that big of a shock; you'd be wrong.'

## Staying on

'Think about options for after you finish your studies from time to time. Do you want to stay in your country of study or move back home; perhaps you want to move to yet another country? Factor in distance from relatives, relationship partners, cost of living, language barriers, cultural attractiveness and opportunities for career progression. I would suggest not waiting until the last year of your degree to do this but have it as an ongoing conversation with yourself as you continue to explore and learn.'

*GRE is now available as a computer-based test in London, Peterborough, Birmingham, Leeds, Manchester, Edinburgh, and Dublin. See www.ets.org/gre for details.

*University of Missouri (www.missouri.edu) is a public research university and a member of the Association of American Universities (an association of 61 leading research universities in the USA and Canada).*

# Chapter 7
## Studying in Canada

If you're looking to get more for your money than in the UK and considering a country with a good quality of life where you may be able to stay on afterwards, Canada has a lot to offer. As many as 2,025 UK students are already out there enjoying the benefits (OECD Education at a Glance 2012).

## The education system

The education system in Canada is run by a separate Ministry of Education in each province or territory. Each region has consistent standards and it is fairly easy to move between them. Courses are taught in English or French although some institutions teach in both languages.

The academic year runs from September to May and is divided into two semesters. Fall term runs from September to December and winter term follows from January to May. Some institutions offer a trimester system, with an additional summer term starting from May onwards, although there may be more limited programme choice at this time. Although it is possible to join courses in the second (and sometimes the third) term, September intake is the most common.

## University study

More than 10,000 undergraduate and postgraduate degree programmes are available at a range of public and private (not-for-profit) universities and university degree-level colleges. The majority of universities in Canada are public. Canada's education system is considered to be of high quality, with investment in research and development at universities in Canada almost twice that of any other G8 nation. Canada can also boast eight universities in the 2012–2013 Times Higher Education World University Rankings Top 200. Bachelor's, master's and doctoral degrees are comparable in level to those from the UK.

### How to find a course

The official Study in Canada portal is a good starting point for your research; it features a course finder for international students and links to information from the 10 provinces and three territories, as well as links to the individual institutions, www.educationau-incanada.ca.

The Association of Universities and Colleges of Canada (www.aucc.ca) features a course search, as well as university profiles, facts and figures, and information on quality assurance.

### Accreditation and quality

You can check that your chosen institution is accredited by using the Directory of Universities, Colleges and Schools in the Provinces and Territories of Canada. You can find this at www.cicic.ca (Canadian Information Centre for International Credentials). The listing includes all public and accredited institutions, as well as some private establishments.

### Undergraduate study

Bachelor's degrees from Canada take three or four years to complete. In some cases, an honours degree is part of the degree programme; in other cases, it is taken as an extra year of study.

You will generally be looking at four years of study for an honours degree.

Four-year applied bachelor's degrees offer a more vocational option, combining academic study with the development of the more practical skills needed for employment. If you're looking to incorporate work experience, co-op programmes are similar to sandwich courses in the UK, providing the opportunity to work as well as gain academic credentials. It is worth noting that certain competitive fields may not always be widely available to international students; your university will be able to advise you of any issues.

## Differences from education in the UK

A key difference in Canadian education is that the degrees tend to be much more general than you would expect in the UK, particularly when compared to England, Wales and Northern Ireland. Although there will be certain programmes you must study to achieve your major, you will have the option to study a range of additional subjects. For the first two years you might be choosing programmes from general sciences or general arts, for example, before starting to specialise.

> **66** My best subject in school was maths and so that's what I decided to study. However, I have always had a wide range of interests so I wanted the flexibility to do other things as well. **99**
>
> *Lauren Aitchison, University of Waterloo, Canada*

> ❝ In Canada, we have mid-term exams and many
> smaller assignments due throughout the year.
> School also goes all year round if you want it to, although
> most people don't take classes in the summer semester. You
> have to obtain a certain amount of credits to gain your
> degree and each class you take is worth a certain amount of
> credits (usually three). ❞
>
> *Alex Warren, University of British Columbia, Canada*

Higher education in Canada takes place in universities, university
colleges and community colleges. Some universities are research-
intensive, with others focusing purely on teaching, in contrast to
the UK, where all universities tend to carry out both teaching and
research. The institution's website (or the institution's staff) should
reveal what type of institution it is.

### Associate degrees

Some students may choose to take their first year and second year
at a community college, studying for an associate degree, before
transferring to a university to achieve a bachelor's degree. Colleges
tend to offer applied (rather than purely academic) studies,
smaller classes (university classes can be large, particularly in
years one and two) and lower tuition fees. There is some snobbery
and colleges are sometimes considered to be the second choice to
university. Associate degrees take two years on a full-time basis
and are broadly equivalent to a Certificate of HE in the UK.

### Entry requirements

Much as in the UK, each university sets its own admissions
requirements and publicises the minimum qualifications required.
High-school graduation in Canada is at a similar level to A levels
or Advanced Highers in Scotland; universities will generally be

looking for applicants educated to this level. Community colleges may have slightly lower entry requirements. Your institution will be able to tell you more, including whether they have any additional requirements, for example, for competitive or specialist subjects.

If you intend to study in French, the institution will talk to you about the level of French they require and whether an assessment of your skills will be necessary.

## Postgraduate study

Postgraduate courses are available at some, but not all, universities in Canada and include master's and doctoral degrees. Postgraduate study in Canada includes coursework, although less than at undergraduate level, alongside research. The courses tend to be based around seminars and will involve large amounts of structured reading, particularly in the early years.

Most master's degrees take two years to complete and don't always require completion of a thesis. Doctoral degrees (for example, PhDs) last between four and seven years, with a dissertation forming an essential component of the qualification. It is sometimes possible to move straight from an undergraduate honours degree to a doctoral degree. In these cases, the doctoral degree will often incorporate the master's degree.

> What we know as 'postgraduate study' in the UK is more commonly known as 'graduate study' in Canada and the USA.

For those intending to follow a regulated profession like law, medicine or social work, a licence to practise is granted following success in academic study and a relevant internship.

## *Entry requirements*

Institutions will normally require an honours degree for
progression to postgraduate study, although some exceptions
are made for those with substantial work experience. Three-year
degrees from the UK (and other parts of the European Higher
Education Area) should meet the general entry requirements for
postgraduate study in Canada.

## Academic recognition

Your chosen institution may already know and understand
the qualification you are applying with; in which case, they
may accept your certificates without further evaluation. If the
qualification is unfamiliar, or if they are less experienced at
dealing with international qualifications, you may need to pay
to have your qualification evaluated. Talk to the admissions staff
to see whether evaluation is required, as you may save yourself
some money if you don't need this service. The Canadian Centre
for International Credentials (www.cicic.ca) will provide further
information on how to proceed.

# Applying

Your first step when applying should be to contact the
international office requesting application documentation. They
should send you information about the application procedure
and timescale, along with requirements for the evaluation
of qualifications, the costs of study and the visa-application
processes.

Alberta, British Columbia and Ontario each have a centralised
application service, while Quebec has a number of different
regional systems. You will find that many individual institutions
require direct application. Applications may be paper-based or
online. Applications will incur a fee, often well in excess of the £23

required by UCAS. If you are applying to a number of universities in various provinces, you may have to pay more than once. Remember to factor in this cost when working out the costs of study. Careful research and narrowing down your choices should help to reduce these costs, and the additional work required by multiple applications.

Application-deadline dates vary between provinces and between individual institutions. International applicants are normally required to apply between December and early spring for September start, in the autumn for January start, and around January for start dates in the summer. Graduate-application deadlines may be earlier, particularly for the more competitive courses.

Start planning for your application a good year in advance. Bear in mind that evaluation of qualifications, the need to sit admissions tests and the time taken for international post may slow the process down considerably. You should expect a decision around four or five months after the deadline date, although this will also vary between institutions.

## The application form

The application form itself is likely to be quite a small part of the application process, requiring basic information about the applicant's:

- personal details
- contact details
- education
- test scores
- relevant professional experience (where applicable)
- referees.

Further documents required in support of an application could include:

- transcript
- letter of intent/statement of purpose
- essay or sample of writing
- letters of reference
- proof of immigration status.

A CV, medical form and portfolio may be required for certain courses. Similarly, a criminal-records check will only be required in certain cases.

There will be an initial deadline date for the application and a later date for the provision of the supporting documentation. Some institutions won't consider an application until all documents are received, so send all documents promptly to improve your chances.

## Transcript

A transcript is an academic record produced by your school, college or university. It might include details of your education and progress from year 10 in England and Wales, year 11 in Northern Ireland or S3 in Scotland. It will include exam and mock-exam results, internal-assessment results and predicted grades; it should include any special awards or recommendation, as well as an explanation of any problems or anomalies in your educational attainment.

## Letter of intent or statement of purpose

This is a key part of the application and may determine whether you are accepted. Use the statement to explain your interest, any relevant experience and what you hope to achieve with the qualification. You need to demonstrate your suitability and your potential. Try to analyse your experiences and remember to back up any claims you make about your strengths with examples. Explain any discrepancies or gaps in your education.

At postgraduate level, you should incorporate an outline of the research you intend to undertake. Consider what interests you about this area of work, how you intend to approach the research and illustrate how the research will fit in with the focus of the department.

The statement needs to be well written and free from spelling and grammatical errors. Two typed A4 pages should be sufficient.

## Letters of reference

A letter of reference should be a positive document that provides details of your skills, strengths and achievements; a detailed, targeted letter is much more helpful than a general one. You will need to find two or three academic staff who know you well and can comment on your capabilities and really sell you.

Provide your referee with details of the courses you are applying for, along with a copy of your statement and transcript. You could suggest some of the key skills you would like them to draw attention to.

The referee will need to illustrate their own academic competence and background. The referee should provide specific examples of your strengths, since any claims should be backed up by relevant evidence. It may be useful for your referee to compare your achievements and skills to others that they have taught.

Give your referees around one month to compile the letters. It is helpful to gently follow them up to check that the letters have been completed. Thank them for their efforts; you may need to use their services again.

Tips, sample references and standard reference forms are available on university websites. See the University of British Columbia, www.grad.ubc.ca/prospective-students/application-admission/letters-reference, and McGill University, www.mcgill.ca/law-admissions/undergraduates/admissions/documents/#LETTERS, for some examples.

## Admissions tests

Canada does not have a standardised university entrance exam; universities have their own admissions requirements. In most cases, UK students shouldn't need to take admissions tests for undergraduate courses.

Entrance exams required by Canadian graduate schools include the GRE (Graduate Record Examination), which can be taken across the world (www.ets.org/gre). It is available as a computer-based test in the UK and costs US$175 (£110). Other tests include the Graduate Management Admissions Test (GMAT) for business studies (www.mba.com), LSAT for Law School (www.lsac.org) and MCAT for Medical School (www.aamc.org/students/applying/mcat).

Different universities use the results from these tests in different ways. In some cases, the result will be a deciding factor; in others, the result will be just one of a number of considerations. Ask your chosen institution how they use the results and what kinds of scores previous applicants have achieved.

You are likely to do better in these tests if you are prepared for the style of questioning and any time limits for completion. Books and courses are available to help you prepare. You can take tests like the GRE more than once, but the costs can end up being quite substantial if you do so.

## What next?

If you are successful in gaining a place at a Canadian college or university, you will be provided with a letter of acceptance. The next step will be to apply for a study permit.

### *You could study . . .*

### Associate of Arts degree Geography

Camosun College, Victoria, British Columbia
Two years
Apply by 1 August
Annual fees C$13,000 (£8,185)
Monthly living costs of around C$1,000 (£630)

### BEng Engineering

McMasters University, Hamilton, Ontario
Four years
Apply by 1 April
Annual fees C$27,500 (£17,315)
Annual living costs C$11,000 (£6,927)

### MA Drama (research)

University of Alberta, Edmonton, Alberta
Two years
Apply by 6 January
Annual fees C$18,300 (£11,523)
Annual living costs C$10,000 (£6,297)

# Visas

A study permit is required for anyone who will be studying for more than six months in the country; you will need to apply to the Canadian High Commission in London. To gain a study permit, you will need to prove that you can pay your tuition fees plus living costs of around C$10,000 (£6,297) per year. You will also need to be in good health and without a criminal record. Follow all instructions carefully and allow around 10 weeks for processing. There is a processing fee of C$125 (£79).

There are different immigration requirements if you study in Quebec, where a *certificat d'acceptation du Québec* (CAQ) from the Immigration Service of Quebec is required prior to entry to Canada. See www.immigration-quebec.gouv.qc.ca/en/immigrate-settle/students/index.html.

If your chosen university or college welcomes lots of international students, the staff should be experienced in supporting applicants through the immigration procedures.

Further information on the procedures and how to apply can be found at www.cic.gc.ca/english/study/index.asp.

# Costs and help with finances

Canada promotes itself as being more affordable for international students than the USA, Australia and New Zealand.

## Costs

Tuition fees across the provinces and territories of Canada vary. According to Imagine Studying in Canada (the Council of Ministers of Education), university tuition fees range from around C$8,000 to C$26,000 (£5,037–£16,369) per year, with college fees of between C$5,500 and C$15,000 (£3,463–£9,444) per year. In 2012/2013, international students paid undergraduate fees averaging C$18,641 (£11,738). International full-time postgraduate students paid an average of C$13,163 (£8,288) per year (www.statcan.gc.ca).

> **❝** The cost of study has been a lot more expensive but now that the fees in the UK have gone up, the difference is much less. The fees are approximately C$8,000 (£5,037) per semester. I also received an entrance scholarship and a second scholarship in my second year. **❞**
>
> *Alex Warren, University of British Columbia, Canada*

Some research-based postgraduate study is subsidised and the fees can be lower than undergraduate fees. To calculate more specific costs for the courses and institutions you are interested in, the Imagine Studying in Canada website has a useful cost calculator at www.educationau-incanada.ca/educationau-incanada/template-gabarit/education_cost-cout_education.aspx?view=d.

To compare the cost of living in Canada to the rest of the world, try the Numbeo Cost of Living Ranking at www.numbeo.com. Canada is ranked number 17 of 90 countries, suggesting that it is cheaper than the UK, Australia and New Zealand.

## Help with finances

If you're looking for a scholarship to help offset the costs of international study, be prepared to start your research early, more than a year ahead. Consider how you will support yourself, as scholarships are limited, highly competitive and may not cover the full costs of your studies.

Talk to your chosen university about any scholarships they offer and take a look at the Canadian government's website as a starting point, www.scholarships-bourses.gc.ca/scholarships-bourses/index.aspx?view=d.

Scholarships include the Canadian Commonwealth Scholarship
Program, Vanier Canada Graduate Scholarships and Trudeau
Scholarships. There are more opportunities for postgraduate than
undergraduate study.

Other sources of information include:

- Canadian Bureau for International Education: www.cbie-bcei.ca/?page_id=1692
- Commonwealth Scholarships: http://cscuk.dfid.gov.uk/apply/scholarships-uk-citizens
- Scholarships Canada: www.ScholarshipsCanada.com.

# Cultural differences

Canada is considered to be a tolerant and multicultural society
and it welcomes students from across the world. Canadian
culture shares much with its neighbour, the USA, but there are
differences. The province of Quebec is French-speaking and
culturally quite different from the rest of the nation. Parts of
Canada show a particularly British influence, including Toronto
and Victoria.

Adjusting to the sheer size of Canada can be a shock, as well as
getting used to the long, cold winter in much of the country.

> **❝** I knew it was cold in Canada but the UK really
> doesn't prepare you for a Canadian winter. I wish
> I knew to invest in a good winter coat and pair of
> snow boots! **❞**
> *Lauren Aitchison, University of Waterloo, Canada*

Citizenship and Immigration Canada has some helpful information on culture shock, as well as on adjusting to life and the weather in Canada at www.cic.gc.ca/english/newcomers/after-life-shock.asp.

# Working while studying

Full-time degree-level students can work on campus at their university or college without any special permission. You will need a work permit to work off campus; the permit allows you to work up to 20 hours per week during term-time, and full-time in the official holidays. If you are taking a spouse or partner with you, they can apply for a work permit too.

Citizenship and Immigration Canada should tell you all you need to know about working while studying, co-op programmes and internships, and working after graduation, www.cic.gc.ca/english/study/work.asp.

# Staying on after study

The Canadian authorities have a number of programmes that allow students to stay on in Canada after completion of their studies. Remember that these schemes change from time to time and may even have changed by the time you complete your studies.

### Post-graduation work-permit programme
Graduating students can apply for a permit of up to three years, depending on the length of their studies, see www.cic.gc.ca/english/study/work-postgrad.asp.

### Canadian experience class
Graduating students have the opportunity to apply to stay on in Canada permanently; you will need to meet various conditions including at least one year's Canadian work experience in a

managerial or professional occupation or the skilled trades. See www.cic.gc.ca/english/immigrate/cec/index.asp for details.

### Provincial nominee programme

If you are considered to offer the skills, education and experience to make an immediate economic contribution to your province, you may be able to gain residence under this scheme, www.cic.gc.ca/english/immigrate/provincial/index.asp.

If you are leaving Canada, you can still remain connected through the Global Canadian Alumni Network. The nearest Canadian embassy or High Commission will be able to tell you more.

# Pros and cons of study in Canada

Pros

- Good quality of education.
- High investment in research and development.
- Opportunities to stay and work after graduating.
- Possibility of emigrating after graduating.

Cons

- Certain competitive fields may not always be widely available to international students.
- Different systems in place in the different provinces.

## Student story
## Lauren Aitchison, University of
## Waterloo, Canada

Lauren Aitchison spent her childhood in the UK, but decided to venture further afield for her university education. 'I decided to study overseas because I wanted a change. I wasn't excited about the courses and universities in the UK but I was about Canada. It was also an opportunity to meet new people and get out on my own. It's really improved my confidence in my decisions.'

It turns out that Canada was the obvious choice for Lauren. 'I have Canadian citizenship and my parents also studied at Canadian universities so it made sense to at least check it out. You get a great education for a cheaper fee. Also with extended family in the country, I have been coming here for holidays all my life, so it wasn't a massive culture shock. My grandma lives an hour from my university so I try to visit her as much as possible.

'My best subject in school was maths and so that's what I decided to study. However, I have always had a wide range of interests so I wanted the flexibility to do other things as well. University of Waterloo is known for its maths and engineering faculties and is one of the top universities in Canada. They also have the only mathematics faculty in North America. This means that I graduate with a Bachelor of Mathematics instead of a Bachelor of Arts or Science like at most other universities. I am getting a good education here where I take mostly maths courses but, for my course, I have to take a certain amount of breadth courses or electives. This way I can take other subjects that interest me like psychology, economics, and history.

'I think my heart was always set on going to Canada. I only visited one university in the UK despite applying to five. The courses didn't really excite me. I then went on a trip to Ontario with my mum to visit some of the universities. I also did some research online. In Canada, there is a magazine called MacLeans that ranks the universities under different categories such as teacher quality and student happiness. I went to this for information first. From there, I just used the university websites to look at courses offered.

'Ontario has a similar application process to UCAS in the UK. It is called OUAC (Ontario Universities' Application Centre). My careers adviser at school didn't know anything about the application process so I just threw myself into it and figured it out as I went along.

'I applied to three universities in Ontario: Toronto, Western, and Waterloo. Waterloo was the first university that sent me an information package and the others followed after. From there it was all about the waiting. No one wants to get rejections but in a way I was hoping that I would get some so it would narrow it down for me. I ended up getting into seven of the eight universities I applied to.

'One major factor in choosing my university is what we call the co-op programme. Waterloo has the biggest co-op programme in the world that we know of. Co-op is a chance for students to take what they learn in the classroom and apply it to the workplace, much like an internship but better. Students alternate four-month work terms with four-month study terms and complete up to six work terms in maths. During your work terms you are like a normal employee, not simply an intern. You have a high level of responsibility and are expected to bring something to the table. You are also paid during your term. Students can earn between C$25,000 and C$80,000 (£15,743 and £50,376) if they are employed for all of their work terms, and then they come out with up to two years' work experience. It's something different for the CV.

'The high-school-education system in Canada seems to be a bit more relaxed than that in the UK. I think, because of this, students coming from Canadian schools find university more of a shock. I found the transition pretty easy. The professors teach with similar methods to teachers in school using things such as PowerPoint and writing on the board. In maths, we get weekly assignments from each class for the first two years, which is just like school. The obvious difference is the class sizes are a lot bigger. Coming from the UK, I had studied some areas of maths that were covered in first year (this was nice because the first few lectures weren't as daunting) but there were also some things that I hadn't learnt that others from Canada had. The first year is about getting everyone on the same page, which I can imagine is similar in the UK.'

There is plenty of support on offer too, should you need it. 'Academically there is lots of support available. There are upper-year tutors for help with assignments, and professors are very approachable. I also like to use my advisers. There are advisers for each course and for the co-op programme who can answer your questions or direct you to the person who can.'

Lauren is finding Canada to be the cheaper option for her studies, but this won't necessarily apply to every student. 'With the increase in UK university fees, Canada is actually cheaper for me. I pay on average C$7,000 (£4,408) for eight months of tuition. However, I am a Canadian citizen so I do not need to pay international fees that are considerably higher. They vary depending on programme but can be around C$20,000 (£12,595). This is a bit more expensive than education in the UK.'

She didn't experience too many challenges when adjusting to life overseas. 'Adjusting wasn't too hard. Everyone is starting university new in the first year and I wasn't the only international student either. It's easy to meet new people. The only bit I find difficult is keeping in contact with family and friends back home. With the time difference, it's especially difficult.

'In Canada we have additional holidays to those in the UK, like Thanksgiving and Family Day, which give us some long weekends. These are hard sometimes because everyone goes home and I don't get to see my family as much as others.

'I haven't had any negative experiences as such, more like difficulties that I've had to adjust to. For example, I have a car here and when it breaks down, I can't call my dad to help. I need to take it to the garage myself. Little things like that aren't too hard but make you realise that you are growing up. It's scary sometimes.'

# Lauren's top tips

## *Accommodation*

'Stay in a traditional-style accommodation residence. You share a bathroom with maybe 10 people and have small rooms but it's all about the experience. It's a great way to meet lots of people when you first arrive at university, and people who are all new to the experience surround you.'

## *Keeping healthy*

'We have something at our university called the "Frosh 15" (or Freshers 15). It is said that, as a first year, you put on 15 lb staying in residence because there is so much food and not all of it is good for you. So stay healthy, so you are in the best condition to enjoy school!

'University of Waterloo has a health-insurance policy for all students, unless you opt out of it. Lots of things are covered such as dentist visits and contact lenses so I would definitely investigate the insurance plans that your university might have.'

## *Living costs*

'Living costs vary depending on the area in which you are going to be living. Waterloo has lots of student housing so there are a range of prices depending on what you are willing to pay. Our local grocery store has a 10% off for students on Tuesdays, so you'll need to find out things like this to save some money. Every little bit counts!'

## *Scholarships*

'Waterloo offers a lot of entrance scholarships for students coming in with high grade averages and for students who maintain high averages throughout their studies. You need to look into what is offered where you decide to go.'

## *Part-time work*

'I wouldn't get a job until you know your workload. If you have the extra time, then a part-time job is a great way to earn a little bit of spending money and have something extra to add to your CV! It shows that you have good time management as you are able to be in school and hold down a job. See if there are jobs available on campus. I work part-time as a student ambassador for the university and it's really nice to give something back.'

## Lifestyle

'Look into what makes your university town or campus unique. In Waterloo, there are lots of shops and places to eat but there are also cute little places like the town square, which is converted into an ice rink in the winter. And we have a local market where you can buy locally grown food for cheaper prices. Also join clubs or sports teams if you have time. I am on the varsity hockey team and it's given me an automatic group of friends and a good stress relief and break from school.

'I knew it was cold in Canada but the UK really doesn't prepare you for a Canadian winter. I wish I knew to invest in a good winter coat and pair of snow boots!'

## Travel

'If you are going to study in a different country, find the time to travel around the country outside of the university bubble. It helps to broaden your knowledge and gives you a change of scenery from libraries and lecture halls.'

## Plan for the future

'Find your university's career services. Ours helps with CVs, postgraduate studies, entrance into professional schools and advice on what to do after finishing studies. Start thinking about what you want to do early, so that you're not stuck after university without a plan. My course is five years' long so I have two years left to decide. Through co-op I am hoping to find an area I like working in, or at least decide what I don't want to do. In the long term, I would like to come back to London because of its central location in the world but if I find a job I love here, maybe I'll stay in Canada for a few years. It's still up in the air.'

Lauren has many positive things to say about the whole experience. 'One of the best bits is the opportunity to meet new people of all different cultures. The Canadian people are so friendly and open that it really makes you smile. Also you can travel and go to places you've never been before. I've visited

Toronto multiple times and taken trips to places like Ottawa. You can get your local friends to show you around. I've been in Canada so long now it feels like home. I like having two places I can call home.'

*University of Waterloo (www.uwaterloo.ca) is based in the 'Silicon Valley of the North' and is considered to be one of Canada's most innovative universities. It is ranked among the top 250 universities in the world, according to the 2012–2013 Times Higher Education World University Rankings.*

# Algoma University: Profile

## Algoma University

Algoma University is a thriving undergraduate university located in the scenic, lively city of Sault Ste Marie, Ontario, at the heart of the Great Lakes along the Canada–US border.

At Algoma, you will never be in a class of more than 65 students, even in first year! Algoma University offers over 30 undergraduate degree programme options and emphasises a balance of teaching and research priorities to optimise interaction between faculty and students. In addition to the 17:1 student-to-faculty ratio, students benefit from undergraduate research opportunities, student advocacy groups, opportunities for co-operative education, a recreation centre, multiple student-housing options and international exchange programmes. Students enjoy all of this while being a part of a learning community that provides every student with an opportunity to be a leader and to experience success.

With its growth in recent years, the university has embraced capital expansion, including a new student residence, student centre, a new Information Communication and Technology Centre and a brand new Biosciences and Technology Convergence Centre which opened in September 2011. The Downtown Student Centre, opened in the fall of 2010, includes an upper-year residence and the University Medical Clinic.

For more information on attending Algoma University, contact: international@algomau.ca, or call 705-949-2301 ext. 4238, or visit us online at www.experience.algomau.ca

## Algoma University: Case study

### Robert Totime: An Enriching Experience Abroad

Robert Totime understands the value of attending a small school.

As natives of Ghana, Robert and his twin brother Gilbert decided to attend Algoma University after visiting a fair. 'When Gilbert and I chose Algoma, we were looking for a small school in a smaller city, away from too many distractions.' Robert has spoken to friends at larger schools, and knows that he would not have had the same kind of experiences at those schools that he has at Algoma. 'They haven't been exposed to the same types of opportunities or resources that we have available to us here,' he said.

Robert became the business-department representative on the Algoma University students' union in his first year. He went on to become the VP internal in both his second and third years, and is now president of the students' union. He has been the event coordinator and also the vice-president of the Algoma multicultural students association. In addition to working on campus, he has been the assistant to the international student adviser, resurrected the student newspaper, organised a Guinness world-record event, and accompanied international students on camping trips to Niagara Falls.

He's done all this while carrying a full course load!

Robert is proud of the work that he has done here at Algoma University, and credits the environment here for providing him with an opportunity to do as much as he has. 'Algoma has been more than I expected it to be,' he said.

Upon graduation in the spring, Robert plans to pursue a master's degree, and he already knows that his relationships with faculty here will help him with the application process. 'Having access to your professors and being able to get their advice on your schoolwork and your future plans is huge,' he said.

## Seneca College: Profile

# Seneca

At Seneca, thousands of students live their dreams every day by pursuing some of the most exciting careers in the world. Our award-winning programmes range from business and technology to fashion arts, computer science, graphic design, and 3D animation.

Seneca's degrees, graduate certificates and diplomas are renowned for their quality and respected by employers around the world. Our programmes promote collaborative, hands-on learning in real-world scenarios. Many offer internationally recognised professional designations that will prepare you for the working world.

You'll learn from experienced, industry-connected professors who are active in their fields. Their ongoing professional engagement ensures that your programme's curriculum stays up to date and relevant. With guidance from your professor, you'll learn in a variety of situations, from classrooms and laboratories to group work and field visits.

Many Seneca programmes have co-op components, which let you gain real-world work experience while you're in school. We're proud to maintain relationships with a range of organisations in Toronto and across Canada. These relationships improve opportunities for you to engage with the professional community and start your career once you graduate.

We want to make sure that after graduation you're prepared. Over 90% of employers indicate that they're pleased with the Seneca graduates they hire. This means that you'll start your career with a built-in reputation for excellence.

Seneca also maintains relationships with universities in Canada and abroad. These partnerships give you the flexibility to upgrade and expand your academic credentials. For example, the University of Toronto recently announced a unique partnership that allows Seneca students to earn a diploma and a degree at both institutions in just four years.

Put simply, Seneca means success. Whether you choose to return home after graduation or stay in Toronto, studying at Seneca means a respected, high-level education that will bring your career to life.

## Seneca College: Case study

### David Jackson (Huddersfield, West Yorkshire)
### Fire Protection Engineering Technology Diploma
### Programme, Class of 2013

'After earning my bachelor's degree I chose to study Fire Protection Engineering Technology at Seneca College in Toronto. Seneca's reputation in the industry, along with Toronto's global profile, made this an easy decision.

'The Canadian college experience is quite different from higher education in the UK, with an emphasis on practical instruction. My instructors are alumni with industry experience who understand the skills necessary to gain employment after graduation.

'During my first summer I completed a work placement in my field. I received help finding contacts in the fire-protection industry, and advice on my résumé and applying for the correct visas. I worked at a school board in a town north of Toronto where I tested and maintained fire-alarm and suppression systems. The experience gave me insight into my field and the opportunity to experience Canadian life outside of Toronto.

'I also lived in Seneca's halls of residence. The international-student floor created a community environment that made me feel at home in my new city. I worked as a resident adviser, where I organised community events, performed security duties and helped students with any issues and problems.

'For my second year I moved downtown to experience life in the city. Toronto is a vibrant, multicultural place; the number of British people living here surprised me. The city is a collection of distinctive neighbourhoods, including Little Italy and Greektown, and the transit system makes it easy to get around.

'So far I'm pleased with my Canadian college experience. I have one year left at Seneca and hope to remain in Toronto after graduation. Seneca is giving me the tools and the confidence I need to begin a successful career. Once I graduate I'll have a well-respected credential that will help me find a job. I can't wait to get started.'

# Manitoba Advanced Education: Profile

## Manitoba, Canada: An exceptional place to learn

Lay a finger on the centre of a map of North America and chances are you'll be looking at the Canadian province of Manitoba. At 649,947 square kilometres, it's larger than France. While France has 60 million plus people, Manitoba has about 1.2 million. There is room for opportunity in Manitoba.

International education is one of those opportunities. Manitoba is among the best places in the world for affordable, advanced education. Our 11 universities and colleges are modern, professionally staffed facilities. They offer secure learning environments and education recognised worldwide. Student tuition fees are among the lowest in Canada.

Manitoba is a province that enjoys a high living standard, stable economy and an affordable cost of living. Canadian democracy and our charter of human rights benefit all, visitors included. Manitoba's unspoiled natural environments, fresh air, blue skies and four distinct seasons are frosting on the cake.

International students coming to Manitoba have access to student support services, scholarship programs, free health care and housing choices like student residences, off-campus apartments, shared home rentals and home-stays. Students may also apply for off-campus work permits. Post-graduation work permits allow international students from eligible Manitoba colleges or universities to stay and gain valuable work experience for up to three years after graduating.

If real change is on your mind, you should know the Manitoba Provincial Nominee Program allows international student graduates with work permits and jobs to apply to live in Manitoba permanently. Graduates who find jobs in their fields and want to make Manitoba their new home may apply for a Canadian permanent residency visa.

The opportunities are exceptional. Learn more about international education in Manitoba:

Manitoba International Education Branch
1100 – 259 Portage Avenue
Winnipeg, Manitoba R3B 3P4
Phone: 204-945-1126; toll free 800-529-9981
Fax: 204-957-1793
Email: Education-excellence@gov.mb.ca
**www.education-excellence.ca**

# Chapter 8
## Studying in Australia

What makes UK students choose to travel halfway around the world to experience study in Australia? Perhaps it's down to the combination of good-quality education, great lifestyle and reasonable entry requirements. Many UK students are already convinced, with 1,661 of them enrolled in Australia when the last checks were made (OECD Education at a Glance 2012).

## The education system

A significant difference between the UK and Australia is the academic year; in Australia, this runs from February to November. Universities tend to run a two-semester year with semester one running from February to June and semester two from July to November. It is possible to start most courses in July, although some courses, including medicine and dentistry, are only available to start in February. The long summer holiday runs from December to February.

### University study

The style of teaching tends to be slightly different from that in the UK, focused on practical learning to encourage independent thought and discussion. The approach is less formal, but equally challenging. You will need to share your views on subjects and may even be assessed on your class participation. In fact, you will probably be assessed in a range of different ways, in recognition of the fact that individual students learn in different ways.

Independent study and the development of critical thinking are encouraged, much as in the UK. You might find that you have more contact hours and a closer link with the lecturers than you would generally get in the UK.

Nearly all of Australia's universities are public, with only a few private universities. Undergraduate and postgraduate study can be offered at both pass and honours level.

> ❝ I found the facilities more modern than the UK, especially when it came to labs. I do a science so I spent plenty of time there. Teaching is great, where lectures are recorded and made available for students. This makes things so much easier, especially if you are unwell. I would say the content was interesting too, I got to learn more about Australian biology. ❞
>
> *Angela Minvalla, RMIT University*
> *(exchange student), Australia*

## How to find a course

You could start your search with the official Australian government site, www.studyinaustralia.gov.au. Use the handy study wizard to research courses or institutions, check entry requirements and create a shortlist. Study in Australia also includes a mini-site for students from the UK at www.studyinaustralia.gov.au/unitedkingdom.

## *Accreditation and quality*

It is fairly straightforward to ensure that you will be studying with an approved provider. The institutions that are approved to offer degrees and other higher-education qualifications

can be found on the AQF Register at www.aqf.edu.au/
RegisterAccreditation/AQFRegister/tabid/174/Default.aspx.

Australia also has an Act in place to ensure that institutions
taking on international students support them adequately; this
might include helping students adjust to life in Australia as well
as helping them to meet their learning goals. Go to www.cricos.
deewr.gov.au to discover the list of institutions that meet these
requirements.

> **❝** I find it seems to be more personal than at UK
> universities. Our class is quite large, but somehow
> you still manage to feel a personal connection with the
> lecturers; they really try to get to know you and give you
> great feedback on assignments and how you're going
> throughout the year. **❞**
>
> *Kadie O'Byrne, Murdoch University, Australia*

## Academic recognition

If your institution takes lots of international students, they may
understand your UK qualifications and accept you without the
need to compare their standard to those offered in Australia. If
the qualification is not known to them, they may ask you to have
your qualifications assessed. There is no need to get an assessment
done until your institution tells you to; you will have to pay for the
service and it might not be needed. If required, they will put you
in touch with AEI NOOSR (Australian Educational International,
National Office of Overseas Skills Recognition), see www.aei.gov.
au/Services-And-Resources/Pages/AEINOOSR.aspx.

## Undergraduate study

Undergraduate study tends to take three to four years in Australia, with a strong emphasis on coursework. Certain courses, like medicine, can take as long as six years. Unlike the UK, ordinary or pass degrees are the norm, generally taking three years. Access to an honours degree is reserved for those who have achieved particularly well. A bachelor's degree (honours) would normally take at least four years and requires independent research and the completion of a thesis.

The system allows for more flexibility than you get in much of the UK. You choose a major and study a fixed number of relevant courses, but you will also have the chance to study a range of elective courses in different subjects. You might start off majoring in one subject and end up graduating with a major in a different subject, based on your interests and abilities as you proceed through your studies.

> A degree with honours is achieved after completing an ordinary bachelor's degree with high achievement. It is different from an honours degree.

## *Vocational education*

TAFE (Technical and Further Education) and VET (Vocational Education and Training) colleges may also offer some higher-education courses. They tend to offer more vocational courses that prepare you for an industry or trade. Vocational higher-education qualifications include associate degrees and AQF (Australian Qualifications Framework) advanced diplomas, both of which are similar in level to HNDs or foundation degrees in the UK.

## *Entry requirements*

If you have passed three A levels or equivalent study, then you should meet the general entry requirements for degree-level study in Australia. Certain university courses require particular grades and specific subjects to have been studied previously, while some courses will require a selection test or audition. On the whole, grade requirements tend to be slightly lower than in the UK. Programmes like medicine and dentistry are competitive, requiring high-achieving applicants with some relevant experience. Associate degrees or advanced diplomas may have lower entry requirements, although they may require specific experience or relevant previous study.

> 66 The grading process is different. Instead of getting a first, 2:1, 2:2, you are awarded high distinction, distinction, credit or pass on each of your assignments, exams or units. 99
>
> *Vicky Otterburn, Murdoch University, Australia*

## Postgraduate study

A range of different graduate qualifications are available, including graduate certificates and diplomas, master's degrees and doctorates.

- Graduate certificates (one semester) and diplomas (two semesters) are the shortest postgraduate options. They are of a similar level to postgraduate certificates and diplomas in the UK and can be used as a bridge to the study of a new subject at postgraduate level.
- A master's degree by coursework (or taught master's) tends to take two years. It may include a minor thesis.

- A master's degree by research generally takes one year after a bachelor's (honours) degree, or two years after an ordinary or pass degree.
- Doctor of Philosophy (PhD) takes from three years.

The length of your postgraduate study depends on your academic background and the subject you choose to study.

### Entry requirements

The successful completion of an undergraduate degree is the standard entry requirement for postgraduate study in Australia. For some courses, you may also be required to demonstrate relevant work experience or previous research.

Entry requirements vary between institutions and their departments. The institution will be able to tell you more or you can browse institutions, using the study wizard, at www.studyinaustralia.gov.au.

# Applying

There are some centralised admissions services in Australia. For example, the Universities Admissions Centre (UAC) administers applications for a number of institutions in New South Wales and Australian Capital Territory; the service covers undergraduate and some postgraduate courses for international students, but only applicants with the International Baccalaureate Diploma (or qualifications from Australia and New Zealand) are eligible to apply this way. In the vast majority of cases, international offices require direct applications.

You need to apply to university in good time to give yourself a chance to get a visa. Final closing dates might only be a couple of months before the start of the semester, but this isn't going to give you the time to sort out all the other aspects of a move overseas. Certain courses, like medicine and dentistry, require a much earlier application; likewise, if you're applying for a scholarship as well, you may need to start the process much earlier. Ideally, you should be preparing for your application a good year in advance.

## The application form

Contact your chosen institution requesting information about the application process and an application form. Application forms can often be completed online. If paper-based, the application might be sent direct to the institution. Alternatively, you may choose to deal with an agent or local UK representative, depending on the requirements of the university or college.

The application process is more straightforward than the UK system. When applying direct to an institution, you will choose a first preference for your course, along with second and third options. The institution may charge you a fee to apply, ranging from around A$50 to A$100 (£33–£65). Certain fees may be waived when applying online or through some educational agents. The UAC application allows up to six choices, with a processing fee of A$66 (£43).

## Other documents

Alongside the application, you will be asked to provide an academic transcript with details of any qualifications gained, as well as details of units and unit grades. Proof of existing qualifications will be needed. If you are applying before your qualifications have been completed, you are likely to receive a conditional offer and will have to provide proof of qualifications once the results come out.

Some courses, but not all, require a personal statement and an accompanying academic reference.

## Admissions tests

In some cases, an admissions test will be required for certain courses at certain institutions. Your institution will tell you more.

If a test is required, please make sure that you are prepared. Although you may not be able to revise, preparing yourself for the style and time constraints of the test can make a big difference.

### Undergraduate admissions tests

Applicants to medicine, dentistry and health-science courses at certain universities may be required to sit either the UMAT (Undergraduate Medicine and Health Sciences Admission Test, www.umat.acer.edu.au) or the ISAT (International Student Admissions Test, www.isat.acer.edu.au). Both are available in the UK.

Applicants who haven't completed the traditional school leavers' qualifications may be asked to take the Special Tertiary Admissions Test (STAT), (www.acer.edu.au/tests/stat) for their skills to be assessed.

### Postgraduate admissions tests

Postgraduate tests used in Australia include:

- the Law School Admissions Test (LSAT), www.lsac.org
- the Graduate Australian Medical Schools Admissions Test (GAMSAT), www.gamsat.acer.edu.au.

If an interview is required as part of the admissions process, you may be interviewed online or over the phone.

## What next?

If your application is successful, you will receive an offer letter. Once the offer is accepted and the required tuition fees are paid (generally the fees for one semester), you will be sent an electronic confirmation of enrolment (eCoE). You will need this document to apply for a visa.

## *You could study . . .*

### Bachelor's degree in Marine Science

University of Tasmania, Hobart

Three years

Apply up to 4 weeks before semester start date

Annual fees A$21,484 (£13,981)

Annual living costs A$12,000–A$14,000 (£7,809–£9,107)

### Master of Anthropology (coursework)

Australian National University, Canberra

46 weeks

Apply by 12 December for February start

Annual fees A$27,312 (£17,767)

Annual living costs A$26,000 (£16,914)

### Master of Health (Research Studies)/PhD

University of Western Sydney

Three years

Apply by 15 May for February start

Annual fees A$21,450 (£13,954)

Annual living costs A$18,610 (£12,108)

# Visas

In order to apply for a student visa, you will need your eCoE and the ability to financially support yourself throughout the course; this includes the cost of tuition fees, return air fare and A$18,610 (£12,108) living costs. It is important to note that this is the minimum required for the visa; you may need more money than this to live on.

A further condition is adequate health insurance whilst you are in Australia. You will also need to meet certain health requirements and may be required to show evidence of your good character.

> The new streamlined visa process (SVP) means that applications for degrees at participating universities require less evidence and are processed more quickly.

Contact the Australian High Commission in London (www. uk.embassy.gov.au) for the latest application procedures and fees information. You should be able to apply online and fees are £365 (as of July 2012); these charges change twice a year, on 1 January and 1 July. You shouldn't apply more than four months in advance and should normally expect your application to be processed within four weeks. Ask your institution if you need further support; they are likely to have experience in this process.

Further information on applying for a study visa can be found at www.immi.gov.au.

## Costs and help with finances

The cheapest Australian undergraduate degrees may be comparable in cost to those in England, while the most expensive courses far exceed English fees. Scottish, Welsh and Northern Irish students will pay more in Australia than at home. So Australia is not a cheap option, but it does have some great benefits in terms of quality of education, lifestyle and opportunities.

## Costs

Fees vary between different universities. According to www.
studyinaustralia.gov.au, you can expect to pay annual tuition fees
as follows:

- bachelor's degree – A$14,000 to A$35,000
  (£9,110–£22,775)
- master's and doctoral degree – A$15,000 to A$36,000
  (£9,760–£23,424).

Lab-based courses and those requiring specialist equipment are
likely to be at the higher end of the fees' scale, with courses in arts
or business towards the lower end. Remember to consider the cost
of books, materials and field trips too.

> All students in Australia pay a student-service fee of up to
> A$273 (£178) (from February 2012) for campus services and
> student societies.

The strong Australian dollar means that the cost of living in
Australia is currently higher than in the UK, although it also
means that earnings are higher too. Australia is currently listed
at number five out of 90 countries on a cost-of-living ranking for
2012 at www.numbeo.com.

It is a requirement of the visa that you have adequate health
insurance; the cost of overseas student-health cover (OSHC) starts
at a few hundred pounds per year. According to the Australian
Department of Health and Ageing, the average cost of minimum
cover is A$404 (£263) for 12 months. Visit www.studyinaustralia.
gov.au/en/Study-Costs/OSHC/Overseas-student-health-cover for
more details.

> **❝** Accommodation can be costly – I pay more in
> Melbourne than I did in London. Food is incredibly
> expensive, even at the supermarket. Living costs are far
> higher than in Britain, but if you are earning Australian
> wages, it is certainly manageable. **❞**
>
> *Shae Courtney, University of Melbourne, Australia*

The following average costs are provided by www.studyinaustralia.
gov.au:

- loaf of bread – A$2.50 to A$3.00 (£1.63–£1.95)
- two litres of milk – A$2.20 to A$2.90 (£1.43–£1.89)
- newspaper – A$1.50 to A$3.00 (98p–£1.95).

To find out about finances and budgeting in Australia, go to
www.moneysmart.gov.au/managing-my-money.

## Help with finances

If you're hoping for a scholarship to help fund your studies in
Australia, you need to start early and get ready to prove yourself, as
competition is fierce. Scholarships are hard to come by and often don't
cover all the costs, so think about how you will support yourself.

You can make a start by using the scholarship database on
www.studyinaustralia.gov.au. You should talk to your university
about any scholarships that they offer.

You could also take a look at the following websites:

- www.australiaawards.gov.au
- www.kcl.ac.uk/artshums/ahri/centres/menzies/
  scholarships/index.aspx
- http://cscuk.dfid.gov.uk/apply/scholarships-uk-citizens.

# Cultural differences

You will soon discover how multicultural Australia is; with one in four of its population born overseas, you are sure to come across other British people. Adjusting to Australia includes adjusting to its extremes of weather and its vast size. Find out about the climate in the different states and territories when you are deciding where to study.

The way of life in Australia is a bit different too; things are generally more informal and the good weather means that there is more time to enjoy life outdoors.

> ❝ The Australian lifestyle is great! Everyone is so friendly, welcoming and laid back. Sport is a big part of the Aussie lifestyle; there are heaps of regular sports clubs and great facilities to use all year around. In the summer, people have BBQs regularly; you don't rush around because of the heat and spend a lot of time at the beach or around a pool with friends. There are lots of music festivals and events on offer. ❞
>
> *Vicky Otterburn, Murdoch University, Australia*

# Working while studying

The opportunity to start working as soon as you start your studies is a definite benefit of study in Australia. For new students gaining a student visa, there is no need to apply for extra permission to work 40 hours per fortnight in term time. You are permitted to work unlimited hours during holiday periods. There are a range of opportunities in pubs, bars, restaurants and shops, but you will need to balance your study and your work. The national minimum wage is A$15.96 (£10.39) per hour.

You will need a Tax File Number (TFN) from the Australian Tax Office (www.ato.gov.au) to work and to open a bank account.

The Australian Government Department of Immigration and Citizenship (www.immi.gov.au) has the most up-to-date and detailed information.

# Staying on after study

Australia is keen to welcome international students and is making a number of changes to make it even more attractive. In early 2013, a new post-study work visa was due to be introduced. International students with a bachelor's degree or master's degree by coursework from an Australian university, and who are granted a visa, will be able to work for two years in Australia in any type of job. Students with a master's degree by research will be able to sign up for three years' work and doctoral students for up to four years.

For those considering staying on a more permanent basis, Australia has a skilled migration programme targeting those who can contribute to the economy. The requirements and occupations needed vary, so choosing a course of study because it is on the skilled-occupation list is not a guarantee of success; the list may well have changed by the time your course is completed. For the latest details, see the Department of Immigration and Citizenship website at www.immi.gov.au/skilled/general-skilled-migration.

> **66** There are many ways to stay after you have
> finished studying: applying for residency, applying
> for a work visa or a sponsorship by a company based on an
> employment opportunity. The studying is the easy part,
> finding the job is much harder, so many more people are
> going to university these days and it is much more
> competitive for places in the workforce. **99**
>
> *Vicky Otterburn, Murdoch University, Australia*

# Pros and cons of study in Australia

Pros

- Strong reputation for higher education.
- Reasonable entry requirements.
- Good pay for part-time work.
- Possibility of emigrating if you have the right skills.

Cons

- High cost of fees.
- High living costs (while the Australian dollar is strong and the pound is weak).

## Student story
## Shae Courtney, University of Melbourne, Australia

Shae Courtney started his university life in his home town, London, but always had a dream of living in another country. 'I decided to study overseas because I have always been fascinated with Australia. It has been my long-standing goal to live and work overseas and I saw this as an opportunity not only to do this, but to encounter and integrate with another culture.'

His first experience of study in Australia was as an exchange student, but things soon changed. 'I originally came to study in Melbourne via a partnership with my then home university, Queen Mary, University of London. I later ended up transferring my BA English Literature to Melbourne. I applied for a credit assessment to get recognition of my work from the UK. My original degree is actually still on deferment back at QMUL as a safeguard.'

His experience of the transfer was fairly seamless. 'As a British student, A levels are world-renowned for being rigorous qualifications. The transfer process was easy as a result.'

Shae reports favourably on the level of support he has received from his new university. 'The University of Melbourne depends heavily on international students from across the world and increasingly so from developing Asian nations. With such a large body of international students, pastoral care is of a high standard.

'There is little or no financial support from the university. There is, however, a high degree of academic support unrivalled by many British universities.' Shae does find the cost of living expensive in his adopted home. The Australian dollar is currently strong which makes everything pretty pricey. 'Accommodation can be costly – I pay more in Melbourne than I did in London. Food is incredibly expensive, even at the supermarket. You'll find that fruit and veg are cheapest at markets. Forget no-frills air fares. Travel in Australia is expensive, even public transport around the city, but petrol is cheap.

'On the whole, the costs of studying here are favourable, particularly if you look at the fees for undergraduate study from 2012 entry forward. There are also a suite of bursaries and grants available from the university. Living costs are far higher than in Britain, but if you are earning Australian wages, it is certainly manageable.'

Shae has been able to work while he has been in Australia. 'Most students on a student visa are entitled to work approximately 20 hours per week during term time on or off campus. You'll need a Tax File Number which is available from the Taxation Office.'

Adjusting to the Australian way of life hasn't been a problem. 'It is easy to assimilate if you are British in Australia. Shared history and common values mean there is much commonality between the two nations and their peoples.'

Australia also offers the possibility of staying on after your university studies end. 'Depending on your visa circumstances, you may be able to apply for a Skilled Graduate Visa. This is seen as a possible pathway to permanent residency.'

So were there any negative aspects to his decision to study in Australia? 'None. The only drawback is the distance between Australia and Britain. Family ties pull me back to the UK.'

Shae used a number of sources of information to help him find out about studying abroad. Here are his top four:

- Foreign and Commonwealth Office, www.fco.gov.uk
- DFAT (Australian Department of Foreign Affairs and Trade), www.dfat.gov.au
- Smartraveller, www.smartraveller.gov.au
- Lonely Planet, www.lonelyplanet.com.

And the best thing about Shae's experience hasn't been the weather or the laid-back Aussie way of life: 'The best thing about studying overseas is the warm welcome I have received from the Australian people. I have some superb friends here and have made robust professional networks over the past two years.'

*University of Melbourne (www.unimelb.edu.au) is Australia's second-oldest university, ranked number 28 in the Times Higher Education World University Rankings 2012–2013. It is an internationally recognised research-intensive university.*

# Chapter 9
## Studying in New Zealand

New Zealand might seem like a long way to go for an education, but many international students choose the country for its safety, quality of life and the option to settle after studies. According to a 2012 survey, over 5,000 UK students are already studying there.

New Zealand is a little larger in area than the UK, but with a population of only 4.5 million.

## The education system

Much as in Australia, New Zealand's academic year runs from late February to November. The academic year incorporates two semesters, each lasting 12 weeks. You can expect breaks mid-semester and at the end of semester one, with a longer summer break after semester two (from November to February). It may be possible to join certain courses in semester two or as part of a summer school starting in January.

At all levels, students in New Zealand are encouraged to develop independent thought and defend their ideas in discussion and debate. Most taught courses are assessed by means of exams and classroom activities, which could include essays, assignments, presentations, projects and practical work. Make sure that you get involved in class activities; your participation may be assessed here too.

All eight of New Zealand's universities are publicly funded. There are also a range of other institutions with degree-awarding powers: polytechnics, colleges of education and wānanga.

* Polytechnics, or institutes of technology, originally specialised in technical or vocational studies, but now offer a range of subjects and research activities.
* Colleges of education, for the most part, offer studies in the fields of early-years, primary and secondary education.
* Wānanga provide mainly vocational educational opportunities that include Māori tradition and culture.

There are also private training establishments offering degree-level education.

### How to find a course

Take a look at New Zealand Educated (www.newzealandeducated. com) to search for programmes at universities, institutes of technology, and polytechnics. The site also features a scholarship search option, as well as useful information about study and life in New Zealand.

### Accreditation and quality

New Zealand has strong quality systems for education. In order to verify that your course or provider is accredited, you can search for approved qualifications and recognised institutions at the New Zealand Qualifications Authority website (www.nzqa.govt. nz/search). Private training establishments (PTEs) have to be registered in order to be included on this list.

Six of New Zealand's eight universities can be found in the 2012–2013 Times Higher Education World University Rankings Top 400, with one of its universities featured in the Top 200.

As an international student so far from home, you need to know that you will be well supported. The New Zealand Ministry of Education has a code of practice that all institutions accepting international students must adhere to. The code requires clarity and accuracy in the information you receive before you apply; ensures that international students have access to welfare support and information on life in New Zealand; and explains grievance procedures, should things go wrong. It should help you to make an informed choice on where to apply and give you a realistic idea of the support you can expect once you arrive. For more details, go to www.minedu.govt.nz.

## Undergraduate study

Bachelor's degrees in New Zealand tend to take three years to complete, although some subjects take longer, up to six years for a Bachelor of Medicine. Students must successfully complete each year before moving on to the next. High achievers may opt for an additional year of study to gain an honours degree, or choose a course of at least four years with honours already incorporated.

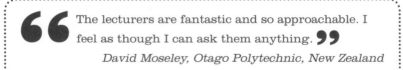

The lecturers are fantastic and so approachable. I feel as though I can ask them anything.
*David Moseley, Otago Polytechnic, New Zealand*

You can often be flexible in the direction your academic studies take you, having the opportunity to try out a range of subjects. It is not unusual for the major subject you choose when you apply to end up being different from the major subject you graduate in. Your university will guide you through the process of choosing

the right core and elective subjects to achieve a major in your
desired subject.

> Stage 1 or 100-level courses are taken in the first year, stage
> 2 or 200-level courses in the second year, and stage 3 or
> 300-level courses in the third year.

It is possible to transfer credit and move between different
institutions at tertiary level.

## Vocational education

Qualifications in technical and vocational education are available
at polytechnics, institutes of technology or in the workplace; some
opportunities are available through universities and wānanga.
Level-6 national diplomas could be compared to qualifications
like HNDs or foundation degrees in the UK. If you decide to move
from a national diploma to a relevant degree, it may be possible to
transfer credit or to gain exemptions from the initial stages of the
degree programme.

## Entry requirements

Entry requirements in New Zealand tend to be lower than in
the UK, as the smaller population means less of a demand for
places. The grades required tend to reflect the academic level you
will need to cope with the demands of the course. In most cases,
you will need to have gained three A levels, or equivalent; some
universities ask for three Cs at A level and there are additional
grade requirements for certain courses.

At the University of Auckland, New Zealand's highest-ranking
university, students need to achieve a minimum of CCC at A
level to be considered for entry in 2013. There are additional
course-specific requirements, for example, a minimum of CCC for

Bachelor Education (Teaching), BBC for Bachelor Architectural Studies, and BBB for Bachelor (Hons) Engineering. They are not currently accepting international applicants to Bachelor Pharmacy, or for direct entry to Bachelor Medicine. If you are applying with alternatives to A levels, contact the university's international office via www.auckland.ac.nz/uoa/is-contact-auckland-international.

## Postgraduate study

At postgraduate level, you might choose to study for a:

- postgraduate certificate
- postgraduate diploma
- master's degree
- doctoral degree.

All of these are of a comparable level to the same qualifications in the UK. Postgraduate certificates take one semester to complete, with postgraduate diplomas taking one year. Master's degrees tend to take two years (or less, if you have achieved an honours degree) and can be based on the completion of a thesis or have more of a focus on coursework. Doctorates would normally take three years to complete.

> If you are not ready for postgraduate study, perhaps because of your achievements at undergraduate level or maybe because you are changing subject, you could consider a graduate diploma.

### Entry requirements

An undergraduate degree from a recognised institution is required to undertake postgraduate study in New Zealand. You generally need a master's degree to join a doctoral degree, although applicants with a bachelor's (honours) degree with a first or upper-second classification may also be considered.

## Distance learning

New Zealand has a range of distance-learning providers offering education at degree level, including the Open Polytechnic of New Zealand (www.openpolytechnic.ac.nz) and Massey University (www.massey.ac.nz/massey/learning/distance-learning). Most tertiary institutions offer blended learning, delivering their education in a range of different ways (including online) to meet their students' needs.

# Applying

Institutions in New Zealand require direct application, so the first step should be to contact the international office at the universities where you would like to study. They will provide all the information you need on how to apply and show you how to access the relevant application forms. They may charge an application fee. Some students choose to use the services of an agent, rather than dealing direct with the institutions.

Ideally, you should start the research process more than a year in advance, to allow time to apply for scholarships, apply for a visa and make the arrangements to move. You should plan to make contact with the universities at least six to eight months beforehand. Closing dates for applications to start in semester one (February) normally fall between September and December; to join programmes in semester two (July), you should apply by April or May. Restricted-entry or competitive courses often have an earlier closing date and some may only have a February intake.

## The application form

The application forms tend to be a lot shorter and simpler than the UCAS form in the UK. You will need to provide personal details, information on your previous and current academic studies and your career plans. You will be asked for a first and second choice of degree, along with details of your intended major(s).

Applications are paper-based or online. If they are online, you will still need to allow time for certified or witnessed documents to be posted or couriered to New Zealand.

## Other requirements

Other documents required include academic transcripts (with details of education and qualifications) and certificates. Academic references and written statements may be requested, along with portfolios and other evidence for certain courses. The institution will also ask for a copy of your passport. Copied documents often need to be certified or witnessed by someone in the legal profession or in another position of responsibility.

In addition, postgraduate applicants may need to provide two references and a CV, and may be asked to submit a research proposal.

In some cases, an interview over the phone or online may be necessary for undergraduate and postgraduate applicants.

## Academic recognition

If your qualifications are unfamiliar to the international office, you may need to pay for an International Qualifications Assessment through the New Zealand Qualifications Authority: www.nzqa. govt.nz/qualifications-standards/international-qualifications/apply-for-an-international-qualifications-assessment.

## What next?

If your application is successful, you will receive an offer of
admission. The next step will be to apply for a visa.

### *You could study . . .*

**Bachelor of Wine Science**
Eastern Institute of Technology, Hawke's Bay
Three years
No application deadline
Annual fees NZ$17,700 (£9,025)
Weekly living costs NZ$200–NZ$300 (£102–£153)

**Master of Antarctic Studies**
University of Canterbury, Christchurch
Two years
Apply by July for February start
Annual fees NZ$32,200 (£16,418)
Weekly living costs NZ$300–NZ$350 (£153–£178)

**Doctor of Music**
University of Auckland
Three years
Applications accepted throughout the year
Annual fees NZ$6,013 (£3,065)
Weekly living costs NZ$380–NZ$480 (£194–£245)

# Visas

Once you have accepted an offer of admission and paid your
tuition fees (or the appropriate deposit), you can start to apply for
a student visa. You are also likely to have to provide a chest X-ray,
police certificates (or criminal records check) and accommodation
details, along with evidence of funds for living costs and air

fare. For courses of over nine months, you will need access to NZ\$15,000 (£7,648) (as at November 2012) per year to cover your living costs alone; you may need more than this to live on. You will also need to take out adequate health insurance to cover you during your stay in New Zealand.

When you apply for a visa, if you hope to work, tick the boxes under 'variation of conditions' requesting permission to work up to 20 hours a week during the academic year and full-time during the Christmas and new-year holidays.

For full details of how to apply, rules and regulations and the latest fees, go to Immigration New Zealand (www.immigration. govt.nz). Further information can be found at the New Zealand High Commission in London (www.nzembassy.com/united-kingdom). You should allow four to six weeks for processing, although many applications are processed within 25 days. The fee is currently £135.

Most international offices have lots of experience in helping students through these processes. They will know the problems that previous applicants have encountered and should support you to make a successful application for a visa.

Once you have a visa, you will need to follow certain requirements in order to retain it, such as attending your course and achieving certain standards. Your visa will only last for a maximum of one academic year, so you will need to reapply for subsequent years of study. You may be able to renew it online through your institution in subsequent years.

# Costs and help with finances

New Zealand is unlikely to offer a cheaper option for education at undergraduate level; some of the cheapest university undergraduate fees in New Zealand are comparable in cost to the most expensive in the UK. At postgraduate level, the costs can be higher than in the UK, although there is an incentive to study PhDs, making New Zealand a very attractive proposition.

## Costs

Individual tertiary institutions set their own fees, which will vary depending on the course you choose. According to New Zealand Educated (www.newzealandeducated.com), annual tuition fees for undergraduate study range from NZ$18,000 to NZ$25,000 (£9,178–£12,748). Fees for courses at polytechnics or institutes of technology may be lower than NZ$18,000 (£9,178) per year, making them a more affordable option.

Postgraduate tuition fees for international students can be as much as NZ$40,000 (£20,398) per year. However, international PhD students pay the same fees as students from New Zealand, starting at around NZ$5,000 (£2,550) per year.

Although you will be required to prove access to NZ$15,000 (£7,648) per year for visa purposes, New Zealand Educated suggests allowing as much as NZ$20,000 (£10,199) for living costs. It includes some helpful indications of costs on its website, www.nzeducated.com/int/en/guide/on_arrival/living_costs. In comparison to the rest of the world, New Zealand is ranked number 12 of 90 countries on a 2012 cost-of-living ranking at www.numbeo.com; the UK is listed just below at number 13.

Remember to budget for medical and travel insurance; international students are legally obliged to hold this throughout their period of study in New Zealand.

**Help with finances**

A range of scholarships are available, although you will need to compete with other applicants. Apply early, follow all the guidelines and be prepared to supplement any scholarship with other sources of funding; most scholarships will not cover all costs. Scholarships include the Commonwealth Scholarship and Fellowship Plan, and international doctoral research scholarships.

You can search for scholarships at www.newzealandeducated.com/int/en/institutions_courses/scholarships. This searches options including national and university-specific awards. Talk to your university or polytechnic about the range of scholarships they administer.

Take a look at the Commonwealth Scholarships website for details of their scholarships, awards and fellowships, http://cscuk.dfid.gov.uk/apply/scholarships-uk-citizens.

# Cultural differences

New Zealand is a multicultural nation with an informal way of doing things. One in seven New Zealanders is Māori, so their language and culture forms an important part of the national identity. In New Zealand, you can expect an outdoor lifestyle with the opportunity to get involved with sports and a range of cultural activities.

Although there will be similarities to the UK, don't assume that life will be the same; there will be cultural differences. It is helpful to find out about the culture and way of life in New Zealand in order to prepare yourself for a successful transition. Talking to other people who have already made the transition can be helpful. There are many websites for expats that might help in this process. Your university's international office may be able to help too.

# Working while studying

If you have ticked the relevant boxes on the student visa application (variation of conditions), you may be allowed to work up to 20 hours per week during academic term, and full-time during the summer holidays. Make sure you have permission before you start working and follow the visa requirements to the letter. Your right to work can normally be found on your student visa. You can apply for a variation of conditions at a later date, if necessary.

Don't assume that you will find work immediately. It can be hard to find the right job to fit in with your studies and your visa requirements. You will also need to consider how you balance your academic studies and your working life. Take a look at Student Job Search for opportunities in your area, www.sjs.co.nz. You will need an Inland Revenue Department (IRD) number too. Find out more at www.ird.govt.nz/how-to/irdnumbers.

# Staying on after study

If you hope to stay on in New Zealand after finishing your studies, there are a number of schemes currently in operation. The government is keen to retain young people with the right skills and knowledge to contribute to the New Zealand economy. If you hope to emigrate, you may decide to choose your subject based on skills-shortage areas at the time you apply; don't forget that these lists are subject to change and may well be different by the time you complete your studies.

If you don't have a job offer, you have the following options.

- **Graduate job search work visa**
  Recent graduates from tertiary institutes in New Zealand can apply for a visa of up to 12 months giving them time

to search for a skilled job (and to work on a temporary basis while searching). On finding a skilled, long-term job, you can apply for a graduate work experience visa for two to three years. You will need to provide evidence that you can support yourself financially.

- **Skilled migrant category visa**
  This is a points-based residence visa, with points gained for a job offer, experience, qualifications and so on.

There are a number of options if you are offered a job considered to be in a shortage area.

- **Essential skills visa**
  The essential skills visa allows those with a job offer to work in New Zealand (provided a New Zealander cannot be found to do the job).
- **Long term skills shortage list (LTSSL) work category**
  If offered a job on the LTSSL, you can apply for a 30-month work visa; after two years, holders of this visa can apply for a resident visa.
- **Skilled migrant category visa**
  A job offer will enhance the points you can gain on this points-based residence visa.

For information on all these options and more, see www.immigration.govt.nz/migrant. The information is complex and subject to change. Your university may be able to put you in touch with relevant sources of support for this process.

# Pros and cons of study in New Zealand

Pros

- Range of internationally recognised qualifications.
- Support for international students.
- Reasonable entry requirements.
- Possibilities to stay on and work afterwards.

Cons

- Current costs of living.
- Far from home.

## Student story
## David Moseley, Otago Polytechnic, New Zealand

David Moseley is a passionate outdoor enthusiast. So much so, he packed his bags and travelled from the United Kingdom to picturesque Otago in New Zealand, to experience an area that is packed full of activities for the adrenaline junky.

'University fees in the UK tripled, so I thought "why not come to New Zealand for around the same amount?" ' David says.

The 19-year-old is based in the city of Dunedin, a coastal beauty spot and education hub, home to about 125,000 people. Because 25,000 of those residents are students, Dunedin offers a study experience unlike many other cities in New Zealand. Most students live in the north of the city around the campuses of Otago Polytechnic and Otago University, creating a truly unique student community.

David is in his second and final year of a Diploma in Outdoor Leadership and Management at Otago Polytechnic's Otago Institute of Sport and Adventure. This hands-on programme allows students to tackle a range of outdoor pursuits, and allows them to strengthen and develop technical, professional instruction and leadership skills relevant to adventure sports.

'I have always loved the outdoors and have quite a lot of experience in mountaineering, rock climbing and kayaking. This programme is just perfect for me because it encompasses everything I want,' David explains.

'I absolutely love it and can't say a single bad word about it. It doesn't feel as though I'm actually studying, I'm just having loads of fun!'

But at the same time, David admits he is learning a lot – and he has nothing but praise for the teaching staff at Otago Polytechnic. 'The lecturers are fantastic and so approachable,' he says. 'I feel as though I can ask them anything.'

Between a buzzing student social life and a raft of adventure opportunities in Dunedin, nearby Queenstown and Central Otago, David has no problems keeping his weekends full. 'I live in student accommodation in Dunedin so there's always something going on there! And town is so accessible, you can just walk everywhere.

'I love getting out amongst the breathtaking scenery. As part of the course we spend a lot of time in Central Otago, and it's amazing. The rugged landscape and the mountains are just beautiful.'

David is starting to plan for life after study and he already has a job lined up with a New Zealand sea-kayaking company once he completes the two-year programme.

'I love New Zealand – it's the adventure capital of the world!'

*Otago Polytechnic (www.otagopolytechnic.ac.nz) prepares learners for successful and fulfilling careers in a wide range of trades, industries and professions. Offering a combination of theory and real-world learning, the institution works closely with industry and business. The polytechnic has a 91% student-success rate – the highest in New Zealand.*

# Chapter 10

# The rest of the world

You might imagine that you wouldn't find students from the UK studying right across the globe; well, prepare to be surprised. Although a less common choice than Australia or the States, some UK students opt for South Africa, Qatar or Singapore as their place of learning. This chapter introduces you to some of the countries you might not have considered for your studies.

## Countries where English is an official language

### Hong Kong

Hong Kong is a special administrative region of China, offering a cosmopolitan lifestyle and a gateway to China. As Hong Kong was under British rule for many years, English is still an official language. Street signs and announcements on public transport are in English, Cantonese and often Putonghua (Mandarin).

Now under Chinese rule, Hong Kong has its own currency and political system and a separate identity from the rest of China.

### *Higher education in Hong Kong*

In 2012, four-year bachelor's degrees replaced the three-year option, bringing Hong Kong into line with most international universities; some joint degrees or specialist fields will take a year or two longer. These reforms did result in increased demand for places in 2012, but additional spaces have been made available to help cope with this. Ordinary and honours degrees are available, along with associate degrees at a lower academic level. Master's degrees will take one to two years, and doctorate degrees a minimum of three years to complete.

---

If you are interested in opportunities in China, you will find that degrees from Hong Kong are compatible with Chinese qualifications. Beginners' courses in Cantonese and Putonghua will be available; some programmes even offer the chance of a year in Beijing or Shanghai.

---

The academic year runs from early September to May, with orientation activities taking place in late August. The year is split into two equal semesters. Hong Kong features 15 degree-awarding institutions made up of a combination of public and private establishments. Higher education is split between universities, polytechnics and technical institutes.

To find out more about studying in Hong Kong or to search for a course or an institution, go to Study HK (http://studyinhongkong. edu.hk/eng).

## Applying

Entry requirements vary, but satisfactory performance at A level should meet the general requirements for undergraduate-level study. For example, the University of Hong Kong (currently placed above London School of Economics and Political Science (LSE) and the University of Manchester on the 2012–2013 Times Higher Education World University Rankings Top 200) asks for a minimum of three Es at A level (not including languages) to meet the general academic requirements. There may be additional subject requirements and you will need GCSE English Language at grade C. The University of Hong Kong also looks for evidence of second-language ability (evidenced by a grade E or better at GCSE) and state that they 'value all-roundedness'.

An honours degree is required for entry to postgraduate study.

Application deadlines vary, but may be as early as December or as late as May for a September start. Applications should be made direct to your chosen university and are likely to include:

- personal statement
- reference
- predicted grades plus previous educational achievement
- research statement (for postgraduate research).

## Costs

According to Study HK, annual tuition fees on government-funded programmes range from HK$75,000 to HK$120,000 (£6,106–£9,768).

Accommodation in university halls of residence is reasonably priced, but space is at a premium in Hong Kong and private rental can be astronomical. As Study HK explains, 'If you live in university-provided residence halls or hostels, you'll pay a modest HK$5,000 to HK$20,200 (£407–£1,644) per semester; expect to pay that much per month if living off-campus.' Most institutions prioritise accommodation for international students; some universities even guarantee it.

When weighing up living costs, Study HK estimates, 'HK$30,000–HK$60,000 (£2,442–£4,884) per year for additional costs, including food, leisure, transportation, and personal items, depending on how extravagantly you plan to live.' Hong Kong comes in at number 28 of 90 countries on a cost-of-living ranking for 2012. Compare that to the UK, which is listed at a pricier number 13 (www.numbeo.com).

Scholarships are available, although opportunities are limited and most, although not all, are restricted to those displaying academic excellence. See Study HK for a list of scholarships or talk to your institution for further details.

Four of Hong Kong's 15 degree-awarding institutions can be found in the Times Higher Education World University Rankings Top 200 2012–2013.

## You could study . . .

### BBA (Hons) Accountancy
Hong Kong Polytechnic University
Four years
Apply by 15 January
Annual fees HK$110,000 (£8,952)
Weekly living expenses HK$1,180–HK$1,310 (£96–£107)

### MSc Environmental Management
University of Hong Kong
One year
Apply from 1 March
Annual fees HK$100,000 (£8,138)
Annual living expenses approximately HK$75,000 (£6,104)

## Visas
Once you have been accepted and have found a place to live, you can then apply for a student visa. This should be arranged through the university which will normally act as your local sponsor to support the visa application. You'll need to provide proof

of academic qualifications, proof of accommodation and proof of finances. There is no specific amount required by the Hong Kong Immigration Department; your university will be able to give you an idea of appropriate amounts to cover academic and living costs.

For more information on visas, go to www.immd.gov.hk. The application can take up to eight weeks to be processed and will need to be renewed every year. Your institution will be able to support you through the process.

## Working while studying

Although a student visa doesn't normally allow work alongside study, there may be opportunities to take internships, campus-based work or work during the holidays. Talk to your university about these procedures and whether you can apply for a 'no objection letter' allowing certain conditions of employment.

After you complete your degree, you can apply for a 12-month stay without a job offer.

## Pros and cons of study in Hong Kong

Pros

- High proportion of highly ranked institutions.
- A gateway to China.
- English as an official language.
- Chance to experience a different culture.
- Modern, efficient and cheap public transport.

Cons

- Private accommodation is small and expensive.
- Air pollution and humidity.
- Densely populated.

## South Africa

Why South Africa? The Rainbow Nation offers diversity, culture and an outdoor lifestyle combined with a great climate and low cost of living. More than 150 UK students are currently taking advantage of what the country has to offer (OECD Education at a Glance 2012).

### Higher education in South Africa

Higher education is offered at universities, universities of technology, and comprehensive universities. Traditional universities offer academic study, while universities of technology focus on practical or vocational options; comprehensive universities offer both. There are some private universities in South Africa. The languages of English and Afrikaans are both used.

Bachelor's degrees take at least three years (up to six years for medicine), with an additional year of study to achieve an honours degree. A master's degree takes at least one year, while doctorates require a minimum of two years' research.

The academic year runs from February to November. Higher Education South Africa (www.hesa.org.za) has links to all the public universities, where you can browse the courses on offer.

South Africa has one university in the 2012–2013 Times Higher Education World University Rankings Top 200, and four in the top 400.

### Applying

Applications should be made direct to your chosen institution, which will often charge an application fee. They will advise you how to get a certificate of exemption to validate your international qualifications. Two A levels plus three GCSEs at grades A* to C (or four Scottish Highers plus one Standard Grade) should meet the general requirements for undergraduate programmes in South Africa. For further details, see the South African Matriculation Board website (www.he-enrol.ac.za/qualification-country). There will be additional requirements for specific subjects. A bachelor's (honours) degree should meet the general entry criteria for a master's degree.

While postgraduate-research programmes may be flexible about when you can apply, you will need time to apply for a study permit and to prepare for the move. South African post can be slow, so you should apply as early as possible. Deadline dates for undergraduate and taught postgraduate courses vary; expect to apply at least six months before the course starts, maybe earlier if you're also applying for a scholarship.

## Costs

Fees vary depending on what you study and where. For example, the University of Western Cape charges between ZAR30,000 and ZAR40,000 (£2,128–£2,837) per year for its courses, recommends ZAR12,760 to ZAR16,390 (£905–£1,163) per year for a single room, ZAR19,800 (£1,404) for food and from ZAR4,400 (£312) for books and stationery. International term fees or residence fees may also be payable. The international office will be able to tell you more about the costs at your chosen university.

> My tuition fees were more than in the UK as I was an international student. However, that was more than compensated for by the relatively low cost of living in Cape Town compared to London. For this reason, my overall cost of living and studying in Cape Town for a year and a half was about 50% less than it would have been had I studied in London.
>
> *Nick Parish, master's student, South Africa*

In a 2012 cost-of-living ranking produced by www.numbeo.com, South Africa is listed at number 37 of 90 countries, much lower than the UK and much of Europe.

*You could study . . .*

**BA Cultural and Heritage Tourism**
University of Kwazulu-Natal, Durban
Three years
Apply by 30 September for February start
Annual fees ZAR71,100 (£5,040)
Annual living expenses around ZAR70,000 (£4,966)

**Master's in City Planning and Urban Design**
University of Cape Town
Two years
Apply by 30 September for February start
Annual fees ZAR67,690 (£4,803)
Annual living expenses ZAR88,000 (£6,236)

*Visas*

Once you have received a written offer, you will need to apply for a study permit at the South African High Commission (www.southafricahouseuk.com). There is a £35 processing fee and an expected turnaround time of 30 working days. You will need to prove that you can support yourself financially and will be asked for a medical report and a police certificate (or criminal records check), as well as proof of medical cover. The study permit will need to be renewed every year.

*Further information*

International Education Association of South Africa (www.studysa.co.za) has a helpful guide for international students.

## *Pros and cons of study in South Africa*
Pros

- Great climate.
- Low cost of living.
- Outdoor lifestyle.

Cons

- Crime rate.

## Malaysia
Malaysia has hundreds of higher-education institutions to choose from and strong links with the UK. Many overseas universities have chosen to base campuses there, including institutions from the UK such as the University of Nottingham, Liverpool John Moores, and Newcastle University (Medicine).

Other institutions offer dual degrees incorporating UK qualifications. For example, BEng (Hons) Electrical and Electronic Engineering from INTI International College, Penang is awarded by University of Bradford.

## *Higher education in Malaysia*
The academic year in Malaysia is changing to a September start to bring it into line with the northern hemisphere; certain courses also have intakes in January or May. In Malaysia, a bachelor's degree takes three to four years to complete, with the exception of courses like medicine and dentistry, which take five years. A master's degree will take between one and three years and can be coursework-based, research-based, or a combination. A minimum of two years' subsequent study can lead to a doctorate.

Courses taught in English tend to be restricted to private or international universities at undergraduate level. At postgraduate level, there should be English-medium options at public universities too. Only selected private institutions approved by the Ministry of Home Affairs are open to students from overseas; you will need to check that your chosen university has the appropriate permissions to recruit international students. All public universities can recruit from overseas.

Study Malaysia (www.studymalaysia.com) has a course search, along with useful information about education, costs and the country itself.

## Applying

International applicants will need to apply direct to their chosen institutions, either online or via a paper application. A personal statement will be a key component of the application. You should apply by the required deadline date and at least six months before you are due to commence your studies.

## You could study . . .

**BA (Hons) International Business Management**
University of Nottingham Malaysia Campus, Semenyih
Three years
Application deadline not provided
Annual fees RM37,950 (£7,795)
Monthly living expenses approximately RM975–RM1,345 (£200–£276)

**MSc Philosophy of Science**
University of Malaya, Kuala Lumpur
From one year
Apply by 30 July for February intake
Annual fees RM8,496 (£1,745)
Monthly living expenses RM700–RM1,000 (£144–£205)

## Visas

Your university will apply for a student pass on your behalf; once this is granted, you will also receive a multiple-entry visa. More information is available from Study Malaysia at www. studymalaysia.com/education/art_apply.php?id=immigration. You will be required to pay a personal bond of RM1,500 (£308) to your institution, which is refunded when you finish your studies.

## Costs

Tuition fees vary from institution to institution. Study Malaysia suggests that undergraduate fees range from RM33,000– RM140,000 (£6,779–£28,760) (for pharmacy) at private universities and from RM50,000–RM450,000 (£10,271–£92,440) (medicine) at overseas university branch campuses. These costs are for the entire programme, not per year. The annual average undergraduate tuition fee is RM20,000 (£4,108).

Postgraduate research degrees at public universities cost from RM1,800–RM6,000 (£370–£1,232) per year at master's level, and RM2,700–RM8,000 (£555–£1,643) for PhDs.

The fees for a UK degree might be only slightly lower in Malaysia, but if you choose to study overseas, you will benefit from the lower cost of living and the international experience. Living costs are considerably lower than in the UK, with an average cost of living of RM15,000 (£3,080) per year. Malaysia is rated number 64 out of 90 countries on a cost-of-living index for 2012 (www.numbeo. com). Information on funding and scholarships can be found at www.studymalaysia.com, Commonwealth Scholarships (http:// cscuk.dfid.gov.uk/apply/scholarships-uk-citizens) and from your institution.

## *Pros and cons of study in Malaysia*

Pros

- Reasonable tuition fees for Malaysian degrees.
- Opportunity to gain degrees from USA, UK and Australia in a country with a low cost of living.
- Chance to experience a different culture.
- Tropical climate.

Cons

- No world-renowned Malaysian universities.
- Need approval of your institution before you can work during term-time.
- Not all universities are open to international students.

## Singapore

Neighbouring Singapore may be small, but it is a hot spot for financial services, an important trading centre in the heart of Asia and home to the world's busiest port. Its education system is well recognised around the world and comparable in level to education in the UK. English is widely used, particularly for education and business, and most courses are taught in the language.

### *Higher education in Singapore*

The academic year runs from the beginning of August to early May and is divided into two semesters. Bachelor's degrees are available at ordinary level (after three years' study) and with honours (after four years). Most master's degrees take one year, with a minimum of three years required to complete a PhD.

Singapore has four autonomous public universities and a publicly funded institute of technology (which provides an industry-focused university education):

- National University of Singapore
- Nanyang Technological University
- Singapore Management University
- Singapore University of Technology and Design
- Singapore Institute of Technology.

You will find one private university, SIM University, along with a number of other private institutions and international universities with a campus in Singapore.

> Singapore might only have a handful of universities, but two of them can be found in the Times Higher Education World University Rankings Top 200 2012–2013.

To search for a course or find out about an institution, go to Singapore Education, http://app.singaporeedu.gov.sg. The resources section on this website has links to many other useful sites. Contact Singapore (www.contactsingapore.sg) has a lot of information on living in Singapore.

## Applying

At undergraduate level, universities will be looking for good passes in three A levels, so you should be aiming to apply with grades at C or above. In some cases, particularly if you're applying before you know your results, the universities will require the SAT or ACT admissions tests. (For more information on the SAT and ACT, see the US-UK Fulbright Commission website, www.fulbright. org.uk/study-in-the-usa/undergraduate-study/admissions-tests.)

At postgraduate level, you are likely to need a 2:1 in an honours degree combined with GMAT (www.mba.com) or GRE (www.ets. org/gre) admissions tests for specific subjects. See individual universities for entry criteria and test requirements.

Applications should be made direct to the university's admissions or international office. Undergraduate applicants can select up to five potential courses. As part of the application, you might have to write a short essay on your achievements or reflect on any positions of responsibility. Postgraduate-research applicants will need to write a research proposal. At both undergraduate and postgraduate level you will need to provide references.

The university will charge you an application fee from around S$15 (£7.70) upwards. You can apply from September or October.

At the National University of Singapore, you will not be eligible for competitive courses like dentistry, law, medicine or nursing if you apply with predicted grades. If this is the case at your chosen university or with your chosen course, wait until you have your actual grades to make the application; this might mean waiting for the next intake, but can also result in exemption from certain admissions tests.

## Costs

Tuition fees in Singaporean universities are high, but are subsidised by the government through the tuition-grant scheme. This scheme is open to international students on the condition that you work for three years after graduation for a Singaporean company; this can be deferred for specific reasons including further study. You can find out more at the Ministry of Education website (www.moe.gov.sg) or from your university.

The National University of Singapore (ranked above the London School of Economics and Political Science and the University of Edinburgh on the Times Higher Education World University Rankings Top 200 2012–2013) charges fees for undergraduate degrees ranging from S$27,200 to S$116,100 (£13,967–£59,617) (for medicine and dentistry). These fees fall to between S$13,730 and S$40,010 (£7,050–£20,544) when the tuition grant is included.

At postgraduate level, Singapore Management University will charge S$24,080 (£12,365) for master's degrees and S$17,200 (£8,833) for PhDs in 2012/2013: this includes the tuition grant. Without a tuition grant, you would be looking at fees of S$40,180 (£20,634) (master's) and S$28,700 (£14,736) (PhDs).

Additional fees may be payable for the students' union, exams and health services.

Scholarships are available and can be searched for on the Singapore Education website (www.singaporeedu.gov.sg), at the Ministry of Education website (www.moe.gov.sg) or discussed with your university. Some loans may be available.

Singapore Education (www.singaporeedu.gov.sg) estimates living costs of S$750 to S$2,000 (£385–£1,027) per month. It falls at number 19 of 90 countries listed on a cost-of-living ranking (www.numbeo.com), so is considered less expensive than the UK at the moment.

## You could study . . .

### Bachelor's degree in Sociology
Nanyang Technological University
Four years
Apply from 1 October
Annual fees S$13,730 (£7,050) with tuition grant, S$27,290 (£14,014) without
Monthly living expenses S$955–S$1680 (£490–863)

**Master of Engineering (dual degree)**
Singapore University of Technology/Massachusetts Institute of Technology
Two years (one year in Singapore, one in USA)
Apply by 15 December
Full scholarship awarded covering tuition fees and monthly allowance

## Visas

You will need a student pass to study in Singapore. Your university will register you on the Immigration and Checkpoints Authority online registration system (SOLAR) and you will then need to complete an online application. There is no required amount of money that you need to provide evidence of, so you should talk to your university about an advisable amount. You won't receive the student pass until you arrive in Singapore, so you will first be granted a social-visit pass at the airport.

Find out more at the Immigration and Checkpoints Authority (www.ica.gov.sg) or the High Commission for the Republic of Singapore in London (www.mfa.gov.sg/london).

## Working while studying

International students can work up to 16 hours per week under certain conditions and with the approval of the university or polytechnic that you are studying in. You would need to talk to your institution to request a letter of authorisation.

On graduating, if you are successful in finding a job, you will need to obtain an employment pass before you can start working. For more details, see the Ministry of Manpower (www.mom.gov.sg).

## Pros and cons of study in Singapore

Pros

- Chance to experience another culture.
- Modern city-state with a high standard of living.
- Tropical climate.

Cons

- Densely populated.
- Competitive entry.
- Need approval of your university before you can work in term-time.

## The Caribbean

A number of UK students head off to the Caribbean for their studies, particularly for medical or dental programmes, with over 60 medical schools listed there. Many opt for international universities with a base in the Caribbean that prepare students for a medical or dental career in countries like the USA, Canada or the UK. This list might include St George's University Grenada, Ross University, the American University of the Caribbean, and Saba University School of Medicine. St George's recruits from the UK and prepares students for medical practice in a number of countries, including the UK, whereas the other institutions tend to have more of a North American focus.

St George's University has around 60 UK students, mainly in the School of Medicine. Within the School of Medicine, the pass rates are currently over 96%, although the fees are very high. You could be looking at tuition fees from US$46,000 (£28,994) per year. The university has intakes in August and January and you should apply direct.

There are also local universities offering courses, most notably the University of the West Indies (UWI), a regional university representing 15 countries with four sites across the Caribbean. Its fees at undergraduate level are around US$15,000 (£9,455) per year, with the exception of medicine, which is around US$24,000 (£15,127).

Undergraduate degrees tend to take three to four years, followed by a two-year master's degree and a three-year PhD. Make sure you check the validity of any professional qualification with the relevant professional body. If you intend to practise medicine in the UK, you should check requirements with the General Medical Council. For a list of the relevant professional bodies in the UK, see the website of the National Contact Point for Professional Qualifications in the UK at www.ecctis.co.uk/uk%20ncp.

Unfortunately, there isn't one single source of information to find other recognised universities. You could use the High Commission websites in the UK; for example, the Jamaican High Commission in the UK, at www.jhcuk.org/citizens/universities, lists UWI, University of Technology, and Northern Caribbean University. You could also use accreditation organisations like the University Council of Jamaica, the Barbados Accreditation Council, and the Accreditation Council of Trinidad and Tobago. Find contact details for these and other accreditation bodies at CANQATE (Caribbean Area Network for Quality Assurance in Tertiary Education), www.canqate.org/Links/RelatedLinks.aspx. Once you are sure that your university is recognised and accredited, you can go to their website for the latest information on courses, fees and how to apply.

## *You could study . . .*

### BA African and African Diaspora Studies
University of the West Indies, Mona Campus, Jamaica
Three years
Annual fees US$15,000 (£9,455)
Living expenses not provided

### Master of Science in Biology
Northern Caribbean University, Manchester, Jamaica
Two years
Annual fees approximately US$10,000 (£6,303)
Living expenses not provided

## *Pros and cons of study in the Caribbean*
Pros

- Tropical climate.
- Low cost of living.
- Chance to gain medical training relevant to more than one country.

Cons

- A range of education systems on offer with no single reliable source of information.
- High costs for medical and dental studies.

# Countries where English isn't widely used

Across the rest of the world there are options for those wanting to study in English. Even in places where English is not widely spoken you will find pockets of opportunity for UK students. We will explore a few of those countries here.

## China

The Chinese government is investing heavily in its higher education and is keen to attract international students although the numbers of non-Chinese students are low at the moment. The growth of China as an economic force means that awareness of Chinese culture and language is likely to be an important asset.

### *How to find a course*

You can search for degree programmes on the CUCAS (China's University and College Admission System) website, www.cucas. edu.cn. Once your search brings up a list of courses, you can select those taught in English. The Chinese Ministry of Education also holds a list of English-taught programmes in Chinese higher education, as well as information on scholarships; visit www.moe. edu.cn/publicfiles/business/htmlfiles/moe/moe_2812/200906/48835. html. You'll find more opportunities at postgraduate level rather than at undergraduate level.

### *Higher education in China*

The academic year runs from September to mid-July and international students should apply between February and April.

Bachelor's degrees normally take four years to complete, master's degrees take two to three years, and doctorates take from three years; all are similar in level to those offered in the UK.

Traditionally, the style of teaching in China has been more teacher-centred than in the UK. You may find that this is less of an issue on English-taught courses aimed at international students.

### *Applying*

A-level study is generally required for undergraduate courses, with a bachelor's degree (plus two references) required for master's study, and a master's degree (plus two references) for doctoral study.

Applications can be made direct to universities or online through CUCAS. If applying through CUCAS, additional documentation (copy of passport, academic transcripts and police certificates (or criminal records check), for example) can be scanned or clearly photographed for submission. CUCAS charges a service fee of US$50 (£32) for up to six applications, with applications processed within two to four weeks. Institutions also charge an application fee before they will issue the school-admission notice required for a visa; they will normally take a further four to eight weeks to process an application.

## You could study . . .

### Bachelor's degree in International Economic and Trade Finance
Jinan University, Guangzhou
Four years
Apply by 1 July
Annual fees RMB24,000 (£2,425)
Monthly living expenses RMB623–RMB1,247 (£63–£126) (accommodation) and RMB400 (£40) (food)

### Master's degree in Cell Biology
Zhengzhou University, Henan Province
Three years
Apply by 24 September for October start
Annual fees RMB24,000 (£2,425)
Annual accommodation costs RMB8,000–RMB18,250 (£809–£1,844)

## Visas
For study in China of over six months, you will need an X-visa. You can apply through the Chinese Embassy. Go to www. visaforchina.org for more details.

## Costs
CUCAS advises of tuition fees around RMB12,500–RMB25,000 (£1,261–£2,522) per year and living expenses of around

RMB31,200 (£3,152), although other organisations suggest that
more money will be needed. Costs will vary depending on the type
of lifestyle you want to lead. China is listed as number 79 of 90
countries on the Numbeo cost-of-living ranking for 2012; it is the
lowest-ranked country for cost of living featured in this book.

> **"** The city of Ningbo itself was much cheaper than
> the UK and the cost of living was a fraction of what
> I would spend in the UK. **"**
>
> *Lewis McCarthy, University of Nottingham Ningbo, China*

Full and partial scholarships are available through the China
Scholarship Council (www.csc.edu.cn/Laihua). If you are proficient
in a Chinese language, you may be eligible for a Chinese
Government Scholarship. Search for scholarships on the Ministry
of Education website (www.moe.edu.cn) and through CUCAS
(www.cucas.edu.cn).

There are age restrictions for international students hoping
to study higher education and apply for certain scholarships
in China.

- Undergraduate applicants should be under 25.
- Master's degree applicants should be under 35.
- Doctoral applicants should be under 40.

## Pros and cons of study in China

Pros

- An increasingly powerful world economic force.
- Investment in higher education.
- Chance to experience a new culture.

Cons

- Language barrier outside the classroom.
- A new setting for international students.
- Issues around censorship and political restrictions.

## Saudi Arabia

Although most courses are in Arabic, there are opportunities in English at certain Saudi universities. For example, Saudi Arabia's first international university, King Abdullah University of Science and Technology (www.kaust.edu.sa), opened in 2009 and offers postgraduate courses taught in English.

### Higher education in Saudi Arabia

Public and private universities in Saudi Arabia are overseen by the Ministry of Higher Education. Bachelor's degrees run for a minimum of four years, master's degrees take two years, and doctorates from three years. Qualifications are of a similar level to those in the UK. For a list of universities, go to the Ministry of Higher Education website at www.mohe.gov.sa (click the letter E in the top left for an English version). Some institutions are not open to women.

### Life in Saudi Arabia

Saudi Arabia is a Muslim country where Islamic law is strictly enforced. Life differs greatly from that in the UK; mixed gatherings are not customary and alcohol is not permitted. Recreation activities for men centre on sport, with many activities for women restricted.

### Applying

Applications should be made direct to your chosen university.

### Costs

Tuition fees vary, with individual universities setting their own. Scholarships and fellowships are available; talk to your chosen university about what is on offer.

Saudi Arabia is listed at number 23 of 90 countries on the Numbeo cost-of-living ranking for 2012 (www.numbeo.com). The UK is at number 13.

## You could study . . .

### Master's degree in Computer Science
King Abdullah University of Science and Technology, Thuwal
Two years
Apply by 15 January
Full fellowships awarded covering tuition fees and living expenses

### Visas
Once you have been offered a place, you should then start the process of applying for a visa or entry permit. For details, go to the Ministry of Foreign Affairs website at www.mofa.gov.sa or www.saudiembassy.org.uk.

### Pros and cons of study in Saudi Arabia
Pros

- Investment in higher education.
- Chance to experience a new culture.

Cons

- Saudi universities (and Middle Eastern universities in general) are not well represented on the world university rankings.
- Social and recreational activities may be restricted, particularly for women.

## Qatar
If you're interested in the Middle East, but prefer the familiarity of a UK or US degree, you could take a look at Qatar. Qatar's Education City is a huge complex of education and research

facilities and includes universities from the USA, France and the UK. Find out more at the Qatar Foundation for Education, Science and Community Development at www.qf.org.qa/education/ universities or at Education City at www.myeducationcity.com.

As it is a hub for elite international universities, your experience will vary according to which institution you choose. You can opt for a UK degree or choose a degree from another country. The tuition fees, style of teaching and who will award your degree will be determined by your chosen university.

Student life is likely to be different in Qatar, where the sale of alcohol is limited and modest dress is expected. Social activities might be more focused on campus activities, cultural events and shopping malls rather than all-night clubbing.

## You could study . . .

### MSc Conservation Studies
UCL Qatar, Doha
Two years
Apply by 2 August
Annual fees £8,250
Approximate monthly living expenses QAR3,000 (£519)

## Pros and cons of study in Qatar
Pros

- Investment in higher education.
- Chance to experience a new culture.

Cons

- Different student life.

## Japan

Japan has 3.4% of the world's higher-education students (OECD's Education at a Glance 2012), but they tend to come from other eastern Asian countries like China, the Republic of Korea, and Taiwan. The government is seeking to attract more international students; they have chosen to invest in higher education and are also extending the study options available in English.

A group of universities known as Global 30 has been set up to boost the number of international students in Japan. They receive extra funding and are developing an increasing number of degrees taught in English.

- Doshisha University
- Keio University
- Kyoto University
- Kyushu University
- Meiji University
- Nagoya University
- Osaka University
- Ritsumeikan University
- Sophia University
- Tohoku University
- University of Tokyo
- University of Tsukuba
- Waseda University.

Find out more, including links to all these universities, at Japanese Universities for Motivated People (JUMP), visit www.uni.international.mext.go.jp/global30.

### Higher education in Japan

Currently, most institutions in Japan require proficiency in Japanese, but there are some exceptions. A number of Japanese universities offer master's and doctoral degrees in English, although the options are more limited at undergraduate level. JASSO (Japan Student Services Organisation) has a list of university degree courses offered in English, see www.jasso.go.jp.

There are far more private than public universities. Japan has some international universities and overseas universities with campuses in Japan.

The academic year starts in April and is run as a two-semester system, April to September, and October to March, with holidays at intervals throughout the year. It should take you four years to complete a bachelor's degree; the first two years offer more general studies, while the final two years allow you to specialise. Study at master's level tends to take two years, with a further three years required for a doctorate.

You should apply direct to your chosen university; you may be required to sit an entrance exam.

> Some 479 UK students chose Japan for their higher-education studies, according to OECD's Education at a Glance 2012.

## Costs

Study in Japan (www.g-studyinjapan.jasso.go.jp) suggests average monthly costs, including fees, of JPY138,000 (£1,072). The cost of living in Tokyo will be higher, so you should check individual universities for local costs. The Study in Japan website also has lots of information on scholarships, living and accommodation costs.

University accommodation is substantially cheaper than private rented accommodation, so check whether your chosen university will guarantee accommodation for you. In private accommodation, in addition to rent, there are deposits and 'thank you' money to be paid, which can be around four months' rent (and sometimes more).

Japan has a reputation for being expensive; it is ranked number 3 out of 90 countries on the cost-of-living ranking (www.numbeo.com), with only Norway and Switzerland coming in higher.

## You could study . . .

### BA Liberal Arts (Japanese Society and Global Culture)

Doshisha University's Institute for the Liberal Arts, Kyoto
Four years
Rolling admission (early deadline of 24 August for April entry)
Annual fees JPY1,109,000 (£8,613) (including admission and facilities fees)
Monthly living expenses JPY121,000 (£940)

### MA International Development

International University of Japan, Niigata (private)
Two years
Apply by 18 February for April entry
Annual fees JPY2,200,000 (£17,085) (including admission fees)
Minimum monthly living expenses JPY94,000 (£730)

## Visas

You will need a student visa in order to study in Japan; your university will act as a sponsor for the visa process and should obtain a certificate of eligibility for you. This will need to be processed at the Embassy of Japan (www.uk.emb-japan.go.jp) in the UK (or the country where you are resident). Student-visa holders need the approval of their university and the immigration office to be able to work.

For information on study in Japan, go to www.studyjapan.go.jp/en.

## *Pros and cons of study in Japan*

Pros

- A culture which combines tradition and cutting-edge technology.
- Drive to increase numbers of international students.

Cons

- Language barrier outside the classroom.
- Relatively few western students at present.
- The need to factor in additional fees for study and accommodation.

Hopefully, the information about these countries will have whetted your appetite and given you a starting point for your research. Of course, the countries profiled here are not the only options open to you; many other countries are keen to attract students from the UK. If you are interested in studying elsewhere in the world, you can use the information in this book (see Chapters 2, 3 and 4) to help ensure that the education you opt for is the right step for you.

## Student story
## Lewis McCarthy, University of Nottingham, Ningbo and Shanghai Jiao Tong University, China

'I thought studying overseas would be a great opportunity to spend time living in a different country and culture. I decided not to take a gap year after my A levels and thought that by taking a degree that included a year abroad, I could combine the experiences of gap-year travelling with academic study.'

Lewis was interested in China from the start. 'I chose to learn about China as it is a very different culture to the UK and Europe – the country is also growing in economic and political influence. I believe an understanding of China enhances my career prospects and differentiates me from other graduates.

'I looked at various universities and a range of courses, but it was Nottingham's degree in Management with Chinese Studies that fit me best. A key factor was that Nottingham has its own campuses in China and Malaysia, the opportunity to study at those was too good to pass up. Crucially, I could study at a world-class British university abroad, while other universities only offered programmes abroad at 'partner' universities. A further important consideration was that it was a three-year course, rather than the four-year courses offered elsewhere. This meant I potentially saved a year's worth of student borrowing.'

This wasn't the only way that Lewis managed to cut the cost of learning. 'At Nottingham's campus in Ningbo, the fees and accommodation were around half the price (at the time of study 2009/2010). The city of Ningbo itself was much cheaper than the UK and the cost of living was a fraction of what I would spend in the UK.'

Application for his year out was straightforward, with everything either dealt with or supported by the University of Nottingham. Even applying for a visa wasn't too problematic. 'The application was a relatively long-winded process, but the staff in the Chinese visa centre were exceptionally helpful. Even though I had not filled in part of my form, they telephoned me and, with my permission, completed it on my behalf so it didn't need to be sent back to me again. They also processed and mailed the visa and passport back quickly.'

When Lewis first arrived in China, he found that he wasn't quite as prepared as some fellow students. 'I felt Nottingham could have provided more support, I think part of the problem was that my course was officially part of the Business School, not School of Contemporary Chinese Studies. I got the impression when arriving that those on the Chinese Studies course had been given more guidance and clue as to what to expect.'

But Lewis didn't let this hold him back and he adjusted well to life in China. 'When I first arrived, everything seemed so new, different and interesting that it felt more like a holiday than living somewhere else. By the time that feeling had worn off, I was already settled and accustomed to most things. Still, I know some people who did experience homesickness, miss certain food and get irritated by cultural differences: people not queuing and no concept of personal space, for example.'

Lewis went on to have such a positive experience in China as an exchange student that, after graduating, he went back to China to study Mandarin at Shanghai Jiao Tong University. 'Living in Shanghai was considerably more expensive than Ningbo; however, it was still cheaper than the UK. Rent in Shanghai is roughly half that in London. The cost of study in Shanghai was £2,000 or £3,000; however, the Chinese government offered various non-means-tested scholarships that covered all of these costs plus accommodation, as well as providing a small stipend for living.

'The university application process was simple, I applied by downloading forms via their website, filled them in and emailed back. Once they had confirmed that they had space on their course, I paid some fees via a bank transfer and that was it!

'Shanghai didn't provide much support. I was emailed welcome packs but, beyond that, it was up to me. This was not a problem. The city is cosmopolitan and easy to navigate, there were many helpful students on campus who assisted me when I asked or looked lost.

'On the Chinese-language course you are left to your own devices, although the school does occasionally have events that you can attend. That said, the staff and teachers were all very helpful, they were forthcoming in offering their contact details in case we (the students) ever needed help or things explaining in Chinese. On campus there were also sports facilities that were free to use without the need to book, such as a running track, football field, tennis courts, outdoor gymnasium etc.'

There were some differences to get used to, particularly the style of teaching. 'The teaching differs hugely, the emphasis is on rote learning, a lot of information may be covered in a lesson and you are expected to put in several hours outside class time to learn and memorise what is covered in class.'

Lewis has faced a few negative experiences along the way. 'Pickpocketing, having food stolen while on a train and witnessing mass brawls have all occurred in the two years I have spent in China. However, providing you are aware of risks and use some common sense, you should be fine. There are risks in any country. On the whole, China is probably the country that I have felt safest in for travelling, living and walking home late at night.'

'During the time abroad, you will be exposed to so many different opportunities and possibilities that you would not receive at home: travelling to different areas and regions, eating local delicacies, work opportunities, home-stays with local friends etc. Meeting new people will also give you different perspectives on your own views and a much better insight into local culture, history and customs than can be taught in class. Meeting new people doesn't simply extend to those of the locality that you are studying in either, some of my closest friends now are compatriots and international students who I studied abroad with.'

As it turns out, Lewis's decision to spend a year in China might even have changed his life. 'After I finished at Shanghai, I was accepted onto a master's degree at the London School of Economics. I decided to study "China in a Comparative Perspective". My experiences of China have been overwhelmingly positive and I cannot wait to learn more about the country.'

## Lewis's top tips

### Accommodation
'If you search for private accommodation in China, as I did the second time I went there to study, be prepared to look at many houses each day with estate agents whisking you off by car or bike for viewings. If possible, try to be clear about what you want and where you want to live. There should be someone in the office who speaks a little English, otherwise you can use Google or Baidu Translate.'

### Food
'Don't be squeamish! As long as you're not vegetarian, be willing to try everything. The food is possibly the biggest thing to get used to in China. It is nothing like western versions of Chinese food. Expect to see all body parts of animals (nothing is wasted) and lots of different tastes and types of cooking. In China, it is customary to share several dishes per meal rather than have a single dish each.'

### Living costs
'If you are making food yourself, try to buy meat and vegetables from the same place as the Chinese do – usually markets – it will be infinitely cheaper than western supermarkets which have imported products that are generally very overpriced.

'If you want to live a western lifestyle in China, be prepared that it might cost more than you think, and potentially more than it would in the UK. Rent and travel will be much cheaper but buying western food and drinking in (some) bars could be more expensive. Maybe this is more of a problem in Shanghai, rather than other cities. I didn't find it a problem in Ningbo.'

### Scholarships
'China Scholarship Council (http://en.csc.edu.cn) and Hanban (http://english.hanban.org) offer some excellent scholarships.'

## Working while studying

'It is illegal to undertake any work on a study visa in China. There is always demand for English teachers and it pays anywhere between £10 and £20 an hour. Just check the conditions of the visa you are on.'

## Lifestyle and culture

'Chinese culture stretches back nearly five-thousand years and the Chinese are very proud of their culture. Reading about the culture and history is a good way of preparing yourself and understanding some things when you arrive, just expect it to be different from how you imagine. It is very different from the UK.

'The lifestyle is great, a bit of disposable income can go quite far in China and you can go out for meals and eat at nice restaurants relatively cheaply. Foreigners are well respected within China and you should not have problems with locals, many will be warm and chatty, eager to make new friends.'

## Travel

'You don't need to speak as much Chinese as you think to be able to travel in China. All of the tourist areas will have English translations and if you travel to areas that are off the well-worn track, passers-by will often help you if you seem lost.

'It is a country the size of a continent, so be aware that customs and lifestyles may be marginally different in other places across China. The food will certainly change as each region has its own preferred tastes and delicacies.'

## Options for after you finish your studies

'There are work options, such as teaching, after your study. It is also fairly easy to find work in international or Chinese companies. A grasp of Mandarin will put you in a much stronger position, but it is not always deemed compulsory.'

*University of Nottingham (www.nottingham.edu.cn) was the first foreign university to set up an independent campus in China when it opened its doors in 2005. All teaching is in English and degrees are awarded by the University of Nottingham.*

*Shanghai Jiao Tong University is a public research university, ranked amongst the top 300 universities in the world (Times Higher Education World University Rankings 2012–2013).*

*Lewis recommends www.echinacities.com and shanghaiist.com if you want to find out more about life in China.*

# Chapter 11

## Further research and resources

### Before you go

UK Council for International Student Affairs (UKCISA), Country Contacts
www.ukcisa.org.uk/ukstudent/country_contacts.php

Prospects Country Profiles (postgraduate focus)
www.prospects.ac.uk/country_profiles.htm

UK National Academic Recognition and Information Centre (NARIC)
www.ecctis.co.uk/naric/individuals
Information on the comparability of international qualifications

National Contact Point for Professional Qualifications in the United Kingdom (UKNCP)
www.ecctis.co.uk/uk%20ncp

Foreign and Commonwealth Office
www.fco.gov.uk
Find an embassy or seek travel advice by country

iAgora

www.iagora.com/studies

Students review and rate their international universities


SteXX

www.stexx.eu

Student review and rate their European universities


Association of Commonwealth Universities

www.acu.ac.uk


Citizens Advice

www.citizensadvice.org.uk

For information on how studying overseas might affect your status in the UK


HM Revenue and Customs

www.hmrc.gov.uk

Information on tax when you return to the UK

## International course search

Find a master's/MBA/PhD

www.findamasters.com

www.findanmba.com

www.findaphd.com


International Graduate

www.internationalgraduate.net

Search for postgraduate opportunities worldwide

## International university league tables

The Times Higher Education World University Rankings

www.timeshighereducation.co.uk/world-university-rankings

QS Top Universities

www.topuniversities.com/university-rankings

Academic Ranking of World Universities

www.arwu.org

*Financial Times* Business School Rankings

http://rankings.ft.com/businessschoolrankings/rankings

## Costs and funding

Numbeo

www.numbeo.com

Cost-of-living comparison

Expatistan

www.expatistan.com

Cost-of-living comparison for cities worldwide

Professional and Career Development Loans

www.gov.uk/career-development-loans/overview

International Student Identity Card (ISIC)

www.isic.org

Student discounts worldwide

Student Finance England

www.gov.uk/student-finance/overview

Student Awards Agency for Scotland

www.saas.gov.uk

Student Finance Wales

www.studentfinancewales.co.uk

Student Finance Northern Ireland
www.studentfinanceni.co.uk

Marie Curie Scheme
www.ukro.ac.uk/mariecurie/Pages/index.aspx
Fellowships and grants for research

Commonwealth Scholarships
http://cscuk.dfid.gov.uk/apply/scholarships-uk-citizens

## Insurance
European Health Insurance Card (EHIC)
www.ehic.org.uk

Endsleigh Insurance
www.endsleigh.co.uk/Travel/Pages/study-abroad-insurance.aspx

STA Travel Insurance
www.statravel.co.uk/study-abroad-travel-insurance.htm

## Blogs and diaries
Third Year Abroad, The Mole Diaries
www.thirdyearabroad.com/before-you-go/the-mole-diaries.html

Samuel Knight in Groningen
www.samstudyingabroad.tumblr.com

Residence Abroad Blogs (University of Manchester)
www.llc.manchester.ac.uk/undergraduate/residence-abroad/blogs

Maastricht Students
www.maastricht-students.com

The Student World Blog

www.thestudentworld.com/news_and_blog/article/preparation_for_
studying_abroad#.UFrwCK6Dfcs

## Short-term study overseas

Study China

www.studychina.org.uk

INTO China

www.intohigher.com/china

IAESTE

www.iaeste.org

Fulbright Commission

www.fulbright.org.uk

Summer schools at US universities

EducationUSA

www.educationusa.info/pages/students/research-short.php

Short-term exchanges in the USA

Third Year Abroad

www.thirdyearabroad.com

## Distance learning

International Council for Open and Distance Education (ICDE)

www.icde.org

Study Portals (search for a distance-learning course in Europe)

www.studyportals.eu

Distance Education and Training Council (USA)

www.detc.org/search_schools.php

## Educational agents and marketing consultancies

A Star Future

www.astarfuture.co.uk

Study Options

www.studyoptions.com

Degrees Ahead

www.degreesahead.co.uk

Mayflower Education Consultants

www.mayflowereducation.co.uk

PFL Education

www.preparationforlife.com

M & D Europe

www.readmedicine.com

Pass 4 Soccer Scholarships

www.pass4soccer.com

## Admissions tests

Scholastic Assessment Test: SAT

www.sat.collegeboard.org

American College Test: ACT

www.act.org

Undergraduate Medicine and Health Sciences Admission Test: UMAT

www.umat.acer.edu.au

International Student Admissions Test: ISAT
www.isat.acer.edu.au

Special Tertiary Admissions Test: STAT
www.acer.edu.au/tests/stat

Graduate Management Admission Test: GMAT
www.mba.com

Graduate Record Exam: GRE
www.ets.org/gre

Dental Admissions Test: DAT
www.ada.org/dat.aspx

Law School Admissions Test: LSAT
www.lsac.org

Medical College Admission Test: MCAT
www.aamc.org/students/applying/mcat/

Graduate Australian Medical Schools Admissions Test: GAMSAT
www.gamsat.acer.edu.au

Health Professions Admission Test (Ireland): HPAT
www.hpat-ireland.acer.edu.au

# Studying in Europe

Study Portals
www.studyportals.eu
Search for courses and scholarships in Europe

STUDYING ABROAD

PLOTEUS (Portal on Learning Opportunities throughout the
European Space)
www.ec.europa.eu/plateus/home_en.htm

A Star Future
www.astarfuture.co.uk/what_to_study.html
Search for courses taught in English in Europe and beyond

EUNICAS
www.eunicas.co.uk
Search for courses taught in English

GES Database
www.study-info.eu/index.htm
Search for courses taught in English

EURAXESS
www.ec.europa.eu/euraxess
Research opportunities in the EU

PromoDoc
www.promodoc.eu/study-in-the-eu
Doctoral study in the EU

European Commission, University in Europe
www.ec.europa.eu/youreurope/citizens/education/university

European Commission, Study in Europe
www.ec.europa.eu/education/study-in-europe

Eurodesk
www.eurodesk.org.uk
Information on European work, study, travel and volunteering

Europass

www.europass.cedefop.europa.eu

Documents to make your qualification and skills easily understood across Europe (CVs, diploma supplements and so on)

Erasmus

www.britishcouncil.org/erasmus-about-erasmus.htm

Erasmus Mundus

www.ec.europa.eu/education/external-relation-programmes/doc72_en.htm

## Austria

www.oead.at/welcome_to_austria/education_research/EN

## Belgium

www.highereducation.be (Flemish community)

www.studyinbelgium.be (French community)

## Cyprus

www.highereducation.ac.cy/en

www.kktcenf.org/en/ (Turkish Republic of Northern Cyprus)

## Czech Republic

www.studyin.cz

www.msmt.cz (Scholarships)

## Denmark

www.studyindenmark.dk

www.en.iu.dk/education-in-denmark (Danish Agency for Universities and Internationalisation)

www.optagelse.dk/vejledninger/english/index.html (Danish Co-ordinated Application System, KOT)

www.su.dk/English/Sider/foreign.aspx (State Educational Support, SU)

## Estonia

www.studyinestonia.ee

## Finland

www.studyinfinland.fi

www.universityadmissions.fi (applications to university)

www.admissions.fi (applications to polytechnic or university of applied sciences)

## France

www.campusfrance.org/en

www.cnous.fr (National Centre for University & Student Welfare, student life and student costs)

## Germany

www.study-in.de/en

www.hochschulkompass.de (HochschulKompass, institution search)

www.daad.de (German Academic Exchange Services, DAAD)

www.uni-assist.de/index_en.html (uni-assist, application service for international students)

## Hungary

www.studyhungary.hu

## Ireland

www.educationireland.ie

www.hetac.ie (Higher Education and Training Awards Council)

www.icosirl.ie (Irish Council for International Students)

www.qualifax.ie (course search)

www.postgradireland.com (postgraduate search)

www.cao.ie (Central Applications Office)

www.pac.ie (Postgraduate Applications Centre)

## Italy
www.study-in-italy.it

## Latvia
www.studyinlatvia.lv

## Lithuania
www.lietuva.lt/en/education_sience/study_lithuania
www.skvc.lt/en/content.asp?id=235 (Lithuanian Centre for Quality Assessment in Higher Education)

## The Netherlands
www.studyinholland.nl
www.studyinholland.co.uk
http://info.studielink.nl/en/studenten/Pages/Default.aspx (Studielink for applications)
www.ib-groep.nl/International_visitors/EU_EEA_students/Grant_for_tuition_or_course_fees.asp (Department of Education, grants and loans)

## Norway
www.studyinnorway.no
www.nokut.no (Norwegian Agency for Quality Assurance in HE, NOKUT)

## Poland
www.studyinpoland.pl

## Portugal
www.dges.mctes.pt/DGES/pt (General Directorate for HE)

## Slovakia
www.studyin.sk

## Slovenia
www.slovenia.si/en/study

## Switzerland

www.swissuniversity.ch

www.crus.ch/information-programme/study-in-switzerland.
html?L=2

## Spain

www.universidad.es/en

www.educacion.es (Ministry of Education)

www.uned.es (UNED, for evaluation of qualifications)

## Sweden

www.studyinsweden.se

# Studying in the USA

Fulbright Commission
www.fulbright.org.uk

EducationUSA
www.educationusa.info

College Board
www.collegeboard.org

College Navigator
www.nces.ed.gov/collegenavigator

National Association of Credential Evaluation Services (NACES)
www.naces.org

Common Application
www.commonapp.org

Hobsons Virtual Events

www.hobsonsevents.com

US virtual student fairs

## Scholarships and financial aid

Edupass

www.edupass.org/finaid/databases.phtml

International Education Financial Aid

www.iefa.org

International Scholarships

www.internationalscholarships.com

US Citizenship and Immigration Services

www.uscis.gov

# Studying in Canada

Study in Canada

www.educationau-incanada.ca

Association of Universities and Colleges of Canada

www.aucc.ca

Canadian Information Centre for International Credentials

www.cicic.ca

Citizenship & Immigration Canada

www.cic.gc.ca/english/study/index.asp

Immigration Québec

www.immigration-quebec.gouv.qc.ca/en

Statistics Canada
www.statcan.gc.ca

International Scholarships
www.scholarships-bourses.gc.ca/scholarships-bourses/index.
aspx?view=d
www.cbie-bcei.ca/?page_id=1692
http://cscuk.dfid.gov.uk/apply/scholarships-uk-citizens
www.ScholarshipsCanada.com

# Studying in Australia

Study in Australia
www.studyinaustralia.gov.au
www.study-in-australia.org/uk

Australian Qualifications Framework
www.aqf.edu.au

Australian Good Universities Guide
www.gooduniguide.com.au

Australian Educational International, National Office of Overseas
Skills Recognition (AEI NOOSR)
www.aei.gov.au/Services-And-Resources/Pages/AEINOOSR.aspx

Australian High Commission in London
www.uk.embassy.gov.au

Department of Immigration & Citizenship
www.immi.gov.au

International Scholarships
http://cscuk.dfid.gov.uk/apply/scholarships-uk-citizens
www.australiaawards.gov.au
www.kcl.ac.uk/artshums/ahri/centres/menzies/scholarships/index.
aspx

Finances and budgeting
www.moneysmart.gov.au/managing-my-money

Australian Tax Office
www.ato.gov.au

# Studying in New Zealand

New Zealand Educated
www.newzealandeducated.com

New Zealand Qualifications Authority
www.nzqa.govt.nz/search

Universities New Zealand
www.universitiesnz.ac.nz

Immigration New Zealand
www.immigration.govt.nz

New Zealand High Commission in London
www.nzembassy.com/united-kingdom

Student Job Search
www.sjs.co.nz

Inland Revenue Department
www.ird.govt.nz/how-to/irdnumbers

# Studying in the rest of the world

## Hong Kong
Study in Hong Kong
http://studyinhongkong.edu.hk/eng

Hong Kong Immigration Department
www.immd.gov.hk

## South Africa
International Education Association of South Africa
www.studysa.co.za

South African Matriculation Board
www.he-enrol.ac.za/qualification-country

South African High Commission in London
www.southafricahouseuk.com

## Malaysia
Study Malaysia
www.studymalaysia.com

## Singapore
Singapore Education
www.singaporeedu.gov.sg

Contact Singapore
www.contactsingapore.sg

Ministry of Education
www.moe.gov.sg

Immigration and Checkpoints Authority
www.ica.gov.sg

High Commission for the Republic of Singapore in London
www.mfa.gov.sg/london

Ministry of Manpower
www.mom.gov.sg

## The Caribbean

Jamaican High Commission in London
www.jhcuk.org/citizens/universities

Caribbean Area Network for Quality Assurance in Tertiary
Education (CANQATE)
www.canqate.org/Links/RelatedLinks.aspx

## China

China's University and College Admission System
www.cucas.edu.cn

Chinese Ministry of Education
www.moe.edu.cn

China Scholarship Council
www.csc.edu.cn/Laihua

Chinese Embassy
www.visaforchina.org

## Saudi Arabia

Ministry of Higher Education
www.mohe.gov.sa

Ministry of Foreign Affairs
www.mofa.gov.sa

Royal Embassy of Saudi Arabia in London
www.saudiembassy.org.uk

## Qatar

Qatar Foundation for Education, Science and Community
Development
www.qf.org.qa/education/universities

Education City, Qatar
myeducationcity.com

## Japan

Study in Japan
www.studyjapan.go.jp/en

JUMP (Japanese Universities for Motivated People)
www.uni.international.mext.go.jp/global30

JASSO (Japan Student Services Organisation)
www.jasso.go.jp

Embassy of Japan in the UK
www.uk.emb-japan.go.jp

# Aarhus University: Profile

AARHUS
UNIVERSITY

Aarhus University is a young, modern university established in 1928. It has grown to become a leading public research university with international reach covering the entire research spectrum.

## Top reasons to choose Aarhus University

### Top 100 university
Aarhus University is consistently ranked as one of the world's top universities – for instance it was ranked as number 51 by crown indicator in the 2012 Leiden Ranking.

### Research-based teaching
At Aarhus University, teaching is done by active researchers. Interaction and dialogue between lecturers and students are considered central to the learning experience.

### No tuition fee for EU students
At Aarhus University, no tuition fee is charged for full degree students from EU/EEA countries and Switzerland.

### World leader in national higher education
Denmark was ranked as one of the world's top five national higher education providers in the 2012 Universitas 21 Ranking.

### Programmes in English
Aarhus University offers 67 complete programmes in English at Bachelor and Master's level. Furthermore, all PhD programmes are in English.

### International university
More than 10% of Aarhus University students are international and represent over 100 nationalities.

### Highly satisfied international students
91% of international students were satisfied or more than satisfied with their overall learning experience at AU. 85% described the support and guidance by the International Centre as good or excellent.

### Professional service and guidance
The International Centre offers a full orientation and introduction programme, as well as professional support and guidance throughout your time at AU.

### Free career counselling and job bank
AU offers career counselling and a job bank free of cost for international Master's students and graduates.

### Safe, secure, equal
Denmark is widely cited as one of the world's most liveable places. It also has the world's highest level of income equality according to the OECD.

# Windesheim University: Profile

## High quality education in English

Do you want to study in Holland and study in English? Are you interested in creating a more sustainable world? Have you always dreamed of studying and working in an international atmosphere?

Windesheim Honours College (WHC) offers a Bachelor of Business Administration (BBA) degree with a specialisation in either Communication and Media or Public Health. We are a public university; therefore EU students pay home-stay fees. We offer an intensive four-year programme with highly qualified and experienced staff from all over the world.

This unique programme combines traditional BBA subjects with a specialisation, in the field of Communication and Media or Public Health. For more information about the curriculum check the website: www.windesheimhonourscollege.nl/education/curriculum

The aim of the programme is to become project manager, by bringing different stakeholders together to manage a project. This can be on governmental, NGO or corporate level. The programme is set up to provide students not only with a chance to learn the theory but also to put it in practice as well, for example at internships and project weeks.

All cases and projects are based on real-life examples and in some cases put into use in real life. In 2010 two first-year students won a national competition for their project to help solve the housing problem in South African townships and travelled to Cape Town to meet with potential business partners. More recently, students worked on a project in collaboration with a Dutch NGO; the 1% club in a co-creation day hosted at WHC.

## STUDYING ABROAD

In years one and two students will stay in Zwolle, the Netherlands and in their third and fourth year they will choose electives at a partner university. This can either be in the Netherlands or abroad. Students also need to complete two internships. While at Windesheim Honours College students will be part of an international community, they are living in the residence as well as studying together. We pride ourselves on personal contact between staff, lecturers and students.

Do you want to find out more about us? Visit our website www.windesheimhonourscollege.nl or email us at honourscollege@windesheim.nl.

## University of Twente: Profile

**UNIVERSITY OF TWENTE.**

### High-tech, human touch

The University of Twente combines high-tech research with a human touch: our 3300 scientist and other professionals work together towards solving real-life problems with cutting edge research. This research is used directly in our Bachelor of Science, Master of Science and PhD programmes in Engineering, Behavioural and Social Sciences.

Our commitment to integrate social and engineering sciences is reflected in high level teaching and research. Our innovations are brought to the market by over 750 spin-off companies. Currently 5,500 bachelor and 2,500 master students are enrolled in UT programmes. The UT offers 36 Bachelor's and Master's degree programmes taught entirely in English.

### Multidisciplinary education

The University of Twente provides multidisciplinary education and encourages students to take an international perspective. Studying at the University of Twente means being active in education and research groups and learning from one another. Teachers must inspire and arouse genuine interest and affection for their subject.

### Campus life

The University of Twente is the only true campus university in the Netherlands and provides an academic and social setting in which you can quickly become an active member of a thriving community. The UT offers a variety of on-campus services: a medical centre, counselling facilities, a hotel, religious support and much more. You can buy meals or simply gather at the campus restaurants, cafés or bars. The campus hosts over 50 student-run sports and cultural associations as well.

## Top-level research

With 12 research universities in the top 200 universities in the world, the Netherlands is the country with the highest density of top-level research and teaching facilities (Times Higher Education, 2011). This, combined with a population of which 98% has excellent command of the English language, means that the Netherlands welcomes you for your higher education!

For more information please visit www.utwente.nl.

# University of Twente:
# Case study

*Usman Salim, Pakistan, International Business Administration:*
'I would not only recommend it but would encourage students to study abroad. The experience of studying abroad will be a major contributing factor in their personal growth and will give them a broader perspective of the world. University of Twente provides a very stable learning environment as well as providing state of the art facilities to its students.'

*Antonia Raileanu, Romania, European Studies:*
'The campus gives you the opportunity to practice various sport activities such as: horse riding, climbing, indoor and outdoor swimming, zumba, beach volleyball, basketball etc.

'I would definitely recommend UT as one of the best universities. It gave me the chance to grow, to consider many other options, to discover opportunities and more important, to aim for more.'

*Shinwoo Back, South Korea, Advanced Technology:*
'Some might wonder whether this multidisciplinary structure is too vague, sacrificing depth in one subject for a wider knowledge. However, I feel the Advanced Technology course provides a rigorous and solid preparation for any Master's program – and I would wholeheartedly recommend it to anyone with a passion for technology, who's looking for a challenge.'

*Agung Adi Priyanto, Indonesia, Business Information Technology:*
'Since the UT is a member of 3TU I was expecting to study at one of the best technical universities in the Netherlands. The number of international students here is quite high. Student activism is difficult to combine with your study, but manageable. I am the board member of the Indonesian Student Association in Enschede (PPIE).'

*Pantelis Bampoulis, Greece, Nanotechnology:*
'During the introduction week, the UT administrative staff took care of all the necessary procedures such as the enrollment, housing, doctor, bank

account etc. The introduction week not only helped me with arranging all these formalities but also gave me the possibility to meet new people, make new friends and get to know the life in UT and Enschede.'

## Wetsus Academy: Case study

'Everybody has a dream and people start to dream from their childhood. All children dream of becoming a singer or a dancer . . . Actually all dreams are very important, otherwise you will not go further.

'After I completed my bachelor studies, I knew that I would like to broaden my knowledge in the water field as I had been inspired by a teacher of Waste Water treatment, who demonstrated the value, importance and magic of water. I was lucky to find the Master's programme of Water Technology at Wetsus Academy in the Netherlands.

'In the beginning I was talking about the dreams . . . So, one of my dreams was to experience life in a foreign country. For this reason I decided not to continue my studies in my native country but to study in the Netherlands.

'The time in the foreign country was challenging but also really great. In my opinion, leaving "a comfort zone" teaches you to know yourself and the world better than you knew before. Moreover, it opens one's eyes to a big and colourful world and teaches that sometimes you have to look at things in a bit different and easier way than you used to.

'First of all, I met people from the entire world, who made my stay very special. It taught me to be flexible, patient and understanding. Second, I had really nice teachers: they came from three different universities in the Netherlands (Groningen, Wageningen and Twente) and were friendly and easily approachable.

'In addition, the studies are self driven, well structured and focused on problem solving. It teaches you not to accept everything you hear or read but it encourages you to develop your own ideas.The teachers were easy going and keen to help solve or explain problems, even if they were not present at Wetsus Academy all the time. Third, it was possible to see how new technologies are developed and implemented in reality. It showed me that it is possible to create a value from the things which you have never expected to use in your life. Moreover, this Master's programme gave me the opportunity to be a part of an investigation of new technologies during my master thesis and internship period.

'Actually I am very happy that I finished this Master's programme and if someone were to ask me "would you do it again?" my answer would definitely be yes. I would advise anyone who has a chance to study in a foreign country and has some hesitations – to just go for it.

'When I completed my Master's programme, I was working on "Carbon capture and storage project" in Finland. Currently, I am working at Algae Biotechas as a researcher.'

*Inga Grigaliunaite*

# Glossary

**Academic transcript**

A record of academic progress from around Y10 (Y11 in NI, and S3 in Scotland) onwards, including exam results, unit grades, internal assessments, academic honours and explanations for any anomalies.

**American College Test (ACT)**

The ACT is used to determine academic potential for undergraduate study.

**Associate degree**

A two-year programme of higher education, often in a vocational subject such as hospitality or health.

**Bologna process**

A system to make higher education comparable and compatible across the EHEA, through use of mutually recognised systems and a clear credit framework.

**Community college (USA)**

These colleges offer two-year associate degrees, with the possibility of transferring to a university to top up to a full degree; a cheaper option than going straight to a US university.

**Co-op programme**

Period of paid work experience linked to a university course, rather like a sandwich course in the UK.

**Core**

The compulsory foundation for university study (used in North America and a number of other countries); students choose from a broad range of subjects.

**Diploma mobility**

Taking an entire degree overseas, as opposed to a study-abroad or exchange programme.

**Diploma supplement**

A detailed transcript of attainment in higher education, recognised across the EHEA and beyond.

**eCoE (electronic confirmation of enrolment)**

The eCoE is issued by Australian colleges and universities as proof of enrolment and is required to apply for a student visa.

**ECTS**

European Credit Transfer and Accumulation System, aiding the transfer of students between institutions.

**EHEA**

European Higher Education Area; the countries where the Bologna process is utilised.

**Elective**

An optional course taken at university.

**English medium**

Education with English as the language of instruction.

**Europass**

Helps people to study, work or train across Europe, by presenting skills and qualifications in a standardised format that is easily understood in a range of countries.

**Freshman year**

First year (USA).

**Frosh**

Another name for a fresher or freshman. Frosh week is similar to freshers' week in the UK.

**Graduate Australian Medical Schools Admission Test (GAMSAT)**

Used to determine academic potential for postgraduate medical courses.

**Graduate Record Exam (GRE)**

Used to determine academic potential for postgraduate study.

**International Teacher Education for Primary Schools (ITEPS)**

Primary teaching qualification recognised in Denmark, Sweden, Norway, the Czech Republic, Turkey and the Netherlands.

**Junior year**

Third year (USA).

**Letter of intent**

A statement demonstrating why you should be considered for your chosen course, used by the universities to distinguish between applicants. It may also be described as a letter of motivation, a statement of purpose or a personal statement.

**Letter of motivation**

A statement demonstrating why you should be considered for your chosen course, used by the universities to distinguish between applicants. It may also be described as a letter of intent, a statement of purpose or a personal statement.

**Letter of recommendation**

Reference letter to a potential university, most often (but not always) from a member of academic staff who can comment on your ability and potential.

**Major**

Your main subject area, for example, history, engineering or nursing.

**Mid-term**

An exam taken midway through the academic term.

**Minor**

A secondary subject area or a specialism of your major.

**Nollning (Sweden)**

The introduction of new students to university life, much like freshers' week in the UK.

**Numerus clausus (Germany)**

A competitive system for courses that have more applicants than places.

**Numerus fixus (the Netherlands)**

A fixed number of places are available on a course.

**OECD**
Organisation for Economic Co-operation and Development.

**Orientation**
Events and activities for new students, like freshers' week in the UK.

**Personal statement**
A statement demonstrating why you should be considered for your chosen course, used by the universities to distinguish between applicants. It may also be described as a letter of intent, a letter of motivation or a statement of purpose.

**Polytechnic (New Zealand; Finland)**
An institution providing professional or work-related higher education, in conjunction with business and industry; also known as a university of applied sciences.

**Research-intensive or research-based university**
An institution involved in extensive research activity and doctoral education.

**Research proposal or research statement**
The outline of an applicant's plans for research, including area of interest and rationale.

**Scholastic Assessment Test (SAT)**
Used to determine academic potential for undergraduate study.

**Semester**
The two periods into which the academic year is divided in some countries.

**Senior year**
Fourth year (USA).

**Sophomore year**
Second year (USA).

**Statement of purpose**
A statement demonstrating why you should be considered for your chosen course, used by the universities to distinguish between applicants. It may also be described as a letter of intent, a letter of motivation or a personal statement.

**Study-abroad programme**
A term often used to describe an exchange programme or short-term overseas study.

**Tertiary education**
Education following secondary level; it includes university education, as well as other post-18 education such as vocational training.

**UNESCO**
United Nations Educational, Scientific and Cultural Organization.

**University college (Denmark, Norway and Sweden)**
An institution providing professional undergraduate degrees in areas like engineering, teaching or business.

**University of applied sciences (Finland and the Netherlands)**
See Polytechnic.

**Wānanga**
An educational establishment in New Zealand that teaches degree-level courses in a Māori cultural context.

# Index of advertisers